Long Before the Dodgers

Long Before the Dodgers

Baseball in Brooklyn, 1855–1884

by James L. Terry

McFarland & Company, Inc., Publishers
Jefferson, North Carolina, and London

Library of Congress Cataloguing-in-Publication Data

Terry, James L., 1949–
    Long before the Dodgers : baseball in Brooklyn 1855–1884 /
by James L. Terry
        p.   cm.
    Includes bibliographical references and index.
    ISBN 0-7864-1229-1 (softcover : 50# alkaline paper) ∞
    1. Baseball—New York (State)—New York—History—
19th century.   2. Brooklyn (New York, N.Y.)   I. Title.
GV863.N72N4895   2002
796.357'09747'23—dc21   2002000122

British Library cataloguing data are available

On the front cover: First New York–Brooklyn All-Star game
at Fashion Course, July 20, 1858 (from cover of *New York Clipper*,
July 24, 1858).

Manufactured in the United States of America

McFarland & Company, Inc., Publishers
  Box 611, Jefferson, North Carolina 28640
  www.mcfarlandpub.com

For Elaine, Eugene and Faye

Contents

Introduction

The most glorious year for Brooklyn baseball fans of a certain age is undoubtedly 1955. In the World Series that year the Dodgers defeated the New York Yankees to win their first championship in 55 years. The seventh-game victory on October 7, a 2–0 shutout pitched by Johnny Padres, touched off an unprecedented borough-wide celebration. Doris Kearns Goodwin, who was 12 years old at the time, recalls traveling with her mother into Brooklyn that evening to meet her father to join the celebration. After dining at Junior's, a landmark deli and popular eatery of Dodger players, the family took the subway to downtown Brooklyn. Tens of thousands of delirious fans filled Montague Street in front of the Bossert Hotel where the Dodger players were gathering. The scene was a veritable lovefest, as Dodger players came outside the hotel to mingle with the crowd and thank the fans for their support. Kearns Goodwin recalls:

> No one wanted the night to end. When my father turned to ask my mother how she was holding up, she replied she felt twenty again. He led us to the foot of Montague Street, where a promenade overlooking the East River offered a view of the Statue of Liberty and the lights of Manhattan. Ever since the day in 1898 when Brooklyn had given up its proud history and independent status to merge with New York City, Brooklynites had lived in the shadow of Manhattan. Each new slight—including the demise of the famed *Brooklyn Eagle* earlier that year—only reinforced the perception of second-class citizenship. But this night was Brooklyn's night. This night, Brooklyn, not Manhattan, was the center of the world.*

Although the Dodgers played only two more seasons in Brooklyn before moving to Los Angeles, Doris Kearns Goodwin and countless other

---

*Doris Kearns Goodwin, Wait 'Til Next Year: A Memoir *(New York: Simon & Schuster, 1997)*, 213–214.

writers, documentarians, and now webmasters, have preserved the rich history of the Bums of Flatbush. The Brooklyn Dodgers will forever be a living presence for those too young to have taken the trolley or subway to Ebbets Field. But, aside from historians of baseball and Brooklyn, few people know that 100 years earlier Brooklyn was the center of the nascent baseball world. In 1855, Brooklyn's first organized baseball club, the Excelsiors, began playing on grounds at Third Street and Fifth Avenue, the same location where 29 years later Dodger history would begin. In the 1860s, in the shadow of Manhattan, Brooklyn would boast the best baseball clubs in the land.

This book is a chronicle of the early years of baseball in Brooklyn before the birth of the Dodgers. Brooklyn was involved in many of baseball's "firsts": the first championship clubs, the first paid star player and tragic hero, the first team to make a road trip, the first curveball pitcher, the first player to perfect the bunt, the first enclosed ballparks that charged admission, and the first sports journalist to be elected to baseball's Hall of Fame.

But this story is more than a mere chronicle of baseball achievements. The early history of baseball in Brooklyn offers a unique vantage point to examine the transformation of the game from a recreational pursuit of gentlemen's clubs to a professional spectator sport. It also reveals much about race and gender relations, and the role of the media during this significant transformational period in American history. For Brooklyn, the transition would not be easy. Rooted in the tradition of the male fraternal associations, the Brooklyn clubs were slow in adapting to the business model of professional play. As baseball evolved, the tensions between amateurism and professionalism would be manifested on the fields in Brooklyn.

A few words about method are in order. Unlike most other popular spectator sports, a baseball game is not constrained by a clock. Yet, baseball is not timeless. It is played out in a succession of cycles, from times at bat, to innings, to games, to a series of games, to seasons. Our conception of baseball time is noticeable when failure at any point in the cycle leads to expressions of hope: "Wait 'til the next time at bat," "We'll get them the next inning," "Tomorrow is another game," and the most famous Brooklyn expression, "Wait 'til next year." With some occasional divergences, in telling the story of baseball in Brooklyn I have tried to maintain this cyclical chronology.

I am indebted to many baseball historians who together have provided an excellent framework for understanding baseball's early years. Collectively they have been both a source of information and inspiration.

Although I risk of the sin of omitting the contributions of many, I am compelled to name a few historians whose research and writing particularly inform this study: Henry Seymour, David Quentin Voigt, Melvin L. Adelman, George B. Kirsch, Ted Vincent, William J. Ryczek, Marshall D. Wright, Jules Tiegel, John Thorn, Carl Prince, Frederick Ivor-Campbell, Robert L. Tiemann, Mark Rucker and numerous other contributors from the Society for American Baseball Research.

Although grounded in the accumulated body of baseball research to date, the sources of information for this book come primarily from contemporary local newspapers, national sports weeklies, the annual *Beadle's Dime Base Ball Player* and other publications of Henry Chadwick, and the Spalding Collection maintained at the New York Public Library. For their assistance in accessing or procuring these documents I want to express my appreciation to the knowledgeable and helpful librarians and staff of the National Baseball Hall of Fame Library, the New York Public Library, the Brooklyn Public Library, the Library of Congress and Bobst Library of New York University. I would also like to thank my institutional home, New York University, for granting a sabbatical leave which allowed me the luxury of time for research and writing. Finally, I want to thank my friends and family (especially Elaine, Eugene and Faye) for their encouragement and kind acceptance of my obsession with baseball.

Prologue

Verily Brooklyn is fast earning the title of the "City of Base Ball Clubs," as well as the "City of Churches." As numerous are its church spires, pointing the way to heaven, the present prospect indicates that they may be soon outnumbered by the rapidly increasing ball clubs.
Porter's Spirit of the Times, *June 20, 1857*

It is July in the year of 1862 in the "City of Churches," Brooklyn. You are a clerk in a local bank on Fulton Street. For several years you have been a member of what was called the Jolly Bachelors Club that now goes by the name of its esteemed base ball team, the Excelsiors. It is a Thursday afternoon and you leave work early to join your fellow club members at the foot of Court Street for the 3 o'clock Excelsiors home match with the rival Eckfords of Williamsburgh. Some members will travel by carriage, but you pay the five-cent fair and take the Brooklyn City Railroad's Greenwood horse car from Fulton Street, down Court Street to Hamilton Avenue near the wharfs at the Brooklyn Basin.

When you arrive at the Excelsiors' grounds, you see that a large crowd has already staked out good viewing spots encircling the green playing field. You notice among the spectators fellow club members, players from rival clubs, and local Irish cranks from the neighborhood. At the scorer's table you spot the noted sports writer, Henry Chadwick, whose account of the game you will avidly read the next day in the *Daily Eagle.* Under a tent erected for the occasion, several lady friends of club members enjoy the comfort of the only seats at the grounds. The formally dressed umpire, a player from the Atlantic Club, has just taken his position outside the first base line. Off to one side of the row of spectators behind the catcher's position the "sporting crowd" are wagering on the outcome of the game.

5

Beyond the green field young boys have found a good view from tree branches. And even further out, there appear to be spectators clinging to the masts of ships in the nearby harbor.

The atmosphere is tense. All of Brooklyn is waiting to see if the Excelsiors can recapture their old form of 1860. In that year, the South Brooklyn club had battled the Atlantic club of Bedford for the championship. But, in 1861, the Union cause took priority over base ball and the Excelsiors could not field a first nine for the entire season. Now, led by young Jim Creighton, the pitcher par excellence in base ball, the Excelsiors are ready to capture the championship.

The Eckford Club has won the coin toss and elected to bat first. Your noble Excelsiors, clad in their flannel uniforms of blue pants, white shirts trimmed in blue with a blue "E" emblazoned on the chest, take the field. But already your mind is thinking ahead to the postgame festivities. Your club will host the Eckfords at a sumptuous postgame collation. There will be plenty of food and drink, which will make up for the longwinded speeches by club officials. And with more drinking, even the most reticent club member will join in the singing and merriment. Perhaps you will cap off the evening by taking in the popular minstrel show at Hooley's Opera House.

The odds have already changed on the outcome of the game, as Creighton readies to make his first pitch to the Eckford's leadoff striker. You are ready to cheer the Excelsiors on, proud that your club is one of the best in Brooklyn, and that Brooklyn is "the city of base ball."

CHAPTER ONE

In the Beginning

Contrary to popular myth, organized baseball was born not in the sylvan landscape of Cooperstown, New York, but in the burgeoning urban environment of New York City and Brooklyn.[1] Various games of ball, such as old cat, stoop ball, rounders, and town ball, had been played throughout the country from the time of the nation's early settlement. But the game we know today as baseball was shaped by the forces of modernization that impinged most directly on the rapidly changing urban environment.[2]

Brooklyn at Mid Century

In the early nineteenth century, Brooklyn, which occupied a small corner of Kings County along the East River, was a sleepy bedroom community of wealthy merchants who had amassed their fortunes across the river in Gotham.[3] Most of Kings County was farmland where the largely Dutch landowners continued to own slaves as late as 1827. But, with the opening of the Erie Canal in 1825, New York City and Brooklyn soon developed into the industrial and commercial center of the country. Brooklyn's population and economic growth were phenomenal. Between 1810 and 1840, wealth increased 2,000 percent and the population 1,000 percent.[4] From 1835—when Brooklyn received its city charter—to 1855 the population grew from 24,592 to 205,250, making Brooklyn the third largest city in the nation.

Brooklyn would continue to be known as a bedroom community, with 13 steam ferries carrying commuters across the East River. But, at mid-century, the city had developed its own commercial base and nascent cultural institutions. The East River shoreline from Greenpoint to Red Hook was lined with shipbuilding yards, docks and warehouses with stores for tobacco, hides, wool, coffee, molasses, sugar, salt and grain. The city's diversified manufacturing, based largely in Williamsburg, included distilleries and breweries, sugar refineries, gas works, printers and binders, and factories that manufactured products ranging from hats and clothing to elegant cut glass.

The demand for skilled and unskilled labor lured tens of thousands of European immigrants to Brooklyn. In 1855, 47 percent of the city's population was foreign born.[5] Of these, nearly 60 percent had emigrated from Ireland, while almost 20 percent had come from Germany. With the influx of European immigrants, the proportion of blacks in the population declined significantly. Blacks (free and slave), who had comprised a third of the county's population in 1800, represented only 1.8 percent in 1860.[6] The native class of Dutch patricians and Yankee merchants, also a declining proportion of the total population, continued to control most of the city's wealth.[7]

Such rapid growth did not come without costs. The new immigrants were faced with insufficient and often substandard housing. Many newcomers, from rural origins, had to adapt to an unfamiliar world of urban life and factory labor. In addition, Brooklyn's infrastructure of public services, which was suitable for village life, was slow in adapting to the new urban environment.[8] The baffling arrangement of jurisdictional authority among the county, city and state governments as well as the graft and corruption of machine politics slowed the development of public health services, street improvements, water and sanitation facilities, police and fire protection, and public recreation.[9]

For immigrants and natives alike, the rapidly developing capitalist economy undermined traditional patterns of work and leisure, segmenting people's lives. People sought new sources of social attachment and identity in the impersonal urban environment.[10] New forms of association developed, based on commonalities of social class, occupation, ethnicity, and community. Baseball clubs, as voluntary associations, provided one such basis of social attachment.[10] It is not surprising that these clubs developed along class, occupational and territorial lines. In one sense, they provided an escape from the world of work, but they also were a locus of social bonding and support, not only for club members but also an increasing number of fans, or "cranks," who would identify with a club. Although baseball was a leisure time activity, it was a game congruent with the emergent corporate mentality which valued order, competition, self-control, and discipline.[11] In Steven Gelber's words, baseball "replicated and legitimized the social and intellectual environment of the urban workplace."[12]

At mid-century, technological developments and ideological changes would facilitate the rapid development of baseball in the New York area. Revolutions in communications and transportation promoted the growth of the game. The sporting press, centered in New York, which had largely covered horse racing and cricket, devoted increasing coverage in the late 1850s to baseball. Weeklies, such as *Spirit of the Times*, *Porter's Spirit of the Times*, *Wilkes' Spirit of the Times*, and especially the *New York Clipper*, became promoters of the sport, introducing it to a nation-wide audience. In Brooklyn, the *Daily Eagle*, the *Daily Times*, and the *Daily Union* increasingly provided coverage of baseball matches of local clubs. The development of the telegraph allowed reports of games in the New York area to be sent to newspapers, at first in the Northeast, and eventually throughout the country. When the Brooklyn Excelsiors made their first road trip to upstate New York in 1860, their reputation had preceded them.

The building of intercity and intracity railroads facilitated the expansion of commerce and was also means for baseball clubs and fans to travel to matches across town and between cities. In 1854, the Brooklyn City Railroad purchased the local omnibus (horse drawn stage) companies and began replacing them with horse drawn railroad lines.[13] By the 1860s, horse car lines crisscrossed the city, providing easy and cheap access to baseball grounds in Williamsburg, Bedford, and South Brooklyn.

In the early nineteenth century the ideological message from the pulpit, the press, and the headquarters of business was that physical exercise and sports were useless if not immoral. By mid-century, however, unhealthy working and living conditions in the cities led to a change of attitude of institutional authorities. In the 1840s and 1850s, Brooklyn civic leaders began to take measures to improve sanitary conditions and made plans for public parks that would provide healthful outdoor recreation.[14] Local newspapers and the sports weeklies promoted the physical and spiritual benefits of physical exercise and recreation. A commentary in the July 23, 1846, issue of the *Daily Eagle* by the newspaper's editor championed the game of baseball for its healthful benefits. Walt Whitman, perhaps Brooklyn's first baseball promoter, wrote:

> In our sun-down perambulations, of late, through the outer parts of Brooklyn, we have observed several parties of youngsters playing "base," a game of ball. We wish such sights were more common among us. In the practice of athletic and manly sports, the young men of nearly all our American cities are very deficient—perhaps more so than those of any other country that could be mentioned. Clerks are shut up from early morning till nine or ten o'clock at night—apprentices, after their day's works, either go to bed, or lounge about in places where they benefit neither body or mind—and all

classes seem to act as though there were no commendable objects of pursuit in the world except making money, and tenaciously sticking to one's trade or occupation.... Let us enjoy life a little.... Let us go forth awhile, and get better air in our lungs. Let us leave our close rooms, and the dust and corruption of stagnant places, and taste some of the good things.... The game of ball is glorious...

The Culture of the Early Game

Although historians credit the New York Knickerbockers, established by Alexander Cartwright in 1845, as the first organized baseball club, documentation of the existence of baseball clubs in New York City dates back to the 1820s. A recently discovered communiqué in the April 23, 1823, issue of the *National* Advocate describes a baseball club that played on Saturday afternoons in New York City. "A Spectator" wrote to the newspaper:

> I was last Saturday much pleased in witnessing a company of active young men playing the manly and athletic game of "base ball" at the Retreat in Broadway (Jones') [Broadway, between Washington Place and 8th Street]. I am informed they are an organized association, and that a very interesting game will be played on Saturday next at the above place, to commence at half past 3 o'clock, P.M. Any person fond of witnessing this game may avail himself of seeing it played with consummate skill and wonderful dexterity. It is surprising, and to be regretted that the young men of our city do not engage more in this manual sport; it is innocent amusement, and healthy exercise, attended with but little expense, and has no demoralizing tendency.[15]

Twenty years later, the Knickerbockers would become the model for club organization, and, more significantly, their codification of the game's rules soon became the standard of governance.[16] Beginning in 1842, Cartwright, a bank clerk and volunteer fireman, and a group of his friends played baseball on a field at Madison Square. After being displaced from these grounds, Cartwright organized the Knickerbockers and rented a field and dressing rooms for $75 a year at Elysian Fields in Hoboken, a short ferry ride from Barclay Street in Manhattan.

The Knickerbockers was primarily an exclusive social club created, in baseball historian Harold Seymour's words, as "a vehicle for genteel amateur recreation and polite social intercourse."[17] The clubs membership was comprised of professional men, merchants and white-collar workers who could afford the club's financial obligations and the leisure time to play ball weekday afternoons. Although the club fielded a "first nine" of their better players to play against other clubs, typically the Knickerbocker contests were intraclub matches followed by an evening of food, drink and congenial conversation. Numerous other middle class baseball clubs born in the New York area during the 1850s would follow this gentleman's club model.

The Knickerbocker game rules, printed and widely distributed, would become the standard rules of play in the New York area and eventually throughout the Northeast. The parameters established over a century and half ago, which became known as the "New York game," basically define the rules of the game played today. Some notable differences, however, make the early game seem rather quaint.[18] The bases were set at 42 paces, or roughly 75 feet, and the pitcher stood at least 15 paces from home plate. The pitcher, not confined to a particular space, was required to "pitch" the ball underhand and allow the "striker" to hit the ball. Neither balls nor strikes were "called" (the umpire stood in foul ground on the first base side of the infield) but three swinging strikes resulted in an out. Fielders could make a put-out by fielding a hit ball on one bounce. The completion of the game came not at the end of nine innings, but when one club had scored 21 or more "aces" by the end of a completed inning. Before a match, the club that won a coin toss could choose whether to bat or take the field first. Typically, clubs would elect to bat first. Although teams soon sported colorful uniforms, ball gloves or any protective equipment was noticeably absent.

In addition to the rules of play, the Knickerbockers would establish the social conventions of the early game.[19] The teams were established as fraternal associations whose members would socialize after games and throughout the year. Following matches with other clubs, the home club would host the visitor at a banquet. After dinner, typically officers of each club would make speeches and the game ball would be awarded to the victor. The expression "winning the ball" would come to refer to a victory. Usually singing and other musical entertainment would follow, often lasting well into the night. The entry in the Knickerbocker scorebook for their game with the Excelsiors on August 20, 1858, includes not only the box score to the match but also a note describing the postgame activities:

> After the match both clubs together with a large number of invited guests repaired to Odd Fellows Hall Hoboken where a fine collation had been prepared for them. Speeches were made by various members of the fraternity—and others, songs sung & C & C. Hilarity and good feeling prevailed. The company breaking up at a late hour in the evening.[20]

In the 1860s when teams began traveling to more distant cities, the host club's hospitality would become more elaborate. Representatives from

Knickerbocker and Excelsior teams, 1858. (Spalding Collection, New York Public Library.)

the home club would often escort the visitors to and from their hotel, act as guides on sightseeing excursions, and sponsor more elaborate postgame banquets attended by local dignitaries. This social aspect of the early game was nearly as prominent a feature of interclub contests as the game itself, and the newspaper coverage of matches would usually include descriptions of these extracurricular activities.

Prominent Brooklyn clubs, like the Atlantics and the Excelsiors, might have a hundred members or more, most of whom were spectators and not players. In the press they were referred to, for example, as the Atlantic Base Ball Club or simply the Atlantics. This nomenclature continues today as even major league franchises are still referred to as clubs. Teams might also pick up additional monikers. For example, the Atlantic Club was at times in the press referred to as "the Bedford boys," in reference to the locale of their home grounds.

Typically a club would form, officers would be elected, the location of a home ground would be established, and written invitations would be sent to other clubs proposing a series of matches. As the following item in the *Daily Eagle* illustrates, clubs would send announcements of their club's formation to the local newspapers and sports weeklies in order to make themselves known to the "base ball fraternity."

A Challenge—The undersigned is authorized, by a Nine selected from the firm of Stratten & Chappel, Plumbers, 103 Orange Street, to issue a challenge to play a friendly game of Base Ball, with a Nine selected from any shop in the city of Brooklyn. By addressing a note to me at the above address, a match can be arranged. W.J. Rocae

Who will take it up?[21]

Although the first documented Knickerbocker game was played against the New York Base Ball Club on June 19, 1846, at Elysian Fields, the New York *Morning News* reported a game a year earlier at the same grounds between the New York Base Ball Club and "the Brooklyn team."[22] Elysian Fields, immortalized at least by New Jersians as the birthplace of baseball, was truly an idyllic setting of green pasture owned by Commodore John Cox Stevens on the banks of the Hudson River.[23] Situated on a plot bounded today by Tenth and Eleventh streets, and Hudson and Washington Streets, the site is perhaps best known to New York area residents as the former location of the Maxwell House Coffee factory.

In October 1845, despite a cold northern wind, a large crowd of spectators, including several women, gathered to watch the contest. The Brooklyn team, comprised of several prominent cricket players, was soundly defeated 24–4. Typical of the early matches, following the game both teams joined in a spirited postgame dinner party. As this match illustrates, it was not unusual for players to engage in both cricket and baseball. If, in this 1845 meeting, the Brooklyn cricketers were novices at baseball, in a few short years Brooklyn players would hone their baseball skills and dominate the game in the 1860s.

The First Brooklyn Baseball Clubs

By 1855, New York and Brooklyn each had four prominent baseball clubs. In New York, the Knickerbockers, Eagles and Empires played at Elysian Fields while the Gothams' home ground was in Harlem. Brooklyn boasted the Excelsiors of South Brooklyn, the Putnams of Williamsburgh, the Eckfords of Greenpoint/Williamsburgh, and the Atlantics of Bedford.

Following the example of the Knickerbockers, John H. Suydam and some of his friends of the Jolly Bachelor's Club founded the Excelsiors of Brooklyn in December 1854.[24] Among its members were representatives of some of the oldest and wealthiest families in Brooklyn.[25] Club official and Brooklyn coroner Dr. Joseph Jones would be an influential voice in the amateur baseball association throughout the 1860s. When the Excelsiors left the arena of competitive play, he would fight a losing battle against professionalism. Two club members—Henry B. Polhemus and

Joe Leggett—would be noted for not only their outstanding playing ability, but also for teaching the game of baseball to their business associates in the city of Baltimore.[26] The Baltimore merchants would honor their mentors by naming their club, the first in the city, the Excelsiors of Baltimore.

The Brooklyn Excelsiors played in South Brooklyn, initially on grounds at 3rd Street and 5th Avenue, the site of a major battle in the Revolutionary War, and currently the location of Byrne Park.[27] They later moved to grounds near Carroll Park and by 1859 began playing at grounds "at the foot of Court Street," the present location of Red Hook Park.[28] On the eve of the Civil War the Excelsiors had built one of the strongest baseball teams in the country. But, following the death of their star player, Jim Creighton, in 1862, the club would never be as competitive again. Although club members would continue to play for the pleasure of the game, they would spend more time socializing in their club headquarters in the row house that still stands at 133 Clinton Street.

The Putnam Club of Williamsburg, organized in May 1855, played on grounds at Wheat Hill at the corner of Hooper Street and Lee Avenue.[29] According to William Rankin's 1909 history of baseball, the membership of the Putnams included "some of the leading men in the vicinity of New York in the commercial and social world."[30] The team's pitcher, Thomas Dakin, would be elected the first president of the National Association of Base Ball Players in 1858 and would later become brigadier general in the Brooklyn militia's Fifth Brigade. Because so many members volunteered for military service during the Civil War the club was forced to disband.

During the summer of 1855, two decidedly more working class teams, the Eckfords and the Atlantics, were formed. The Eckfords were comprised largely of shipwrights and skilled mechanics and took their name in honor of Henry Eckford, the prominent Brooklyn shipbuilder who died in 1832. Until 1862, when they moved to the newly constructed Union Grounds, the Eckords played their home matches on ball grounds near the Old Manor House Inn north of Meeker Avenue in Williamsburg.[31] Eckford pitcher Frank Pigeon, in *Porter's Spirit of the Times*, described the Eckfords' first year of play and their first victory:

> Being shipwrights and mechanics, we could not make it convenient to practice more than once a week; and we labored under the impression that want of practice and our having so few players from whom to select a nine would make it almost impossible for us to win a match even if we engaged in one.... Still, we had some merry times among ourselves; we would forget business and everything else on Tuesday afternoons, go out on the green

Brooklyn Eckford Base Ball Club, 1858. (Transcendental Graphics.)

fields, don our ball suits, and go at it with a rush. At such times we were boys again.[32]

The Eckfords finally did receive an invitation to play a match with the Unions of Morrisania (Bronx). Pigeon describes his emotions approaching the contest:

> It would be difficult to describe the sensations we felt that day—such an intense desire to win, and such dread of defeat. We knew that, if badly beaten, we could never succeed in building up a club. Many of our friends would not go to see the match because they did not wish to witness our defeat.

But, much to their surprise, the Eckfords carried the day. Pigeon concludes:

> We did the best we could to keep up our end, and by that means we overdid the matter, and the result was: Eckford, 22; Union, 8. About seven o'clock that evening, nine peacocks might have been seen on their way home, with tail-feathers spread. Our friends were astonished, as well as ourselves, and all felt rejoiced in the result.

It is likely that several of the players celebrated their victory at the Old Manor House, a favorite "watering hole" for local ballplayers.

To the south of Williamsburg, the largely undeveloped community of Bedford was home to a large community of Irish immigrants.[33] With its home grounds in Bedford, the Atlantic club reflected the ethnicity of the community and its working class political ties. The creation of Democratic ward boss and pool hall owner A. R. Samuells, the Atlantics would soon become the top team in Brooklyn and enjoy the greatest longevity of any of the early Brooklyn baseball clubs.[34] According to baseball historian Ted Vincent, the Atlantics were the beneficiaries of significant sums of money channeled through Brooklyn's deputy tax collector, Edward J. Flynn.

The first recorded Atlantic game was with the Harmony of Brooklyn on October 21, 1855.[35] The Atlantics won the match, 24–22, and won the November 5 return match, 27–10. The following year, the Atlantics would merge with the short-lived Harmony and add five players to their roster who would make the club virtually unbeatable: Charley Price, Dicky Pearce, Polkert Boerum, and Matty and Pete O'Brien.[36]

In the next few years, baseball's growing popularity gave rise to the formation of more clubs in Brooklyn. The Continental Club, established in October 1855, shared grounds at Wheat Hill in Williamsburg with the Eckfords. Although they played competively only for a couple of years, the club sponsored the Silver Ball Championship trophy awarded to the championship teams in the early 1860s.

The Pastime Club, which played on the grounds of the Long Island Cricket Club in Bedford, like the Putnams, was comprised of prominent citizens of Brooklyn. Among its members was a prominent Flatbush realtor, the county register, the commissioner of jurors, a prominent sculptor, and the superintendent of the Coney Island Railroad.[37] Like the Putnams, the Pastimes would leave the playing field during the Civil War.

Two other clubs, the Enterprise and the Exercise, are notable for developing players who would become star players for the Atlantics. Organized in June 1856 in Bedford, during the 1860 and 1861 seasons, the Enterprise roster would feature John Chapman, Joe Start, and Fred Crane.[38] The Exercise Club, which played on grounds in South Brooklyn at Third Avenue and Tenth Street, featured both John Galvin and Joe Sprague in its 1861 lineup.[39]

Although initially formed as a "junior club" in October 1856, the Star Club of South Brooklyn would advance to the senior circuit in the 1860s. The Stars, who shared grounds with the Excelsiors, were the dominant junior club in their early years and developed such talented players as George Flanly and star pitcher Jim Creighton. In the late 1860s, the Stars would continue to field a competitive amateur club led by the team's second outstanding pitcher and future Hall of Famer, Candy Cummings.

Another South Brooklyn team, the Charter Oaks, was less competitive but perhaps the most colorful on the field. According to Harold Seymour, the Charter Oaks were the "leaders in sartorial splendor."[40] At a time when team uniforms were usually solid grey or blue, the Charter Oaks were a striking presence on their Carroll Park home grounds wearing pink shirts and white pants with pink stripes.

The Mutuals of New York, the club that would become Brooklyn's major rival across the East River, was formed in 1857.[41] Sponsored by Boss Tweed of Tammany Hall, the Mutuals played their home matches in Hoboken before moving to Union Grounds in Brooklyn in 1862. The club, originally comprised of firemen from Hook & Ladder Company #1, would soon field top players who were given patronage jobs in various city agencies. Surpassing the Atlantics in longevity, the Mutuals would be a charter member of the National League in 1876.

Although clubs tended to form along class lines, the distinction between the "gentlemen's clubs" and the "working class" teams is somewhat misleading. In his study of the occupational structure of baseball club members in New York and Brooklyn from 1856 to 1870, historian Melvin Adelman finds that very few players throughout these years came from either the upper or lower ranks of society.[42] Among Brooklyn players, about half had lower white collar occupations, while a third were skilled craftsmen. Less than 2 percent were unskilled workers, and fewer than 20 percent had professional or higher white collar occupations. In other words, the overwhelming number of players had jobs that allowed them sufficient discretionary income and time to pursue the game, but they were neither manual laborers, nor among the wealthy members of society. By 1860, competitive clubs like the Excelsiors were recruiting club members more for their abilities on the playing field than for their social backgrounds.

In 1856, baseball was being played throughout the New York metropolitan area. *Porter's Spirit of the Times* observed that "Matches are being made all around us, and games are being played on every available plot within a ten mile radius of the city."[43] The proliferation of teams and the growing interest in the game led the Knickerbockers to call a meeting of club representatives in Manhattan in 1857 to form the National Association of Base Ball Players (NABBP).[44] The following year, representatives met to elect officers and draft a constitution. After initially adopting the Knickerbocker rules, the most significant function of this and subsequent annual winter conventions was to approve rule changes.

According to the regulations of baseball's first governing body, players were required to be members in good standing of an NABBP member club at least 30 days prior to a match.[45] They were prohibited from receiving any compensation for playing and were forbidden to bet on any match in which they were involved.

A regulation ball was to weigh between 5¾ ounces and 6 ounces and measure between 9¾ and 10 inches in circumference. It was to be made of India rubber and yarn, covered with leather. The challenging club would furnish the ball that would be presented to the victorious team as a trophy following a match. The bat was to be made of wood and not exceed 2½ inches in diameter. There was no limitation on length. The bases, to be made of canvas, were to be arranged 90 feet apart. The pitcher's plate, to be made of iron, was set at 45 feet from home base.

At the 1858 convention, the outcome of games was changed from the 21-run rule to the completion of nine innings. The following year, a rule was instituted allowing the umpire to call strikes if the striker refused to swing at good pitches. A rule allowing an umpire to call balls was not instituted until the 1864 season.[46] Until 1865, when the "fly rule" was put into effect, outs could be made by catching a hit ball on one bound.[47]

In 1858, when at least 50 senior ball clubs were playing in the New York metropolitan area, Brooklyn experienced a veritable explosion in baseball fever. It seemed that nearly every male inhabitant of the city with the leisure time and athletic proclivities was playing baseball. By the 1860s, larger clubs would field three teams based on level of skill. A "first nine" played in "championship matches" with other NABBP clubs. A "second nine" played against its counterparts on other clubs and provided reserve players for the club's first nine. For a "third nine" or "muffin" team, players of little skill engaged in baseball more as a social occasion than a competitive sport.

"Junior" clubs provided an outlet for the participation of teenage boys and functioned as a training ground for the development of future senior players. Because delegates under 21 years of age were excluded from the NABBP, junior clubs would form their own governing association in 1861.[48] Age, however, was not the sole criteria separating the junior and senior divisions. Skilled players as young as 15 years of age were known to play on senior first nine squads. And, as the *Daily Eagle* observed in an 1864 article, the junior game was not limited to teenagers:

> Passing along 5th Avenue on Saturday, we observed junior clubs playing games in each of the vacant lots adjoining the avenue.... Some of these youngsters could not have been over 10 years old at most, and yet handled the ball very carefully.[49]

In addition to NABBP and junior association play, countless other Brooklynites, struck with baseball fever, took to the diamond. Clubs were often organized according to occupation or workplace. In the late 1850s and 1860s, the *Daily Union* and the *Daily Eagle* published reports of matches comprising firefighters; postal employees; bank clerks; printers;

newspaper reporters, compositors and typographers; ferry employees; city government workers; and actors and theatrical employees. Rivalries were particularly strong among different companies of firefighters, postal workers, and employees of local newspapers.

Many of the formally organized clubs were short-lived and most long forgotten even to the most erstwhile baseball historian. Some took the name of Indian tribes or themes, such as the Hiawatha, Wyondottes, Niagara, and Osceola. Some club names reflected patriotic themes or famous personages; for example, Tippecanoe, E. Pluribus Unum, Jackson, Hickory, Washington, Lady Washington, Liberty, and Union. Others reflected qualities of strength, speed or agility; such as Invincible, Alerts, Live Oak, Reindeer, Eagle, and American Eagle. Still other clubs, like the Unknown and Katy Did, opted for rather unique names.

The baseball clubs utilized vacant lots throughout South Brooklyn (Western District) and the Eastern District (Williamsburg, Greenpoint, Bushwick and Bedford) for playing grounds. The teams were so numerous that often three clubs would share the same home grounds, each allotted two days a week for practice or matches. Local "blue laws" prohibited play on Sunday, the only free day for many working class citizens to either play or attend games.[50] Occasional reports in Brooklyn newspapers, such as the following item in the April 28, 1862, issue of the *Daily Times*, reveal that the police were known to enforce the ban:

> Officer Haslam yesterday espied in Greenpoint some half dozen boys who were engaged in a game of base ball. But the officer although an admirer of the noble game is also opposed to its practice on the Sabbath, so he arrested both the ins and the outs and locked them up for the night. This morning Justice Colahan dismissed them with a warning to have their practice days changed.

Appendix One indicates the location of some of the teams and their home grounds. Usually the grounds were located close to horse car lines for easy access by players and spectators.

Baseball and the Fourth Estate

Coverage of baseball games became a standard feature of local newspapers. Although the *Daily Eagle* provided sporadic and brief reports of matches throughout the summers of 1856 and 1857, in 1858 the newspaper began offering nearly daily reports of matches including box scores, announcements of newly formed clubs, and promotions of significant upcoming games. In its third page section of "News and Gossip," the *Daily Eagle* presented as much if not more coverage of "second nine," junior, and "muffin" events than of "regular" first nine games. The following *Daily Eagle* report of August 27, 1859 is typical of the newspaper's early baseball reporting.

BASE BALL—The Plate Printers in the employ of Johnson, Fry & Co. divided themselves into two sides under the names of Free and Easy and Dusty, and played a match, as follows, on Thursday last:

Free and Easy			*Dusty*		
	O.	R.		O.	R.
Wood, P	8	6	McIntyre, P	2	4
Scrimgeour, C	1	8	Geohaghan, C	3	4
Locraft, 1B	2	7	Abercrombie, 1B	5	2
Skelly, S.S.	1	7	Allen, S.S.	1	6
J. Wood, 2B	3	7	More, 2B	0	7
Smith, 3B	2	0	Stacey, 3B	3	3
Pickett, RF	3	6	Skinner, RF	1	6
Wilson, CF	2	6	Bartlay, CF	3	0
Gifford, LF	4	5	Morphy, LF	3	4
Total		52	Total		36

Scorer for Free and Easy—W. Brocket
Scorer for Dusty—R. Bergen
Umpire—W. Van Pelt, of the Sylvan Club

The batting was excellent. Owing to the darkness only seven innings were played. Home runs were made by Scrimgeour, Gifford and Skelly of the Free and Easy, and by Skinner of the Dusty.

For such extensive coverage, the newspapers relied upon notices and game reports provided by the clubs. The authenticity and accuracy, therefore, was somewhat problematic. In its August 11, 1859, issue, the *Daily Eagle* uncovered a fraudulent report and took pains to chastise the perpetrators:

Some vicious blockhead sends us an account of a bogus Base Ball Club, which might have been a successful hoax were its author not such an egregious ass as to let his auricular appendages stick out. Any Base Ball intelligence intended for the *Eagle* must be authenticated by a responsible name.

Despite the occasional errors that were likely to be made, the extensive coverage of these "sandlot" games legitimated and promoted the sport. In turn, baseball surely promoted newspaper sales. As most novice ballplayers would admit, they love to see their names in the paper. With the regular inclusion of box scores in game reports, each club member would have his moment of glory.

The *Daily Eagle*, established by Brooklyn Democratic Party politicians in 1841, would have a reporter on the scene to cover significant "match games." The formulaic newspaper report would include a description of the scene, with particular comment on the number of ladies attending; a box score; an evaluation of the quality of play of each team; and for important games, an inning-by-inning account of the action. Typically, the report would include an evaluation of the umpire's performance. Often the reporter would moralize on issues of crowd roundiness and gambling, and whether the players exhibited gentlemanly manners and good sportsmanship. An extreme example of moralizing can be found in an August 3, 1859, report of a match between two clubs that exemplified gentlemanly play, the Knickerbockers and the Excelsiors. In a relatively lengthy article of over 400 words, not a single word is given to discussing the match. Rather, the reporter takes the opportunity to discuss at length how "our national game," at once exciting and exhilarating, offers "manly and noble exercise" which any man can play and which the "wives, sisters and sweethearts" can witness with enjoyment. Fortunately, for those interested in the outcome of the match, a box score of the game was appended.

The *Brooklyn Daily Union*, a pro–Republican Party newspaper established in 1863, followed the same formula in its coverage of baseball. But, by 1864 it had surpassed the *Daily Eagle* in the prominence it afforded the sport. The *Daily Eagle*'s baseball reports appeared on page two or three, with exceptional matches making the first page. The *Daily Union*, however, routinely made baseball a page one item during the season, often placing it in the first two or center columns. Like the *Daily Eagle* and the sports weeklies, the *Daily Union* was given to promotional moralizing, as in this June 18, 1864, commentary:

> ...certainly no better means of relaxation could be afforded than baseball offers, both as regards its benefits as an exercise and the unobjectionable character of the game in a moral point of view. It will thus be seen that the "National game of America" was never in a more flowering condition than at present, and never more likely to be played on a permanent footing than this year.

The *Brooklyn Daily Times*, another newspaper with Republican sympathies, also provided coverage of baseball matches. Originally established as the *Williamsburg Daily Times* in 1848, the journal particularly focused on matches in the Eastern District, providing extensive coverage of such teams as the Eckfords.

In their accounts of baseball games, newspaper reporters could also be harsh critics of the quality of play. In an analysis of an 1856 encounter between the Harmony and Continental Clubs of Brooklyn, for example, the *Daily Eagle*'s baseball scribe pulled no punches in evaluating the performance of the players.

> The play was miserably poor, neither party being entitled to be called good players. Bad, however, as was the play of the Harmony Club, that of the Continentals was infinitely worse.—Mr. Brown, the catcher, being the only *good* player amongst the whole. They all require a good deal of practice before attempting to play a match.[51]

No single individual did more to promote and influence the game than Brooklyn's sports writer Henry Chadwick.[52] Born in England in 1824, Chadwick moved with his family to Brooklyn when he was 13. An avid cricket enthusiast, he played the game as a youth and in 1856 began reporting on cricket matches for the *New York Times* and the *Brooklyn Daily Eagle*. But, after watching baseball matches in the mid–1850s, his passion turned to the new sport. He quickly became an expert on the game, and at one time or another reported on games for nearly every major New York metropolitan area newspaper: the *Times*, the *Sun*, the *Herald*, the *Mercury*, the *World*, the *Daily Eagle* and the *Daily Union*.

Chadwick was more than a mere reporter; through his writing he was a promoter and moralist who shaped readers perceptions of baseball. Joining the staff of the *New York Clipper* in 1856, Chadwick's views of the game would be read by a national audience until the turn of the century. He would also edit the annual *Beadle's Dime Base Ball Player*, the weekly *Ball Players' Chronicle*, and the annual *Spalding Guides* from 1881 until his death in 1908. In addition to writing, Chadwick helped to organize the National Association of Base Ball Players (NABBP) and its successor, the National Association of Professional Base Ball Players. He also served on the rules committee of the NABBP, helping to shape the contours of the game.

For better or worse, Chadwick must be thanked for his passion for numbers. He developed the first scoring system for games and the box score that would be a regular feature of newspaper reports of games. He also inaugurated the elaborate compilation of statistics that to this day is a prominent feature of baseball.

From his arrival at the age of 13, Brooklyn would forever be Chadwick's home. After his death in 1908, his body was interred at Greenwood Cemetery, not far from the grave of baseball's first star player, Jim Creighton. Albert Spalding, his friend and associate, encouraged the National Baseball League to finance an impressive monument over his grave, a tribute to Chadwick, but also a tribute to the game that he helped to establish. In 1938, Chadwick was elected as a charter member of baseball's Hall of Fame, the only writer elected before a sportswriter's division was established.

The New York–Brooklyn Rivalry

Just as the baseball epidemic hit the metropolitan area, baseball promoters in 1858 struck on an idea that would capture the attention of New York area baseball fans to the present day, a series of matches between New York and Brooklyn. All-star squads, "picked nines" of the best players representing clubs from the two cities, would square off in a best of three series. The intercity rivalry, later to become the "subway series," was born.

The games would be played at the Fashion Race Course, a neutral site in what is now Corona, New York, not far from the current location of Shea Stadium. The enclosed horseracing track allowed the promoters to charge an exorbitant 50-cent admission charge. This was the first time spectators would pay to watch a baseball match. The proceeds from the matches went to the firemen's fund for widows and orphans.

The first match was scheduled for July 13.[53] Under a threatening sky, 2,000 fans made their way to the track by horse drawn vehicles or by the Flushing Railroad line. But, by game time a heavy storm forced the match's postponement. The disappointed fans would have to wait another week.

On July 20, under more favorable skies, an even larger crowd gathered at the temporary ball grounds. Such a sight had not been seen at a baseball contest. The *Spirit of the Times* reported:

> An immense concourse of people were upon the course before the time announced for commencing the game, and the cry "still they come!" up to five o'clock. Every imaginable kind of vehicle had been enlisted in the service, milk-carts and wagons, beer wagons, express wagons, stages, and the most stylish private and public carriages.[54]

A colorful procession of stages, carrying representatives of the various area baseball clubs, drew the applause of fans as it entered the grounds. Among the more impressive were the Excelsiors' huge coach pulled by a team of fourteen matched horses and the Eagles' coach featuring a musical band.

Spectators arriving by train had to pass through a group of petty entrepreneurs hoping to capitalize on the event. Tables lined the route

Vol. VI.—No. 14.   NEW YORK, SATURDAY, JULY 24, 1858.   Four Cents.

GREAT BASE BALL MATCH.
ALL NEW YORK VERSUS ALL BROOKLYN.—FASHION COURSE, TUESDAY, JULY 20, 1858.

First New York–Brooklyn All-Star game at Fashion Course, July 20, 1858. From cover of *New York Clipper*, July 24, 1858.

from the station to the ball grounds with card sharks and carnival games of chance such as "try your strength," "guess your weight," and "ring-toss."

Inside the course, the home stretch grandstand was filled. Circling the field, spectators were seated on the ground; behind them, fans stood; and carriages formed an outer loop. The *Spirit of the Times* observed that a large crowd of ladies had turned out, many of whom "seemed to enter into the spirit of the game in a manner worthy of the most ardent devotee, betting kids and other trifles on the result, and applauding heartily at a good catch, a good run, and often a noble *attempt*."

Among the more serious wagering crowd, at game time 20 to 15 odds were offered on Brooklyn. But, there was no rowdy or contentious behavior that would characterize baseball crowds in the coming years. According to the *Daily Eagle*, "The assembly was of the most respectable character. It was composed, in the main, of staid citizens, sober business men of various callings."[55]

At 2:30 P.M., the New York club took the field. The best of New York featured Pinckney from the Unions; Benson and Hoyt from the Empires; and Wadsworth and Van Cott of the Gothams; Gelston and Bixby from the Eagles; and De Bost and Harry Wright from the Knickerbockers. The Brooklyn all-stars included Leggett and Holder from the Excelsiors; Pigeon and Grum of the Eckfords; Price and the O'Brien brothers (Matty and Peter) of the Atlantics; and Masten and Burr representing the Putnams.

Brooklyn took an early 3–0 lead after the first inning, stretching it to a 7–3 margin after three. In the fourth inning, the New Yorkers struck for four runs to tie the game. In the following inning, New York took the lead and held it through the remainder of the game. In the final inning, New York put out Brooklyn on three successive catches to win the first match of the series. The *Daily Eagle* described the scene:

> Then there was a waving of hats and handkerchiefs, shaking of hands, and a general congratulations at the success of the New Yorkers. But, their Brooklyn antagonists did not seem to take it very hard. They smiled good humoredly, and hoped for better luck another year.

The second match of the season was played on August 17 before an even larger crowd, estimated at 5,000.[56] Brooklyn juggled its lineup, replacing Holder and Burr with Oliver and Pearce from the Atlantics. Pigeon, who had played shortstop in the first match, pitched in the second. The changes apparently made a difference in the outcome, as Brooklyn convincingly beat New York 29–8 to tie the series.

In early September, New York won the "rubber" match of the intercity series by a score of 29–18.[57] For the time being, New York could claim bragging rights to having the best baseball players in the metropolitan area, if not the entire country. But, in a short time the entire baseball fraternity would recognize Brooklyn as the championship city of baseball.

At a postgame banquet following a Knickerbocker and Excelsior match in August 1858, players and club members joined in the singing of a tune especially composed for the occasion by Atlantics player Peter O'Brien.[58] In it the names of the top players from New York and Brooklyn, many of whom played in the all-star series, are immortalized. The song captures the spirit of camaraderie and fraternity of these men's associations. Following is as abbreviated version published by Henry Chadwick in 1868.[59]

"Ball Days" in the Year A.D. 1858

I.

Come, base ball players all and listen to the song
About our many Yankee game, and pardon what is wrong;
If the verses do not suit you, I hope the chorus will,
So join with us, one and all, and sing it with a will.

CHORUS

Then shout, shout for joy, and let the welkin ring.
In praises of our noble game, for health 'tis sure to bring;
Come, my brave Yankee boys, there's room enough for all,
So join in Uncle Samuel's sport—the pastime of base ball.

II.

First a welcome to our guests, the brave Excelsior boys,
They play a strong and lively game, and make a lively noise;
They buck at every club, without breaking any bones,
Assisted by their president, the witty Doctor Jones.

III.

They well deserve their motto, and may they ever keep
Their men from slumbering, till their score "foots up a heap;"
And their name will resound through village and through town,
Especially by older clubs, who've been by them done brown.

IV.

They have Leggett for a catcher, and who is always there,
A gentleman in every sense, whose play is always square;
Then Russell, Reynolds, Dayton, and also Johnny Holder,
And the infantile "phenomenon," who'll play when he gets older.

V.

But if I should go on singing of each and every one,
'Twould require another day, till the setting of the sun;
But they need no voice of mine to glorify their name,
Their motto's "Ever Onward," and may it never wane.

VI.

The Nestors and the parents of this our noble game,
May repose on laurels gathered and on records of their fame;
But all honor and all glory to their ever fostering hand,
That is multiplying ball clubs in towns throughout the land.

VII.

Then treat the fathers kindly, and please respect their age,
Their last appearance is not announced, as yet, on any stage;
Some vigor yet remains, as you very well must know—
It shines out like a star in our agile Charles De Bost.

VIII.

Now we'll sing to the Gothams—they hold a formost rank;
They have taken many prizes, and they seldom drew a blank;
Their players are hard to beat, with Van Cott in the race,
And Wadsworth is bound to die on the very first base.

IX.

There's a club called the Eagle, and it soars on very high;
It clipped the parent's wing, and caught them on the fly;
Little Gelston playes behind, and Bixby pitches well,
And Hercules he bats the ball—oh! dreadfully to tell.

X.

And here we have the Putnams—they bear a gallant name;
They are jovial good fellows, as every one will claim—
For Dakin is a trump, as the Brooklyn boys will know,
And with Masten for a catcher, they have a right to crow.

XI.

See the conquering hero comes from the Broad *Atlantic's* ocean,
And the Nestors' hearts do swell with grateful, glad emotion;
They've so many star players, you can hardly name the lions,
But I think you'll all agree they are the O'Briens.

XII.

But we'll cross to the westward, where Empire takes it way,
At our home, the Elysian Fields, this club enjoys its play;
They've Benson, Hoyt, and Miller, Leavy, Thorne and Fay,
All are noted for their even play on every practice day.

XIII.

There's the aspiring Eckford boys, justly considered some;
When they send a challenge, that club looks very *Grum*;
Their *Pidgeon's* ne'er caught napping, and they never are cast down,
With such splendid fielders as Manolt and Ed. Brown.

XIV.

There's a club at Morrisania, that's a very strong bulwark;
It forms a solid "Union" twixt Brooklyn and New York—
They've Gifford for their pitcher, and Booth plays well behind,
And Pinckney, on the second base, is hard to beat you'll find.

XVI.

The young clubs, one and all, with a welcome we will greet,
On the field or festive ball, whenever we may meet;
And their praises we will sing at some future time;
But now we'll pledge their health in a glass of rosy wine.

XVII.

Your pardon now I crave—this yarn is spun too long—
The Knickerbocker's "fiend," you know, he always goes it strong;
On America's game of base ball he will shout his loud acclaim,
And his "tiger" shall be telegraphed to Britain's broad domain.

The End

Over the coming decade, baseball would evolve into a popular spectator sport comprised of a workforce of peripatetic professional performers. The early Brooklyn teams, rooted in the men's club tradition in local communities, would be ill-suited for the new competitive marketplace. But, in those years when the Civil War forever solidified the Union, the clubs from the City of Baseball significantly forged the National game.

CHAPTER TWO

Excelsiors and Eckfords

Although clubs like the Knickerbockers would continue to play only "social matches" in which winning was less important than fraternal recreation, by 1860 intense rivalries developed among many of the NABBP clubs. Lacking a league schedule, clubs arranged matches with each other by written invitation. They would play a home-to-home series against another club, and if necessary, a third "rubber match" would decide the series winner. The better teams were those that could boast the most series victories, but incomparable schedules made this a less than satisfactory means of determining a championship team. This dilemma was resolved in 1860 when a general consensus formed in recognition of the Atlantics as the unofficial reigning champions. Since its establishment, the "Bedford Boys" had yet to lose a series to another club. The first team to win a series from the Atlantics, then, would claim the championship title. Throughout the 1860s, a reigning champion would retain its title until dethroned by a challenger in a best of three series of "grand matches."

The Excelsiors were the first challenger to the title in 1860. In contrast to the Knickerbockers, in the late 1850s the South Brooklyn squad recruited players from other clubs in order to build a competitive team.[1] In 1857, the Excelsiors merged with the Wayne Club of Brooklyn, inheriting in the bargain Joe Leggett, who would become the club captain and a star player. They acquired a prominent first baseman, Aleck Pearsall, from the Aesculapeans, a club comprised of physicians. In 1860, the Excelsiors further strengthened their roster with the addition of George Flanly and Jim Creighton from the Brooklyn Stars, a leading junior club.

Jim Creighton would soon become recognized as baseball's first star player. He began playing in 1858 as a second baseman for the Brooklyn Niagara, a junior club. The following year, he filled in for the Niagaras' absent pitcher in a game against the Stars. Impressed by his performance,

29

Thomas Reynolds   James Creighton   A.T. Pearsall   Jos. B. Leggett   Geo. Whitfield

Jno. C. Whiting   H.D. Polhemus   Ed. Russell   Axel Braman

Personnel of team September 24th 1860 on which date they defeated the All Philadelphians

Brooklyn Excelsior Base Ball Club, 1860. (Brooklyn Public Library, Brooklyn Collection.)

the Stars lured Creighton to their club. In the fall, Creighton's performance in matches against the Excelsiors and Atlantics drew the attention of Excelsior club officials. He signed with the Excelsiors during the winter of 1859, and although it was not publicly known at the time, he was paid under the table to play for the team. Creighton is thus credited with being the first known professional baseball player.

Despite the NABBP ban on professionalism, players throughout the 1860s would be financially compensated in various ways for their services. Some, like Creighton and Al Reach of the Eckfords, were reputedly paid outright; others would be given patronage jobs. At times, star players would receive the proceeds from benefit matches held in their honor. In 1861 the *Daily Eagle* announced a benefit match with a ten cent admission charge to be held at the St. George cricket grounds in Hoboken for Dickey Pearce of the Atlantics and Jim Creighton of the Excelsiors.[2] Harry Wright, then playing with the Gothams, was honored with a benefit in 1863.[3] At the end of the 1864 season the *Daily Eagle* encouraged fans to turn out for a benefit match for Atlantic star Joe Start: "Like a good son and an affectionate brother he supports a mother and sisters, and we trust his many warm admirers will rally on this occasion to give a benefit that will give him a good start for the winter."[4] Beginning in 1862, when admission fees were regularly charged at games, players would receive a cut of the gate receipts.

When the South Brooklyn club opened its season with an intrasquad game in late April, the *Brooklyn Daily Eagle* observed that the addition of Creighton and Flanly gave the Excelsiors "an almost invincible strength."[5] The club's prowess was further confirmed on a barnstorming trip to upstate New York in early July. Traveling by rail, the club embarked on the first intercity road trip, playing against clubs in Albany, Buffalo, Rochester, Troy and Newburgh. The Excelsiors drubbed all opponents. In a telegraphed report to the *Daily Eagle* from Buffalo, the paper's journalist wrote glowingly of the Brooklyn embassadors' performance:

> It is safe to say that no such ball playing was ever before witnessed in Buffalo. The manner in which the Excelsiors handled the ball, the ease with which they caught it, under all circumstances, the precision with which they threw it to the bases, and the tremendous hits they gave into the long field made the optics of the Buffalo players glisten with admiration and protrude.[6]

The Excelsiors owed a large part of their success to their young pitcher, Jim Creighton. Creighton soon became known as the pitcher par excellence in baseball, revolutionizing the position. Pitchers at the time were at the batter's mercy, merely offering the ball to the batter, allowing him to hit it, much like slow pitch softball today. Batters could even request either high or low pitches. Creighton, within the strictures of the rules, baffled the hitters with his wrist throw, low underhand delivery, great velocity and great control.[7] Moreover, he took advantage of the no walk rule to outwit the batter. Reporting on a match against Unions in 1862, the *New York Clipper* described Creighton's method:

> Suppose you [batter] want a low ball and you ask him [pitcher] to give you one, you prepare yourself to strike, and in comes the ball just the right height, but out of reach for a good hit. You again prepare yourself, and in comes another, just what you want save that it is too close. This goes on, ball after ball, until he sees you unprepared to strike, and then in comes the very ball you want, and perhaps you make a hasty strike and either miss it or tip out. And if you do neither and keep on waiting ... being so long at the bat, and being tired and impatient you strike without judgment, and "foul out" or "three strike out" is the invariable result.[8]

The Excelsiors returned in mid–July to Brooklyn to prepare for their much-anticipated series with the Atlantics, who were the odds-on favorite to retain the title. Through the early summer, the Atlantics decisively defeated each foe they faced, beating the Stars 30–11 and the Union Club 15–4.[9]

The first Excelsiors-Atlantics match was scheduled for July 19 at the Exelsiors' grounds at the foot of Court Street. In pregame hype that would become typical of major matches the *Daily Eagle* promoted the "grand match" a few days before the contest, assuring readers that a large police force would be on hand to preserve order and that preferred seating had been set aside for "lady visitors."[10] Readers were even advised of the best transportation routes to the grounds: the Greenwood cars from Fulton Ferry and the Hamilton cars from Hamilton Ferry.

On July 19 a crowd of 7,000–8,000 spectators packed the Excelsiors' grounds.[11] Betting at game time was 10–8 on the Atlantic Club. Much to the chagrin of the Atlantics and their wagering fans, however, the Excelsiors trounced the Atlantics 28–4. The *Daily Eagle*, for once at a loss for words, gave little detail beyond the observation that "the 'Bedford Boys' never played so poorly." The unexpected outcome surely heightened expectations for the return match.

On August 9, two hours before the scheduled 3 o'clock starting time of the second game of the series at the Atlantics' grounds in Bedford, crowds of spectators clogged the streets en route to the game.[12] Riders on the Myrtle and Fulton Avenue cars had to fight for standing-room space. At the ball grounds, carriages and carts lined the roped-off spectator area along the foul lines. There was a carnival-like atmosphere as "cranks" lined up at various food vendor carts or at tents set up to sell beer and other alcoholic beverages. In addition to the 12,000–15,000 spectators, a corps of reporters and artists for the illustrated papers was on hand to document the momentous sporting event.

At game time a throng of fans had spilled beyond the ropes out onto the field and had to be cleared. But, when the Atlantics took the field, the *Daily Eagle* noted "the crowd hushed down to an attentive silence."[13] Calm prevailed through the early innings as Creighton, up to his old form, blanked the Atlantics. But to the delight of the Bedford fans, the Atlantics erupted for nine runs in the seventh inning. The Excelsiors pulled to within one run, 15–14, in the ninth inning, but the Excelsiors' Leggett, trying to stretch a hit into a double, was thrown out by the Atlantics' outfielder Pearce. The Atlantics had held on to win, and their faithful erupted. According to the *Daily Eagle*, "the shout that rent the air from the stentorian lungs of the countless friends of the gallant

Atlantics was terrific, and it was with difficulty that they made their way to the club house."

The stage was now set for the rubber match to decide the championship, scheduled for August 23 at the Putnam grounds. Fulfilling a busy schedule the week before the match, the Atlantics squeaked by the Enterprise, 16–14, then soundly defeated the New York Mutual 26–14.[14] As the big game day approached, the *Daily Eagle* predicted a record crowd of 20,000 fans, including delegations expected from Philadelphia, Baltimore, Boston, Albany, Troy, Buffalo, Rochester and Poughkeepsie.[15] A large crowd did turn out at the Putnam grounds, but ominously fewer ladies were in attendance than at earlier games.[16] A general view prevailed that the presence of ladies helped to maintain civility among the spectators. Over one hundred police officers were on hand to maintain order, but they could not contain the verbal boisterousness of the Atlantics' fans. With the Excelsiors ahead 8–6, in the fifth inning a disputed umpire's call favoring the Excelsiors led to a derisive response from the crowd. When the raucous fans continued to vent their displeasure into the sixth inning, the captain of the Excelsiors, Joe Leggett, ordered his men off the field, never to return. The spectators left the grounds unsure of the outcome, although those who wagered on the Atlantics figured they were saved at least for the moment. Although the *Daily Eagle* reported that the match would be completed in private at an unannounced time and location, it never was.

In a letter to the *Daily Eagle*, the Atlantics secretary, F.K. Boughton, defended his club and its fans, arguing that the game should not have been called.[17] Critical of unfair press coverage, Boughton described the behavior of the Atlantic cranks as merely "natural exuberance." Moreover, he implied that the Excelsiors were not tough enough to withstand the pressure. "We wish the public to remember," said Boughton, "that the 'Old Atlantics' are used to these exciting battles, and we would recommend those aspiring to the championship not to be too hasty in leaving the field, as it is a 'poor road to travel' and does not lead to that enviable and coveted position." This response of the Atlantics must have surely galled the Excelsiors. Not only did the Excelsiors refuse to complete the final championship game, they never engaged in another match with the Bedford team.

Although the followers of baseball were deprived of a decisive outcome in the championship series, it was clear to all that the city of Brooklyn was home to the best clubs. In early September, the Atlantics decisively beat the Harlem Club, 28–8. In the same week, the Excelsiors shut out the Empire, one of New York's best clubs, 5–0. In a bit of civic pride, the

Daily Eagle observed that the Empires "would stand but a poor chance with several of our Brooklyn clubs. If we are ahead of the big city in nothing else, we can beat her at base ball."[18]

Later in September, the Excelsiors traveled to Baltimore for its second road tour of the season. They easily defeated the Excelsior of Baltimore, 51–6, and on their return home stopped in Philadelphia to beat a "picked-nine" of top Philly players, 15–4.[19]

The Excelsiors and the Eckfords each finished their seasons with better records than the Atlantics. The Excelsiors had 18 wins, 2 losses, and the one fateful tie with the Atlantics. Their potent offense dominated other teams. Catcher Joe Leggett, infielder John Whiting, and outfielder George Flanly were the three top run scorers in the NABBP.[20] On defense, pitcher Jim Creighton was arguably the best in the game. The Eckfords suffered only two losses in their 17 games, but both were against the Atlantics. Although the Bedford club finished with 12 wins, 2 losses, and 2 ties, it remained the championship club.

In 1861, the Civil War took its toll on organized baseball with many players exchanging their baseball uniforms for military garb. Club membership in the NABBP dropped from 54 in 1860 to only 34 in 1861.[21] The game continued to be played in the New York area, but with fewer clubs engaging in considerably fewer games. With the majority of its members enrolled in the Union army, the up and coming Excelsiors were unable to field a first nine for the season.[22] The club suffered an unusual casualty of the war when they learned that Aleck Pearsall had enrolled as a surgeon for the Confederate cause.[23] The Excelsiors promptly expelled Pearsall from the club, giving up their star first baseman.[24]

Some "under-employed" players were able to keep active in extracurricular play. Polhemus and Flanly of the Excelsiors, for example, showed up on the roster of Pacific Engine Company #14 in a match with their rival Brooklyn fire brigade Atlantic Hose Company #1.[25] Cricketers Creighton, Pearsall, and Brainard of the Excelsiors along with Matty O'Brien of the Atlantics played on a "select 11" cricket match at the Long Island Cricket Club in Bedford.[26] Although their team played no season matches, Creighton, Pearsall and Flanly represented their club on the Brooklyn all-star team in their game with the New York all-stars.[27] Near the end of the season, the Excelsiors' Creighton and Brainard joined the Atlantics but did not see any action.[28] To the disappointment of the Atlantics, however, the Excelsior stars returned to their old club when it returned to action the next year.

The less than exceptional season was highlighted by the New York–Brooklyn all-star match and the championship series between the

Atlantics and the Mutuals. On a cool and cloudy day in late October the best players of Brooklyn and New York met in Newark to vie for the Silver Ball trophy offered by the *New York Clipper.*[29] Despite the prohibition of alcoholic beverages at the Newark grounds, 10,000 fans turned out to watch the contest. Trailing in the fifth innings, Brooklyn rallied to beat their rivals by 12 runs, winning the trophy and bragging rights as the premier baseball city.

The Continental Club of Brooklyn also offered a Silver Ball trophy to the winners of the championship series. On October 3, the nearby Hoboken grounds was the site of the first match between the reigning champion Atlantics and the Mutuals of New York. Although each team carried an undefeated record into the contest, the Atlantics were favored to win. Starved of opportunities to engage in their pastime, the "sporting fraternity" (i.e., gamblers) turned out in large numbers. The *Daily Eagle* described the scene:

> The contest was witnessed by a concourse of persons amounting to at least from six to seven or eight thousand, which filled the fences, the trees, and every available chair and piece of standing ground anywhere near the field; a fair proportion of whom were ladies.[30]

The game turned into a slugfest with the New York club upsetting the favored Atlantics 21–18. In contrast to the vitriolic championship series the previous year, the Mutuals entertained their foes in a postgame banquet where "several hours were spent in singing and numerous other pleasant enjoyments."

Two weeks later, the return match in Bedford was another hitting duel with the Atlantics evening the series in a 52–27 rout. Although the quality of play and drama did not match that of play in the previous year, of perhaps greater significance was astonishing interest and support of Brooklyn fans. An estimated 10,000 spectators turned out for the contest. It is worth quoting at length again the *Daily Eagle*'s report:

> Benches were erected, affording ample accommodation for the ladies, and those of the sterner sex who were so fortunate as to obtain them. Ropes and stakes were used liberally in keeping the crowd from encroaching on the field. A detachment of police was upon the ground to preserve order, and not a single fight, row or disturbance of any kind occurred during the game—within our knowledge. Tents were erected,—the national ensign, the stars and stripes, floating over them in several parts of the field, where refreshments etc., could be obtained. The crowd was not only on the ground, but also several housetops in the vicinity were crowded with spectators. Outside the ring formed by spectators, were numerous carriages and stages and equipages of various kinds from the St. Nicholas and other hotels.[31]

The lateness in the season and the increasingly inclement weather would postpone the deciding match in the series to the following year. Although the Eckfords' 8–4 season's record once again was better than the Atlantics' 5–2 mark, the Eckfords had not challenged the reigning champions to a series. The Atlantics kept the championship title for another year. Although the war had diminished play during the 1861 season, the continuing growth of popularity of the sport among fans was not lost among some budding entrepreneurs who would seek to profit from this potential market in the coming years. In so doing, they would bring baseball one step closer to the commercialization and professionalization of what was becoming known as the "national pastime."

The momentous 1862 baseball season would witness the opening of the first enclosed ballpark which regularly charged admission, the crowning of a new championship club, and the tragic death of the game's star player. Although a snowstorm in early April delayed the opening of spring practice, the *New York Clipper* reported that all the major clubs were nearly back to full strength and were anxious to start the season.[32]

In 1861, Henry Cammeyer, an associate of Tammany Hall's Boss Tweed, leased a six acre tract of land accessible by several horse-car lines between Marcy and Harrison avenues and Rutledge and Lynch streets in Williamsburg with the hopes of creating the first sports muliplex.[33] He envisioned facilities for horseback riding, boating, gymnastics, ice skating and baseball. When his grandiose scheme came to naught, he settled for an ice skating rink in the winter of 1861. Recognizing the growing popularity of baseball as a spectator sport, before the 1862 season he converted the rink into an enclosed baseball park. The grounds were drained and leveled, and a six to seven foot fence erected around the perimeter. A long wooden shed was constructed with benches especially for lady spectators. Other benches for "cranks" were scattered around the grounds, bringing the seating capacity to 1,500. Less fortunate fans had to stand along the sidelines or sit in carriages that were allowed to encircle the field. Cammayer had a clubhouse erected that would accommodate three teams, a saloon building to dispense refreshments, and buildings to handle admissions and to store equipment. An unusual pagoda structure, which skaters had circled on the ice rink, remained as an obstacle in the outfield. Flagpoles were erected which flew the Stars and Stripes and the participating club pennants. Cammayer did not require a rental fee to the home clubs (initially the Eckfords, Putnams, and Constellations), but for the first time regularly charged a ten-cent admission fee to fans. Although spectators were unaccustomed to paying to watch baseball games, the price was not unreasonable for middle class fans.[34]

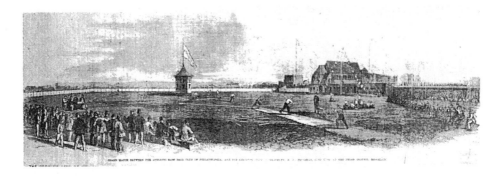

Game between the Philadelphia Athletics and Resolute Base Ball Club of Brooklyn, June 15, 1865, at Union Grounds, Brooklyn. (From *Frank Leslie's Illustrated Newspaper*, July 1, 1865.)

On May 15, Cammayer inaugurated his new Union Grounds with an exhibition game of players representing the three home teams. Two to three thousand fans filled the seats or stood along the sidelines. Although admission was free for the event, several thousand more people lined the embankment outside the park. These "cheap seats" would typically be the preferred vantage point of many fans. In another Brooklyn first, at the beginning of the festivities a band played the "The Star Spangled Banner," the tune that many youth would come to identify as the national anthem of baseball. Although rudimentary, the first baseball park was open for business.

Union Grounds was the site of all three matches of the renewal of the Silver Ball Championship Series. Although the previous year the deciding match for the championship between the Mutuals and the Atlantics was not played, the sponsoring Continental Club of Brooklyn decided that the Eckfords would be the challenger this year.[35] Proceeds from the matches were to be donated to the U.S. Sanitary Commission to aid Civil War veterans and their families. On July 11, the Eckfords defeated the Atlantics in their first game by a score of 20–14.[36]

The second match was played before a crowd of 6,000 fans, many of whom watched from the embankment outside the park. The Atlantics jumped to an early 8–0 lead and went on to an easy 39–5 victory in the slugfest. According to the *Brooklyn Daily Times*, bad decisions by the umpire in the early innings "killed the Eckford boys." Demoralized, the Eckfords' defense fell apart. In the words of the *Daily Times*:

> We have seen a great many games of base ball, and have also seen the Eckfords play quite a number of times, but in all our experience, we never saw

the outfield of a match played in such execrable manner as the Eckford's was played yesterday. It was "awful to behold."[37]

In its coverage of the game, the *Daily Times* also presented an unusual commentary on Henry Chadwick, universally revered today by baseball historians. Although the reporter's comments may have reflected a bit of jealousy, they may also reveal an arrogant side of the "Father of Baseball's" character:

> The "What is it!" who recently returned from an exhibition tour to Philadelphia and Boston was as large as life. We cannot see how this man can so forget his position, as to force himself on ball players in the manner he does. There is a place set apart for reporters and scorers alike; but he ignores this, and flouts himself down on a small stool in the way of the players and umpires—pulls out a large score book and several pencils, and throws a disdainful look towards the other members of the press, as much as to say, "Do you know who I am? Why I am the 'What is it!' author of base ball and cricket, and the only writer on these subjects." The conceit of this fellow runs away with his brains and we must have compassion on him.[38]

The deciding match between the Eckfords and the Atlantics on September 18 drew, according to the *New York Clipper*, "the largest assemblage known in the annals of the game."[39] An estimated 10,000 fans filled the enclosed park and the outside embankment. In a close and well-played battle, the Eckfords won the deciding match of the series and the championship with an 8-3 victory. Like modern day World Series celebrations, champagne flowed in the clubhouse after the game, as the Continental Club President presented the Silver Ball to the Eckfords. Following a round of speeches, the assembled gave an appreciative three cheers to the Continental Club and to Mr. Cammayer.

With little time to savor their victory, the Eckfords a week later met the Mutuals of New York to play the second game of their season series. The Eckfords had taken the first match played in Hoboken, 28-4. With Union ground decorated in colorful bunting and the Eckford's "whip" (pennant) flying for the first time, the Eckfords beat the Mutuals 29-14, sweeping the series in two games and successfully defending their championship crown.[40] The *Daily Times* savored the victory of its local heroes against the "boss of New York clubs." In contrast to the Mutuals who "have been scouring the country for good players ... nearly all [Eckford] players have *graduated* in the club, there being only one in the nine of yesterday that *ever played in a match with any other club*."[41]

As an anticlimax, that same week the Atlantics played the final match of their aborted series with the Mutuals. On an oppressively hot afternoon, before a crowd of 10,000 fans at ball grounds in New York at 63rd Street and 3rd Avenue, the former champion Atlantics lost 16–9. The *Daily Eagle* philosophically commented on the unexpected turn of events:

> There are periods in the records of clubs as well as in the lives of persons, when every faculty appears to droop, and, do what we will, the impending misfortune must and does fall. This is exemplified every day, both in the business and pleasurable worlds. Never more so in the base ball way than recently. Who would have thought the famed Excelsiors would be deprived of the championship by its old ally the Eckford? The Atlantics of this city, until recently the champions, have been defeated by the Mutual of New York, their most formidable antagonist.[42]

But what of the famed Excelsiors? The *Daily Eagle* could not have imagined the tragedy that would befall the club from South Brooklyn. Inactive the entire 1861 season, the Excelsiors returned to play at their home grounds on June 26 in a match with the Charter Oaks. Appearing rusty, they were able to eke out a 20–19 victory as darkness fell.[43]

In July, the Excelsiors traveled to Boston where they showed signs of regaining their old form. In a field roped off on the Boston Common, the Excelsiors defeated the Bowdoin of Boston by a score of 41–15.[44] Five to six thousand people watched Jim Creighton pitch eight innings in the four hour game under a hot sun. Creighton also starred in batting, hitting two home runs and scoring a total of eight runs. Following the game, the mayor of Boston joined other dignitaries and the two teams at a banquet at the Parker House that lasted until midnight.

The following day, the Excelsiors defeated a select nine from two prominent area teams, the Tri-Mountain and Lowell Clubs. Again, the Excelsior put on a show of hitting, defeating the Massachusetts players 39–13. Creighton impressed the fans again when, according to the *New York Clipper*, "[he] hit a ball to right field which was a perfect 'sockdolager.'"[45]

On return to Brooklyn, the Excelsiors found the competition more difficult. On July 26, they were beaten by the Unions, their first loss since 1859 to a team outside Brooklyn.[46] In the game, Creighton delivered an average of 20 to 30 pitches to each batter. But, the Union batters had caught on to his method and patiently waited for a good pitch.

By October, the Excelsiors were slumping further. In a match on October 4 with the less formidable Star Club, they could only manage a 5–5 tie. Surprisingly, Creighton's name did not appear in the box score. Commenting on the team's play, the *Daily Eagle* observed, "The Excelsiors have now become [sic] to be regarded as a half-dead club, and their performance this season has been generally so unexpected that the ball people seem warranted in regarding them as such."[47] On the same day, *Wilkes Spirit of the Times* reported a rumor that Creighton and fellow teammates Flanly and Brainard were moving to the Atlantics.[48] But the worst was yet to come.

On Tuesday, October 14, the Excelsiors would play their last game of the season, and Jim Creighton the final match of his life. In this rematch against the Unions, the Excelsiors won by a score of 13–9. Although no explanation was given in newspaper coverage, Creighton played second base and did not pitch. The *Daily Eagle* reported that Creighton "sustained an internal injury occasioned by a strain while batting."[49] He was taken to his father's home at 307 Henry Street where he died two days later. Other reports, including that of Excelsior club official Dr. Jones, indicate that Creighton's injuries were sustained in a cricket match.[50] Regardless of the exact circumstances, baseball had lost its first star player, and it would be several years before the Excelsiors recovered from the tragedy.

The *Daily Eagle* eulogized Creighton as "one of the best players in the union" and as "the pitcher *par excellence*."[51] But, in addition to his playing skills, "He was warm in his attachments, gifted with a large measure of humor, an enthusiastic and practical musician, and most agreeable conversationalist." At his funeral:

> The remains were encased in a handsome rosewood coffin, with silver mountings, and upon a silver plate was inscribed the name, age, etc. of the deceased—James P. Creighton, 21 years, 7 months, 2 days. The funeral services were conducted at the house, by the Rev. Dr. North, and at four P.M. the funeral cortege moved off to Greenwood Cemetery, where the remains were deposited [in] a lot adjoining the Fireman's Monument. Messrs. Leggett, Polhemus, Lent and Flanly officiated as pall bearers.

The Excelsiors completed their season with a respectable 4–1–1 record. The disappointing Atlantics only managed two victories in their five match games. Two of their three losses were at the hands of the Eckfords. The artisan Eckfords from Williamsburg finished the season with an impressive 14–2 record. They had wrestled the championship from the Atlantics, keeping the crown in Brooklyn.

As the 1863 season opened, four teams were vying for the championship: the Eckfords, Atlantics, Mutuals and Eurekas of Newark. But, before the championship matches began, Brooklyn fans were treated to the first annual visit of the Philadelphia Athletics. The Athletics opened against the Excelsiors at their grounds on June 15. Former outfielder Asa "The Count" Brainard would have the unenviable task of replacing

Creighton as the Excelsiors' pitcher. Brainard would become an outstanding pitcher, earning the nickname "Ace," but while in Brooklyn he would always play in the shadow of Creighton.

The Excelsiors took an early 5–0 lead after three innings and continued to lead 14–7 at the end of seven. But, the Athletics dramatically came from behind to tie the game in the ninth. The Excelsiors scored one run in the top of the tenth, but the Philadelphia club brought two runners across in its half of the inning to win the game. The *Daily Eagle* lamented that the South Brooklyn club missed the pitching and hitting of Creighton.[52] Following the postgame banquet, Excelsior club president Dr. Jones paid tribute to the memory of their fallen hero and led a procession to Creighton's gravesite at nearby Greenwood Cemetery.

On the 17th, the Athletics faced the champion Eckfords. Before the match, Eckford representatives acted as tour guides, escorting the Philadelphia contingent to the Continental Iron Works in Greenpoint, where the famous *Monitor* ironclad had been constructed.[53] The entourage viewed the construction in progress of other ironclads, then toured the navy yard where ships fresh from battle in Charleston Harbor were being repaired.

The teams then converged on Union Grounds, which this year the *Daily Eagle* noted was pleasantly covered in white clover. Appreciative outfielders would also notice that the pagoda building had been moved back toward the outfield fence. Three thousand fans turned out to watch the Eckfords take an early 10–1 lead. The Athletics scored four runs in the fifth inning, but a heavy rain following the sixth inning led the umpire to call a halt to the game, awarding the Eckfords a 10–5 victory. According to the *Daily Times*:

> ...the "Burgh" was proud of the boys ... in the field, at the bat, or on their travels to the bases, they were all equal to the expectations of the large crowd present.[54]

The following day, the usual large and festive fans in Bedford welcomed the Athletics for their match with the Atlantics.[55] The 6000 fans watched a tight match through the early innings before their Atlantics pulled away to a 21–13 win. On the 19th, the Athletics returned to Union Grounds to play their final match in Brooklyn against the Star Club. The Star, which had been a leading junior club, had made the jump to the senior division. But, they were clearly outmatched at this playing level, suffering a 37–17 loss to the Athletics.[56]

The Eckfords and the Mutuals played their first series match in Hoboken on July 22. In a closely played game, the Mutuals were down

10–7 going into the ninth. They scored two runs, but the Eckfords held on to win 10–9.[57]

On August 3 the Mutuals began their series with the Atlantics in Bedford.[58] Three to four thousand fans braved the scorching sun on one of the hottest days of the year. In a four-hour game, tempers of players and fans matched the heat in what must rank as one of the more bizarre games in Brooklyn baseball history. At the end of the first three error riddled innings the score was tied 10–10. The Atlantics took the lead when they scored nine runs in the 6th inning. They took a commanding 26–18 lead into the bottom of the ninth. In his report for the *Clipper*, Chadwick presciently observed, "it has now become a common rule of the game that, until the last man is out and the game is really ended, it is never safe to predict who will be the victor, no matter how sure this or that party may think their chances of success are."[59] Many years later, in more parsimonious fashion, Yogi Berra would simply say, "It ain't over 'til it's over."

In the ninth, the Mutuals' bats came alive, propelling them to within two runs of the Atlantics. The Atlantic fans had become restless, especially those with money riding on the outcome, and as was their fashion began to freely verbalize their discontent. At this point the Mutual players added fuel to the fire by openly taunting the Atlantic players. According to the *Daily Eagle* report:

> ...this would have been harmless enough in its results but for two things, one being the fact that the Atlantics are not angels in regard to good temper, and the other that the large amount [wagers] pending on the result gave it a pecuniary interest that led hundreds to forget that they had nothing to say in regard to the game.[60]

The stage was set for the baffling conclusion of the match. Failing to field a ball hit in his direction, an Atlantic player was heard to say that he couldn't see the ball. In the ensuing confusion, fans who thought the game was being called on account of darkness surged onto the field celebrating what they thought was an Atlantic victory. When the umpire finally straightened matters out and the fans pushed back off the field the game was resumed. The game was now tied. The next Mutual batter struck out, but Dickey Pearce, the Atlantics' catcher, missed the ball. The batter took off for first. Inexplicably, Pearce made no effort to retrieve the ball. The Mutuals' player circled the bases and scored the winning run.

The newspaper reporters were apparently as baffled as everyone else; neither the *Clipper* nor the *Daily Eagle* gave a clear explanation of what had ensued. Chadwick, ever the proponent of sportsmanship and gentlemanly behavior, was, however, incensed over the performance. He called for the end of the championship series format, saying that "they create a feeling of rivalry that results in endless disputes ... and above all they are the means of affording hearty encouragement to that spirit of gambling that knows neither ... truth or justice in its efforts to obtain results."[61]

In an editorial comment later that month in the *Daily Eagle*, printed is the first hint that players may be involved with the gambling element:

> ...in all future games, every player who may be either silly enough to allow his temper to get control of his better judgment, or so regardless of his character as to act in such a manner as to make it apparent that the result of the match is extremely important to him personally, from the pecuniary advantages that will accrue to him in case of a victory, will undoubtedly render himself amenable to the disgraceful charge [of] bribery or of having broken the rules which exclude players from being in any way concerned in any wager laid on the result of the contest.[62]

After the Mutuals won the return match, the rubber game of the series was set for September 24 on neutral turf at the St. George Cricket Grounds in Hoboken.

Meanwhile, the Atlantics would play their series with the champion Eckfords. The first match, played on September 2, got off to an inauspicious start when neither team could agree upon an umpire.[63] A half-hour delay before an official could be chosen would briefly postpone what would be one of the worst performances of the Bedford Club. The Atlantics' bats were silent, their pitching and fielding abysmal, and their fans impatient. After five innings, they trailed the Eckfords by an unbelievable score of 22–0. Although the Atlantics showed some spark of life—rallying for nine runs in the last three innings—it was too little, too late. The Eckfords kept their winning streak alive with at 31–10 victory.

The teams played the return match on September 8 before 8,000 fans at Union Grounds. In what was surely a comparison with the Bedford cranks, the *Daily Eagle* commented upon the demeanor of the Eckfords' home crowd: "One solitary policeman was found to be sufficient to enforce the rules of the ground, so considerate was the intent of the highly responsible assemblage collected for the occaision."[64]

The Eckfords struck quickly in the match, batting around in the first inning and scoring four runs. They never trailed in the contest and came away with a decisive 21–11 win. The Eckfords retained their championship crown.

The following week, the anticipated match between the Atlantics and the Mutuals would be played as a benefit game for Harry Wright rather than a championship match.[65] The Atlantics regained their hitting form, scoring 13 runs in the first inning. This time, the Mutuals could not come back, losing to the Atlantics 42–18. Following the game, the teams were able to put aside their differences and partake of a "hot supper" provided by Harry Wright. In the words of the *Clipper*, "The final result … has been the entire restoration of the good feeling that formerly marked the intercourse of these fine clubs." One wonders if the Atlantics would have been so congenial if the championship had been at stake and they had lost.

The final championship match of the season, between the Eckfords and the Mutuals, was played at Union Grounds on October 6. With the game tied going into the fifth inning, the Eckfords erupted for eight runs and went on to win 18–10. The Eckfords completed the season with a perfect 10–0 record. The *Daily Eagle* presciently observed: "If the Eckfords were to try for years they could not attain a higher or more creditable position than they now possess."[66] The *Daily Times* was particularly prideful of the Eckfords because, unlike most other clubs, they did not participate in the "buying and selling" of players.[67] Ironically, this would be the last game that fans would see the championship lineup intact. Before the next season, Ed Duffy and Tom Devyr would move to the Mutuals and Joe Sprague to the Atlantics. A year later, the Eckfords' star first baseman, Al Reach, would revolve to the Philadelphia Athletics. The Eckfords had indeed attained their highest and most creditable position.

CHAPTER THREE

Reign of the Atlantics

The 1864 season would see the opening of Brooklyn's second enclosed ball park, Capitoline Grounds. Reuben Decker and his associate, Hamilton Weed, following Henry Cammayer's example, constructed a combination ice skating rink–baseball park on 15 acres of farmland leased from the Lefferts estate in Bedford near the Atlantics' old ball grounds. A wooden fence enclosed the field located between Nostrand and Marcy, and Putnam and Halsey avenues.[1] Like Union Grounds' pagoda, Capitoline Grounds featured an inexplicable round brick building in deep center field. In April the *Clipper* reported the regulations agreed upon by the park's proprietors and its first tenants, the Atlantics and the Enterprise clubs.[2] Admission would be ten cents. An additional twenty cents was charged for carriages, representing perhaps the first fee for parking. Neither liquor nor intoxicated fans were allowed in the park. Betting and "loud remarks upon the decisions of the umpire" were also prohibited. And, fans were not allowed on the playing field. Violators of any of the regulations would be "promptly expelled from the park." These "grounds rules" were clearly an attempt to curb the excesses of the notorious Bedford cranks.

As the following *Brooklyn Daily Union* item of July 25, 1864, indicates, the Capitoline owners were an early user of public transit advertising.

> HOW TO TELL WHEN BALL MATCHES WILL BE PLAYED— Messrs. Weed and Decker request us to give notice that hereafter when a ball match is to be played, the red ball used in the skating season will be displayed in the windows of the Fulton Avenue cars. Whenever the "ball is up" therefore know that a match is to be played.

Before the match play season began, in April and May the Brooklyn clubs held a series of "prize games" every Saturday to try out the new pitching rules and to experiment with the "fly game."[3] Bats were awarded to the best hitters in the game and balls awarded for the best fielding. Teams were chosen from whomever showed up at the grounds. These games attracted some of the best players from the top teams and unusually large crowds for mere practice matches. A May 20th game at Star Grounds, for example, attracted a crowd of 2,000 fans who were interested in seeing the experimental game.[4] The Atlantics, however, who had earned a reputation for uncooperativeness among the Brooklyn baseball fraternity, refused to waste their time with experimental practice games. In a "prize game" held at the Atlantic's old grounds in late May, the Bedford team was poorly represented, drawing the ire of both the fans and the other clubs.[5]

When the regular season began, it appeared that the Eckfords and the Atlantics were again the teams to beat. The Atlantics opened their season by convincingly beating the Mutuals 25–16. On June 30, "the ball was up" on the Fulton Avenue cars, when the Atlantics hosted the Empire at Capitoline Grounds. In this first meeting of the two clubs since 1856, the heavily favored Atlantics were barely able to eke out a 13-13 tie before rain ended the contest. The *Daily Eagle* observed that the Atlantic fans and players appeared overconfident against the less skilled team.[6] On a positive note, the newspaper could not resist a favorable comment on the improved crowd behavior at Capitoline Grounds: "The Atlantics, for the first time since their organization, have now a ground that is under the control of the club to the extent of preserving perfect rules and decorum on match days."

In a return match the following week, also played at Capitoline, the Atlantics took control and easily beat the Empire 33–9. The *Daily Eagle* complemented the Atlantics on their serious and aggressive play which had not been evident the week before, "It is really a treat to see the Atlantic nine play as they do now: they work together like a finished machine."[7] The Atlantic machine would not falter through the rest of this season and the next as they easily mowed down every opponent.

The Atlantics' season was highlighted by road trips to Philadelphia and Rochester where the Brooklyn club proved its dominance over the top clubs of other cities. The week before they embarked for Philadelphia, the Atlantics hosted the Brooklyn Star Club. Representatives of the Olympic and Keystone Club of Philadelphia were in the crowd at Capitoline Grounds that day, presumably to finalize arrangements for their upcoming matches and also to scout the Brooklyn club.[8] If they saw any weaknesses in the Atlantics which could be exploited, it would not be evident in the following week's play.

The Atlantics' entourage traveled by steamer to the City of Brotherly Love and took up residence in the American Hotel.[9] A delegation of representatives from other Brooklyn clubs, including the Enterprise, Excelsior, Star, and Eckford, also made the trip to watch the action and take in the sites. In four successive days, Philadelphia fans watched their top clubs succumb to the powerful bats of the Atlantics. Even the contingent of rival Brooklyn clubs must have been amazed at the lopsided Atlantic victories: 64–19 over Camden, 65–10 against the Keystones, 58–11 over the Olympic, and 43–16 against the city's best club, the Athletics.[10]

The victory over the Athletics was particularly noteworthy. The Athletics' star pitcher, Dick McBride, who was serving in the Union Army, was granted a special three-day furlough to return to Philadelphia to pitch against the Atlantics.[11] Without McBride, the score might have been even more lopsided.

The Atlantic players' gentlemanly behavior on and off the field drew the commendation of the *Daily Union*, which noted that they were "as civil on the ball field as in the parlor."[12] In contrast to the club's bad boy reputation in Brooklyn, in Philadelphia the newspaper reported "the Brooklyn public will be gratified to learn that the Atlantic's behavior is noted all over the city."[13]

Off the field, the Philadelphia clubs proved to be excellent hosts, escorting the Atlantics on sightseeing tours and providing nightly entertainment and feasts. The visiting team took in "an excellent negro minstrel entertainment" at the Walnut Street Theatre, and was given a "guided tour of the Mint, the water works, the cemetery and other places of interest."[14] The Keystone Club's hospitality, however, was unsurpassed. The *Daily Union* published a page one feature article that describes an event on par with a state dinner:

GRAND DINNER TO THE ATLANTICS AT ST. JAMES'

The dinner given to the Atlantics by the Keystone Club was truly a magnificent affair. The room was hung with the Club and other flags, and the table was profusely laden with everything in the line of substantials and delicacies. The following is the bill of fare:

Broiled—Spring Chicken, St. James style,
Pickled—Oysters, American style,
Entrees—Tomatoes Stuffed, a la Modern; Fricandeau of Veal, Tomato
    Sauce;
Sweetbreads, braize, a la Jardinière; Rice Croquettes, Lemon Flavor,
Cold Dishes—Superior Sugar Cured Hams; Beef Tongues; Pressed Corn
    Beef;
Beef a la Mode,

Game—Blackbirds, on Toast,
Salads—Chicken and Lobster,
Relishes—Sliced Tomatoes; Sliced Cucumbers; Cucumbers and Onions;
    Pickled Beets; Mixed Pickles; Pickled Onions; Continental Sauce;
    Walnut Catsup; Tomato Catsup; Worcestershire Sauce; Olives; French
    Mustard,
Vegetables—Baked Mashed Potatoes; Succotash; Stewed Potatoes; Stewed
    Tomatoes,
Pastry—Green Apple Pie; Custard Pie; Blackberry Pie,
Dessert—Vanilla Ice Cream; Huckleberries and Cream; Cantaloupes;
    Watermelons; Peaches; Apples; Oranges; Almonds; Raisins,
French Coffee

Following the feast, speeches and toasts by various club representatives lasted until 10 P.M.[15]

By early September, the Atlantics had achieved a 15–0 record. But, the club's checkered past still haunted them. The *Daily Union* hailed the team's success but with a word of caution to the team.

> The Atlantic Club are the pride of Brooklyn players, and their superb nine command the admiration and praise of the entire fraternity. Atlantics, do not tarnish that good name; strive to maintain your superiority, and let Monday's play show that you have risen to the top of the ladder, with no one to thank for it, and only your good play, indomitable perseverance, and gentlemanly behavior the cause of success.[16]

The Atlantics must have taken the advice to heart, because they did continue to win. In late September the club made its second road trip, this time to Rochester to take on two Canadian teams.[17] Once again, the Atlantics put on a demonstration of hitting prowess, defeating the Young Canadians 75–11 and the Ontario Club 54–5. They then traveled to Utica and defeated that city's club in an unusually low-scoring, 4–2.

Following the Utica victory, the Atlantic players returned to their hotel parlor for some musical entertainment.[18] The Eastman Business College Brass Band of Poughkeepsie played some "choice airs." Then some of the Atlantic players displayed their own musical talents. Freddy Crane showed his skill at the piano. Then John Chapman, Joe Sprague and Crane performed as a "whistling trio." The *Daily Union* reporter on the scene, however, failed to comment on the quality of their parlor play.

Following the dinner, which featured entertainment from the Union Glee Club, the players were escorted to the train depot where a brass band and a large crowd of local citizens bid them farewell. The Atlantics boarded a special car provided by the New York Central Road and headed back to Brooklyn, having maintained their winning streak.

Montage of ball players from the New York area and a game played between the Atlantics and Eckfords at Union Ground, Brooklyn, on October 13, 1865. At top center is Brooklyn's tragic hero Jim Creighton; to the left is NABBP president P.C. Vorhis; at the right is the "Father of Baseball" Henry Chadwick. (From *Frank Leslie's Illustrated Newspaper*, November 4, 1865).

In the chill of October, the Atlantics completed their 1864 season undefeated, with a 15–7 victory over the Empire Club.[19] Their perfect record was marred only by a tie earlier in the season with the Empire Club. The Eckfords, in disarray, played poorly throughout the year, finishing with a dismal 1–4 record. They did not even respond to the Atlantics' challenge for a series. The Excelsiors improved their record over the previous year, winning eight and losing three contests. But, they played neither the Eckfords nor the Atlantics during the season. The Atlantics, once again, were the undisputed champions.

In 1865, the Star Club emerged as a contender for the championship. When they began as a "crack" junior club, they were known for developing players such as Jim Creighton and George Flanly. But, when the club moved to the "first nine" level, they were not up to the competition on the field and suffered financial problems. In April the Star members met at their club headquarters at the corner of Court and President Streets to plan the upcoming season. Reporting on the meeting the *Daily Union* noted:

The Star have a full treasury, are out of debt, have a long list of members, and two first class nines, and are ready for challenges from any club in the country. They will soon issue challenges to the most prominent of the metropolitan clubs, including the Atlantic, Excelsior, and Eckford of Brooklyn, and Eureka of Newark.[20]

They also were able financially to make a road trip to Philadelphia in July. In the City of Brotherly Love, they successively beat Camden 54–29, the Olympic 31–22, and the Keystone 37–31. They were outmatched by the Athletics, however, losing 25–14. The *Daily Union* pointed out the Stars major weakness:

All are aware of the fact that there are but few clubs that surpass the Stars in the material of a first-class playing club, and yet there is not one in which the prime element of success—thorough *training and discipline*—is so lost sight of, and so neglected.[21]

In contrast to the rising Stars, the Excelsiors continued to follow the path of the old Knickerbockers. Although the South Brooklyn club moved from their home grounds at the foot of Court Street to Capitoline Grounds, there was no indication that the club would rejoin the ranks of the contending teams. Reporting on a July match between the Excelsiors and the Knickerbockers, the *Daily Union* described the "social game" played by the two "gentlemen's club."

Yesterday afternoon the denizens of Wall Street and its vicinity, who enjoy the privilege of belonging to one or other of these first class ball playing organizations, threw aside, for the time being, their speculative occupations, ignored the oil and gold markets, disregarded the latest quotations of the respective Boards of Brokers, and went over to Hoboken for an afternoon's enjoyment on the green turf of the Knickerbocker's ball grounds... The Excelsior and Knickerbocker Clubs have a sensible arrangement between them to play each year a series of games which the winning of the trophy is made an object of secondary importance in comparison to the playing of a jolly good game of base ball, in which social enjoyment and recreative exercise are the prominent features...[22]

The Eckfords were trying to rebound from the loss of several players from their championship team. They beat the weaker Resolute Club, but lost to the Keystones, Unions, Mutuals, and Atlantics.[23] On September 28, the Eckfords traveled to Hoboken to take on the Mutuals in their return match. To the surprise of the wagering fans, the underdog Brooklyn club pulled off a 23–11 upset victory. The *Daily Union* prematurely hailed the Eckfords for beating the odds: "The victory yesterday was one to be proud of as it was a triumph achieved fairly and honorably, and that won by a club that has fought their way up the past two years against obstacles that would have broken up any ordinary organization."[24]

But, the game would be remembered as the first documented case of "hippodroming": players rigging a match. In its report of the game, the *Daily Union* noted, "Some of the followers of the Mutuals who lost money on the match attributed the defeat to willful misplays." The newspaper dismissed the complaints. Mutual club officials, however, were not so sanguine. The series of passed balls and throwing errors which allowed 11 Eckford runs in the fifth inning convinced them that their catcher, William Wansley, and perhaps others were involved in throwing the match.[25] That evening the officials met and formed a committee to investigate the matter. The committee's work, completed at the end of the season, was expedited when the Mutuals' 18-year-old shortstop, Thomas Devyr, submitted a remorseful letter, admitting guilt in the affair and implicating the catcher, Wansley, and third baseman, William Duffy. According to Devyr, the three were offered $300 by a gambler to "heave" the game. At the end of the season, Wansley and the two former Eckford players, Devyr and Duffy, were expelled from the club and prohibited from playing in any NABBP games.

The affair provided evidence for what many had suspected for several years—that hippodroming was an inevitable result of ubiquitous gambling at baseball matches. But, in his confessional letter, Devyr provides some insight into another side of hippodroming, unrelated to gambling. Citing Wansley's justification for "heaving" the game, Devyr wrote, "We can lose this game without doing the club any harm, and win the home and home game."[26] In other words, players on a dominant team might intentionally lose one of the matches, confident that they could win two of three series matches. With players' income supported by gate receipts, three matches were surely more lucrative than two.

The Atlantics opened their season with a 21–10 victory over the Empire Club in Hoboken. The *Daily Union* presciently noted of the Atlantics, "It is safe to say that the nine does not exist that can win a ball from them."[27] This indeed would again be the year of the Atlantics. In several contests they would come close to defeat, but they managed to come away with the ball in each match during the season. The Atlantics would receive as much press coverage of their off-the-field activities as their game performances, especially their fraternal relations with one Philadelphia club, the Keystones, and their hostile relations with another, the Athletics.

The Atlantics easily won their first three matches of the season. Then, on July 27, they combined a powerful hitting attack with superb

CHAMPIONS OF AMERICA.

Entered according to Act of Congress, in the year 1865, by CHAS. H. WILLIAMSON, in the Clerk's Office of the District Cour' of the United States, of the Eastern District of New York.

Atlantic Base Ball Club of Brooklyn, 1865—This team photograph by Brooklyn photographer Charles Williamson was a forerunner of baseball cards that became popular in the 1880s. During the 1865 season, the Atlantics presented the card-mounted photograph to opposing teams. (Library of Congress.)

pitching to defeat the Empire Club at Capitoline by an incredible score of 65–3.[28] Tommy Pratt pitched flawlessly for the Bedford boys and would have had an unprecedented shutout except for Atlantic throwing errors, which allowed the three runs to score.

The following day, the Keystones of Philadelphia were in town to play the Stars and the Atlantics. Before their match with the Stars, the home club hosted the Keystones to a dinner of lobster salad, which apparently was tainted.[29] Although most of the team became ill, the Keystones were still able to defeat the Stars, 37–34.

The Keystones' stomachs had calmed by the next day when they faced the Atlantics. In what was described by the *Daily Union* as "a poorly played affair," the Atlantics won by a score of 33–13.[30] The newspaper suggested that the players' minds were less on the game than the "pleasant feast afterwards." And, indeed, the Atlantics went all out to entertain their guests. The minds of both the *Daily Eagle* and the *Daily Union* reporters, as well, were more on postgame festivities than the action on the field. Two days earlier the *Daily Eagle* published details of the post-game plans. Each paper provided only minimal coverage of the game itself, but extensive details of what followed.

The Saturday match was scheduled for the unusually early hour of 12:30 P.M. Following the match, the teams boarded two free cars provided by the Brooklyn City Rail Road for the 15-minute ride to downtown Brooklyn. At Fulton and Jay streets, they were met by the superintendent of the Coney Island Rail Road, Frank Quevado, who had an "excursion car" waiting to take the entourage to Coney Island. The ride down, according to the *Daily Union*, was "enlivened by some excellent singing."[31] Upon arrival, the players were provided bathing suits and they all went for a swim. Afterwards, "the whole party adjourned to the Oceanic House, where some grand and lofty tumbling, acrobatic displays on the trapeze, wrestling, boxing, jumping, and in fact all kinds of fun, were indulged in until supper was ready—that important part of the entertainment being duly prepared at 8 P.M."[32]

The proprietor of the Oceanic House, Mr. Barrett, had prepared a feast "fit to set before the Queen." Customary speeches were delivered after the meal by the respective club presidents and by Mayor Wood of Brooklyn, along with presentations of the trophy and game ball to the Atlantics. Then, according to the *Daily Eagle*, "Songs and toasts made the hours pass quickly and pleasantly away, and it was growing late before the party broke up."[33] The Keystone contingent left just in time to catch the midnight "owl train" back to Philadelphia.

The Atlantics' attention turned back to the playing field as they prepared for a more challenging series with the Mutuals. The first match was played on August 3, before a large and contentious crowd in Hoboken. The spectators who ringed the field, appeared intent on rivaling their Bedford counterparts in unruly behavior. The *Daily Eagle* noted:

> The crowd, yesterday, interfered greatly with the fielding, and once they opened for Sid Smith to get out, after kicking the ball away, and then closed up to prevent his return. When Peter O'Brien was preparing to catch a ball, he was saluted with, "You son of a b---, don't hold that." Such expressions tended to show how sympathy manifested itself.[34]

Although the oddsmakers heavily favored the Atlantics, 100 to 60, the Mutuals played the Brooklyn team close, and trailed the Atlantics by only one run, 13–12, at the end of five innings. The Atlantics' side was put out in order in the top of the sixth. In their half of the sixth, the Mutuals tied the game and, with a runner on third and none out, threatened to take the lead when a torrential rain halted the game. According to the *Daily Eagle*:

> A rush was made for the house in order to secure shelter from the storm. Here, the pick-pockets did a thriving business, relieving a large number of their watches, pocketbooks, &c. In the Mutual room, the ball was duly presented and received, the game being decided on the 5th inning.

According to game rules, if an inning could not be completed, the score reverted to the completion of the prior inning. Neither team—both confident they would have won at the completion of nine innings—was happy with the way the game ended. But, the Atlantics had escaped with a 13–12 victory to maintain their winning streak.

A crowd of 18,000 to 20,000 gathered at Capitoline Grounds on August 14 for the anticipated rematch. The *Daily Union* noted that "Every avenue leading to the locality of the contest was crowded with people, the cars being over-loaded for hours, and stages, coaches, and vehicles of every description called into requisition to convey the anxious crowd to the centre of attraction of the day."[36]

Capitoline proprietors Weed and Decker had taken special care in preparing the field for play. The *Daily Eagle* observed:

> The grass has been cropped as low as machinery could accomplish it, the sod has been rolled, the bare spots, from pitcher's to catcher's positions, and the circle around the bases had been moistened and rolled, and the home and pitcher's plates, bases and foul lines were distinctly drawn and whitened... Never did any grounds present as complete, perfect and regular ball field, as the Capitoline yersterday.[37]

A police force of 150 men, led by Inspector Folk, were on hand to protect the players from crowd interference, and the crowd from the pickpockets. As the three o'clock game time approached, the officers cleared the field and the teams readied for play. As tensions mounted, the *Daily Eagle* described the scene: "The crowd pushed far back to their limits, the police forming a square around the crowd, the scorers, reporters and umpire alone allowed inside with the players. There the two nines stood, confronting each other, both looking determined as if they really meant work." A photographer, Mr. Berger, appeared from the crowd with his camera to immortalize the scene. Then, the game began.

The Mutuals took an early 3 to 1 lead at the end of the first inning. But, in the second inning, the Atlantic bats erupted. The Bedford crew batted around, scoring 12 runs. Charley Smith, Joe Start, and Dickey Pearce each had home runs in the inning. In their half of the second inning, the Mutuals countered with five runs, owing largely to Atlantic muffs, including one by Freddy Crane. When the Atlantics noticeably took their mistakes in stride, the *Daily Union* could not resist commenting on the uncharacteristic behavior of the Brooklyn players:

> ...Crane accidentally failed to get hold of the ball in time to pass it either to first or third base, and when he did get hold of it he smilingly passed it to the pitcher. Now this was not the orthodox style of doing things at all; for, according to Atlantic precedent, he ought in the first place to have been growled at and censored by every man in the nine, besides which he should have revenged himself on the ball for not being caught by throwing it as swift as he could, and if the throw had been a wild one, more cause for growling would have been given, and things would have gone on in the orthodox style.[38]

The Atlantics scored five runs in each of the next two innings, and then 11 runs in the fifth, putting the game out of reach. The Mutuals scored 13 runs in the final two innings, but fell short by a final score of 40–23. Following the match, Mutual Club official and New York City Coroner Wildy presented Peter O'Brien with the game ball which was inscribed "Atlantic vs. Mutual, For the Championship." The convincing win by the Atlantics surely erased any doubts about who was the championship team.

With little time to savor their victory, on August 18 the Atlantics traveled to Newark to take on the Eurekas in what should have been a relatively easy match for the Brooklyn team. But, poor batting by the Atlantics and outstanding fielding by the Eurekas kept Newark in contention throughout the game. Trailing 21–15 going into the bottom of the ninth, the Eurekas scored five runs. With the tying run on first base and only one out, an upset appeared to be within Eurekas' reach. The *Daily Eagle* described the dramatic finish:

> All Newark was wild. The women could not sit still; the boys were jubilant, and a constant murmur of excitement was audible. "Look wild," was Pearce's order, and the Atlantics were laid to work. Pennington struck a hard ball to centre field, but Crane was looking for it, and quick as thought he picked it from the ground and sent it in a hurry to Start, making the second out. Now all was still more exciting. Rogers took the bat. Everything depended on him. He made a drive at the ball, which struck just outside the fair line, and Start went for it on the fly. "Foul," was the cry of the umpire. "Get behind it," said Pearce, when Joe Start followed orders, and captured the ball, thus ending the game by a score of 21 to 20, the Atlantic ahead.[39]

Once again, the Atlantics escaped with a narrow victory.

In late August, the Atlantics traveled to Washington, D.C., to take on the Nationals. Following their 33–19 win, the Brooklyn team engaged in some sightseeing, visiting, among other points of interest, the War and Treasury Departments. They then visited the White House where they were honored with a personal audience with the president.

Among the entourage was Henry Chadwick, who reported in the *Daily Union* his conversation with President Johnson. Ever the promoter of baseball, Chadwick took the opportunity to lobby in behalf of the national game:

Mr. Chadwick	"Mr. Johnson, we had hoped to have the pleasure of seeing you present at the tournament."
The President	"Well, Mr. Chadwick, you know what pressing calls I have on my time. I should very much like to have seen the games, but it was impossible for me to leave."
Mr. Chadwick	"Your presence, sir, if but for a few minutes, would have given our game a national stamp, which would have greatly assisted in giving it popularity."
The President	"I see you whipped our fellows badly, sir."
The Rev. Mr. Crane—who was standing near the President—"They played very Finely, though, sir. We had our work to do."	
Mr. Chadwick	"Mr. Johnson, the Excelsior Club Of Brooklyn will visit the Nationals next month, and, if possible, you would confer a great favor on the fraternity at large if you would visit the grounds on the occasion of the match."
The President	"I will try to do so, sir. I should like much to see the game."[40]

On September 21, the Atlantics met the Eckfords for the first time since 1863, beating them by a narrow margin of 28–23. It was becoming apparent that the Atlantics would play well against top teams but would slack off against lesser opponents. Reporting on the Eckford match, the *Daily Eagle* chastised the team for its lack of effort.

> The Champions have grown a little careless in their play, of late, and it is not at all creditable to them. Many go and witness these games, not that they anticipate a close thing, but because they want to see the Atlantics play; and to play poorly and carelessly is to do discredit to club and friends. Whatever is worth doing, is worth doing well, and this maxim should actuate the Atlantics, one and all in every game.[41]

The final week of September, the Atlantics traveled to Boston and were back in their old form. On the Boston Common, they defeated the Tri-Mountain Club by an astounding score of 107–16, and the Harvard Club, 58–22. In their game with the Charter Oaks in Hartford, the

Atlantics came away with a 37–11 victory, but played with a noticeable lack of effort. Again, the *Daily Eagle* called the team to account:

> The playing of the game was not of a very brilliant style, and was entirely spoiled by the "let up" so palpable ... carelessness or indifference in a game, may be satisfactory to some friends, but the masses turn out to see the "champions" play, and they expect a good game, and should have it.[42]

Although the report did not go so far as to charge the Atlantics with hippodroming, it came very close, remarking that in the ninth inning their fielding "play was not good, because they did not want it good."

As the season entered its final month, the Atlantics had yet to play against their chief rival from the Philadelphia, the Athletics. In June, the Atlantics tried to arrange a series when the Athletics made a trip to New York in June. But, the Athletics declined, saying they would return to New York in October. When the Atlantics were in Washington, they again tried to finalize arrangements for a series, but neither team could come to an agreement. Colonel Fitzgerald of the Athletics reportedly told the Philadelphia press that the Atlantics were afraid of the Athletics and would not play them. The *New York Tribune* picked up the story and quoted the *Philadelphia Press* as stating "the declination makes the Athletics the champion club of the United States."[43] This, of course, did not sit well with the Atlantics. Bad blood had developed between the two clubs the prior year when the Atlantics traveled to Philadelphia to play matches with several local teams. The Atlantics had accused the Athletics of intentionally rigging the schedule to their favor, forcing the Atlantics to play the Athletics after they were exhausted from playing the other Philadelphia teams on successive days. William Babcock, president of the Atlantics, wrote a lengthy letter to the *Daily Eagle* detailing the Atlantics' side of the story.[44] After further negotiations, the first match was finally set for October 23 in Brooklyn with the rematch scheduled for October 30 in Philadelphia. But, fate would provide another wrinkle to the story.

On October 20, one of the Atlantics' longtime beloved club members and star players, Matty O'Brien, died.[45] On the evening of the 21st, the club met in special session to draft a series of resolutions paying tribute to O'Brien. One of the resolutions proclaimed that, out of respect to the memory of the deceased, the club would cancel any further matches in the season. President Babcock immediately cabled the information to Colonel Fitzgerald in Philadelphia.

On Sunday, the 22nd, over fifty club members, bearing black crape armbands, marched from Babcock's home to the O'Brien residence for the funeral.[46] They were joined by over one hundred representatives from other New York and Brooklyn clubs as well as the Olympic and Keystone of Philadelphia. Following the service, O'Brien's body was borne to its final resting place in Flatbush.

In its October 23rd edition, the *Daily Eagle* recorded O'Brien's final wishes which would impact the the remainder of the Atlantics' playing season:

> His last thoughts almost were upon the Club, and the game which was to have occurred today, was especially on his mind. He urged upon Charlie Smith, "to beat the Athletics."

Although the Athletics accepted the cancellation of the October 23 match, they appeared intent upon holding the Atlantics to their commitment to play in Philadelphia on the 30th. The *Daily Eagle* reported:

> On Friday [October 27th] some of the Athletics remarked that their nine "would be on their grounds on Monday, fully armed and equipped, and unless good and sufficient reasons for postponement were in the meantime received, *they* would claim the ball." Even a Philadelphia paper announced the game as coming off, after the Atlantic resolutions were made public.[47]

A committee of the Atlantics met on Saturday with Peter and Christopher O'Brien, brothers of Matty, to discuss the family's feelings on the matter. They agreed that having the Atlantics play and beat the Athletics would best honor Matty. The club immediately cabled the Philadelphia Club that they would leave Brooklyn on Sunday at 6 P.M. and play on Monday.

Sunday evening, members of the Keystone Club met the Atlantics at the Kensington Depot in Philadelphia. Although the Brooklyn players enjoyed the companionship of the Keystones, the lack of hospitality by the Athletics was clearly a breach of baseball etiquette and an insult to the Atlantics. Just past noon on Monday, the Keystones escorted the Atlantics by coach to the Athletics' grounds at Columbus and 15th streets. The *Daily Eagle* described what had become a familiar scene at championship matches:

> Within the enclosure, the vast crowd formed a large cordon around the entire circle, to such an extent as to interfere with the fielding at times. Outside the grounds, the entire space as far as the eye could reach, was one dense mass of human beings, all intent on seeing this great encounter. Barouches, buggies, phactors, and vehicles of every description filled up the intervening space. The grand stand within the grounds, was filled with well dressed and good looking ladies, there being not less than 15,000 spectators present.[48]

The game would be a seesaw battle throughout. The Athletics took an early 4–3 lead after the first inning. By the end of three innings they had stretched their advantage to 9–5. In the seventh inning, the Atlantics scored four runs, capped off by a three-run homer by Norton that cleared the outfield fence. With two innings remaining, the game was knotted at 14. The Atlantics added three runs in the eighth and four in the ninth, while shutting out the Athletics in their half of the eighth. The Brooklyn club had a commanding seven run lead going into the bottom of the ninth. The Athletics pushed one run across, but with two runners on were down to their last out. Wilkins, the hard-hitting Athletics shortstop, came to the plate. He fouled the first two pitches out of play. The *Daily Eagle* described Wilkins' final swing:

> Then, making a wicked plunge at the ball, bent on a hard hit, the ball raised high in the air on a foul line to 3d base. Charlie Smith prepared for and gauged it. Will he catch it? All is breathless. He closes his hands on it; then suddenly turns as though he had dropped it, the crowd just ready for an exclamation, when, with the words "Old Long Island is not beat yet," he held the ball aloft, now the trophy of victory. Cheer upon cheer rent the air, and the Atlantics were still champions.[49]

As the *Daily Eagle* concluded, "fortune, fickle goddess, smiled on the Brooklyn boys, and victory was theirs."

As the Atlantics were boarding their coach after the game, Colonel Fitzgerald presented them with the game ball trophy. But, the Keystones rather than the Athletics hosted a postgame banquet for the Atlantics and accompanied them to a minstrel show that evening. The Atlantics caught the midnight train back to Brooklyn where they would have one week to prepare for the rematch in Bedford.

With a fall chill in the air, the final championship match was played at Capitoline on November 3.[50] The Atlantics wasted no time, scoring nine runs in the top of the first inning. The Athletics countered with six runs in their half of the first, four of them resulting from Atlantic miscues. By the end of the seventh inning, the Atlantics had stretched their lead to a commanding 25–16 margin. The Atlantics scored one in the eighth inning, but the Philadelphia club scored eight runs in their half of the inning, capped off by a home run by third baseman Luengene. The Atlantics added one more run in the top of the ninth, and the Athletics came to their last at bats trailing by six. This time the Atlantic pitching and fielding were flawless, as the Athletics were put out in order. As the Atlantic catcher, Frank Norton, caught a foul pop-up to end the game, the crowd rushed onto the field and mobbed their championship team.

The Atlantics had held onto their championship, completing two successive undefeated seasons.

That evening at the postgame banquet held at Montague Hall, the Atlantics were joined by representatives from several clubs, including the Camdens, Nationals, Keystones, Actives, Eurekas, Mutuals, Excelsiors, and Enterprise. But, noticeably absent were the Athletics who refused the Atlantics' hospitality. The Athletics missed not only the sumptuous feast but also the opportunity to take in the popular minstrel show at Hooley's Opera House.

At the end of November, Decker and Weed were anxious to ready Capitoline for the approaching ice skating season, but they held off for a few days to allow one more baseball game. On November 27, the Atlantics played a benefit match against a picked nine from other Brooklyn and New York clubs, with the proceeds going to the Atlantics players.[51] Despite the raw and chilly weather and the 25 cent admission charged, a sizeable number of fans turned out to honor their champions. Keeping their winning streak intact, the Atlantics won 23–7.

The indomitable Atlantics finished the season with a perfect 18–0 record, completing two consecutive seasons without a loss. The Atlantics would not lose again until their second match the following year. From September 8, 1863, until June 14, 1866, the "Bedford boys" did not lose once in the 49 games they played. In the mid–1860s, the Brooklyn Atlantics were by far the best team in baseball.

As the 1866 season approached, Atlantic baseball fans must surely have been shocked to learn that two of their star players, Dickey Pearce and Freddy Crane, had joined the Excelsiors. The deal that the two players made with the "gentlemen's club," however, must have fallen through. By August, Pearce and Crane had returned to the Atlantics, but, because of NABBP rules, could not play for 30 days. This clearly put the Atlantics at a disadvantage for much of the playing season. In another deal, the Atlantics acquired the services before the season of the Eckfords' star pitcher, George Zettlein. The Eckford club, already in disarray, would face another long season.

The changing rosters of the teams clearly had an effect on the clubs' competitiveness. By the end of July, the Excelsiors had lost only one match, and that was a close decision to the Unions. Meanwhile, the Atlantics dropped two games to presumably weaker teams in New Jersey, the Irvingtons and the Eurekas. The rosters also had an effect on fan interest. With Pearce and Crane in the Excelsiors' lineup, a large crowd turned out at Capitoline on June 19 to watch the match between the Stars and Excelsiors.[52] The following day at Capitoline, few spectators were on hand to watch the Eckfords play the Enterprise.[53] Success at the "box office" would rely upon presenting a show with quality teams with name recognition players.

By August the *Daily Eagle* had counted out the Eckfords and the Excelsiors as contenders for the championship.[54] For the Excelsiors, it was a season of lost opportunities. When Pearce and Crane rejoined the Atlantics, the Excelsiors' hopes dimmed. Ironically, in August the team added an 18-year-old pitcher to its roster, Arthur "Candy" Cummings, whose fame would rival that of the Excelsiors' fallen hero, Jim Creighton. In his first game pitching against the Mutuals on August 14, the *Daily Eagle* presciently commented, "he has only to keep on in the way he has

Candy Cummings (left) of Brooklyn Star Base Ball Club. (Transcendental Graphics.)

begun, and he will one day (not far distant) be ranked among the best pitchers in the country."[55] Cummings, a future Hall of Famer, would baffle opposing batters with his new pitching innovation, the curveball.

In 1908, the *Baseball Magazine* published Cummings' account of how he developed the technique. According to "Candy," he came upon the idea in 1863 while throwing clamshells and watching them curve threw the air. He perfected his technique over the next few years while at boarding school in Fulton, New York, and later as a player for the Brooklyn Stars junior club. Although Cummings joined the Excelsiors in 1866, he did not attempt to throw curves until the team made a road trip to Boston in 1867. In Cummings' words,

> It was during the Harvard game that I became fully convinced that I had succeeded in doing what all these years I had been striving to do. The batters were missing a lot of balls; I began to watch the flight of the ball through the air, and distinctly saw it curve... A surge of joy came over me that I shall never forget. I felt like shouting out that I had made a ball curve; I wanted to tell everybody; it was too good to keep to myself.[56]

If Pearce and Crane had remained with the Excelsiors, the club may well have contended for the championship. But without a supporting cast of players, a star pitcher alone was not enough to produce a winning team.

With Pearce and Crane rejoining the Atlantics, the Bedford team was once again favored to retain the crown. In their return match with the Irvingtons at Capitoline on September 24, the Atlantics easily beat the New Jersey team, 28–11.[57] Three days later, they defeated the Eurekas, 30–20.[58] The attention of baseball fans was now focused on the Atlantics' upcoming match at Capitoline with their nemesis, the Athletics of Philadelphia.

On October 15, with game time set for 1 P.M., the crowd in Bedford began to gather as early as 9 A.M. At the opening pitch, 15,000 to 20,000 fans had packed inside the grounds, with many more vying for a vantage point outside. According to the *Daily Eagle*,

> The trees on the Fulton Avenue side were black with boys, of smaller and larger growth, who saved their "quarters" and still had a "very fair sight," although they presented a somewhat ludicrous appearance to the "insiders," who never saw "trees bare such fruit before." Even the roofs of the few houses within "seeing distance" were packed.[59]

Although baseball historians have been able to uncover little information about the demographics of spectators at matches in the 1860s, the *Daily Eagle* made an interesting observation about the diversity of the crowd at this game:

> There were numbers of ladies and gentlemen, and many who language and bearing would place them under the class of "Cyprian." The sea of faces would have made an excellent study for a physiognomist.

Led by the irrepressible Inspector Folk, police officers from at least ten Brooklyn precincts were on hand to maintain order. Although they were effective in maintaining crowd order, they made no effort to enforce the prohibition of gambling at the grounds. By game time, betting was heavy on the Atlantics.

The Atlantics won the toss and elected to bat first. At just past 1 o'clock, the Athletics, clad in their dark blue pants, white flannel shirts and white caps, took the field. The early part of the game was evenly played. The Atlantics took a 4–2 lead after two innings, but the Athletics tied the game in the third. The Atlantics gained a one run lead at the end of four, but again the Athletics evened the score in the fifth inning. By this time, the wagering odds on the Atlantics had dropped precipitously. In the sixth inning the Atlantics scored one unanswered run, but in the seventh exploded for eight tallies. The demoralized Athletics were unable to erase the deficit this time; the Atlantics were the victors by a score of 27–17.

The *Eagle*, perhaps rushed to meet the press deadline, did not report extensively on the postgame activities, other than to say "the usual entertainment of chowder and the etceteras followed." But, it is also likely to infer that the days of elaborate banquets and entertainments sponsored by the host clubs were coming to an end. Especially for competitive teams like the Atlantics and Athletics, their interactions would be confined to the playing field and not the parlor.

The following week in Philadelphia, the Athletics rebounded with a convincing 31–12 win over the Atlantics.[60] Again, through misunderstandings between the two clubs, the deciding third match would be delayed until the next year.

As the season drew to a close, the Atlantics won their deciding matches against the Eurekas and the Irvingtons.[61] Although they could not repeat their perfect seasons of the two previous years, the Atlantics still had not lost a series. Although the Athletics finished the season with a better record, the undecided outcome of their series with the Atlantics allowed the Brooklyn team to retain the championship.

Eighteen sixty-seven would prove to be a watershed year for baseball. The long championship reign of the Atlantics and Brooklyn would come to an end; the "city of baseball" would no longer be at the center of the baseball world. The growth in popularity of baseball after the Civil War throughout the country was making baseball truly a national game. Of the 237 delegates to the 1867 NABBP convention only 24 were from New York State. The western states of Illinois, Ohio, Indiana and Wisconsin had 145 clubs represented, 56 from Illinois alone.[62] Only two years before, New York had over half the 91 convention delegates. The *Clipper* was now reporting on baseball matches from across the country. At the end of the season, baseball's voice, Henry Chadwick, would conclude that "New York has no longer the exclusive right of being considered the centre of the base ball republic, although, without doubt, the *locale* of the strongest clubs."[63]

The composition of the clubs was changing as well. Although players had been paid either directly or indirectly before, players more than ever were going where the money was, revolving from team to team when opportunities availed. Clubs like the Washington Nationals were now capturing the baseball public's attention. Nominally comprised of federal government employees, in 1867 the team was led by George Wright, a player well known to New York area fans. Wright was a prime example of a peripatetic revolver.[64] At the age of 15 in 1862 Wright was a member of the New York Gotham Club. In 1865 he revolved to the Philadelphia Olympics. The following year he returned to the Gothams, but in mid-season jumped to the Unions of Morrisania. In 1867 he became captain of the Washington Nationals. He was listed on their roster as a government clerk, but his office address curiously turned out to be a public park. In 1868, Wright was back with the Unions. The following year he joined his brother Harry with the openly professional Cincinnati Red Stockings.

In 1867, Wright's Nationals, on a western tour, crushed the top clubs in one city after another: Columbus, Cincinnati, Indianapolis, Louisville, St. Louis, and Chicago. Their streak was finally ended when they were upset by the Forest City Club of Rockford, Illinois, led by a 17-year-old pitcher, Albert Spalding.[65] Later that fall, Spalding would move to Chicago. As Spalding tells it, "I went to Chicago, ostensibly, to accept a clerkship in a wholesale grocery, but really to become a member of the Chicago Excelsior Base Ball Club."[66] Although in violation of the NABBP rules, Spalding justified his actions: "the rule prohibiting salaries was ... a dead letter. Most clubs of prominence, all over the country, had players who were either directly or indirectly receiving financial advantage from the game."

The debate over professionalism versus amateur play would rage within the baseball fraternity over the next few years. But, the days when teams of hometown amateur players would represent the best in baseball were nearing an end. Writing in *The American Chronicle of Sports and Pastimes* under the thinly veiled pseudonym "Old Peto Brine," one of the retired Atlantic stars, Peter O'Brien, lamented the changes in the Atlantic Club:

> The fact is, it ain't the club it was, although they play a heap better now than they did then. But somehow or other, there's a difference in the club, and I'm sorry to see that nearly all the old Atlantics are losing interest in the club, and no wonder, when they see men having influence ... who only care for it to get the money out of it. We used to play matches for the honor of the thing in my young ball days; now clubs play for gate money and the betting rings ... if there is one thing I'm down on, it is this "revolving" business ... it seems to me as if some men were in the market all the time.[67]

For a brief moment in 1870, the "Bedford boys," still comprised totally of Brooklyn lads, would stop the clock when they defeated Cincinnati. But Brooklyn fans would wait more than a decade for another championship team. For many of those years, they would have to be content with the sandlot game.

In the summer of 1867 these changes underway were not pressing on the minds of Brooklyn baseball fans. After all, the Atlantics were the champions of America, and as the season began the club was favored to successfully defend the crown. The Atlantics left their Bedford home for Cammayer's Union Grounds.[68] Before the season Cammayer had made some improvements on his ballpark, including additional seating for the fans, a commodious press box with cushioned seats for reporters and scorers, and a reconditioned playing field which the *Clipper* described as "too nice to play on ... a perfect picture of a ground inside the bases." In his deal with the Atlantics and the Mutuals, Cammayer would receive 40 percent of the gate receipts on match games plus expenses. Ticket prices were raised to 25 cents.

The Atlantics began the season with four successive victories, beating the Empire, the Star, and the Eckfords twice. After losing to the Unions in Morrisania, they won their next eight games including a victory over the Athletics.[69] The Atlantics then embarked on a disastrous trip to Philadelphia.[70] In their first match, they were badly beaten by the Athletics, 28–8. Reeling from their lopsided loss, the next day the Brooklyn team barely beat the Quaker City Club, 24–21. Their third match, against the Keystones, ended in a 12–12 tie. In their final game, the Atlantics narrowly defeated the West Philadelphia Club, 36–31. The *Clipper* noted that the Atlantics returned home, "thoroughly disgusted with the City of Brotherly Love."

The situation for the Atlantics would only worsen. The Atlantics tried to cancel the return match with the Athletics at Union Grounds scheduled for September 30, claiming that their team was disabled with too many injuries. The Athletics, however, intent on playing the match, refused the Atlantics' request. On September 30, the Athletics and 2,000 to 3,000 fans showed up at the grounds in Williamsburg. The *Clipper* described the singular turn of events:

> After a long consultation between the officers of the two clubs, word was given that the game would be played, and the large crowd present, who had been waiting patiently for over an hour, filled the seats up and took another rest. It was now found that the "champions" were not going to keep faith in the true spirit of their promise. Instead of playing their first nine, or those of them who were able to play, they stated their intention of putting a "muffin" nine in the field against the Athletics, with the avowed purpose of playing so poorly, that five innings could not be finished, and thus tricking the Philadelphians. No effort was made to disguise this shabby trick, and the members of the Atlantic Club openly talked of it as something "smart."[71]

The disgruntled Athletics refused to participate in what the *Clipper* referred to as farce. Meanwhile, the large crowd of spectators that had paid to see a championship match was growing impatient. The Atlantic players who were present divided themselves into two teams and began playing a scrimmage game. As disgusted with the whole affair as the Athletics, the fans joined the Athletics in exiting the grounds.

One week later at Union Grounds the Atlantics played their fateful rematch with the Union Club of Morrisania. The game, which featured excellent pitching and fielding, was, in the judgment of the *Clipper*, "one of the best—if not the best—ever played."[72] The lead changed hands three times with the Unions leading 14–12 at the end of eight innings. Bob Ferguson led off for the Atlantics in the top of the ninth with a line drive to right field, but the Unions' right fielder, Tommy Beals, "made the most brilliant catch of the game," robbing Ferguson of an extra-base hit. Dan MacDonald then doubled and went to third on a passed ball. The next batter, George Zettlein, struck out but the catcher dropped the third strike and had to throw the batter out at first. On the play, MacDonald came home, drawing the Atlantics to within one run, but with only one out left to give. The *Clipper* describes the final play of the game.

> Kenny made a long hit to extreme centre field, but Austin traveled back for it, squared himself, and amid breathless excitement, made the deciding catch of the game, and the side was out, with the totals of 14 to 13 and the Unions winners... And so the championship, which the Atlantics have held so long, slipped out of their grasp when least expected, and into the hands of a club that has been defeated by the Athletics, Mutuals, Irvingtons, and Unions of Lansingburgh. It seemed hard to realize the fact, so sudden and so unexpected.

The Atlantics easily won their last four games, but they were no longer champions. The *Clipper* noted, "Everything considered, this has been the most unsuccessful season the Atlantics have experienced in several years. They owe their defeats in nearly every instance to overconfidence and the absence of one or two of their best players."[73] But, the *Clipper* failed to recognize that the game was quantitatively and qualitatively changing. Baseball was truly becoming a national sport, and the level of competition was improving. The Atlantics' record was a respectable 19 wins, 5 losses, and 1 tie. But, their days of invincibility were over.

CHAPTER FOUR

The Rise of Professionalism

As the baseball season of 1868 approached it had become common knowledge that players were playing for pay. In their January club meeting, the Atlantics announced that they would field three separate teams for the season: professionals, amateurs, and muffins.[1] The respected authority Henry Chadwick finally acknowledged that "professional ball-playing is a business."[2]

After the first half of the 1868 season, the Atlantics, Mutuals and Athletics emerged as the chief contenders for the championship. The Unions, who many thought had undeservedly captured the crown from the Atlantics the year before, were all but counted out by the press.

In late August, the Atlantics and the Athletics began a new series of matches that many in the baseball fraternity feared would never come off. Following the Atlantics' "muffin ruse" in the rubber match of their series the year before, the Athletics filed breach of contract charges with the NABBP against the Atlantics.[3] The Association, however, ruled in favor of the Atlantics, concluding that they did agree to field a team and play the match. The longstanding animosity between the two clubs was heightened by the affair, and each announced that they would never again meet on the playing field.

Nearly a year later, the Atlantics and Athletics reconsidered their moratorium. The *Clipper* waxed eloquently on the clubs' change of heart.

> Time is a great panacea, however, healing over wounds and obliterating memories of unpleasant events. And so it came to pass that these celebrated clubs—the one the champions of Pennsylvania, and the other the ex-champions of America—forgetting all past differences, resolved to again enter the base ball arena as friendly rivals. How the *entente cordiale* was re-

established we do not know. It is sufficient to know that it is a fixed fact, and we trust their friendly relations will continue through all time.[4]

The pecuniary interests of each club may well have played a greater role in the entente than their desire to establish "friendly relations." Public interest in the longstanding rivalry, heightened by the publicity of the feud, would ensure large crowds at the matches and increase gate receipts. This prospect became evident in Philadelphia the week before the first match, where according to the *Clipper* the major topic of conversation of sports fans throughout the city was the upcoming game.[5]

The Atlantics arrived at their hotel in Philadelphia amid little fanfare late on the evening of August 30. On the following morning, however, large crowds of excited fans gathered on the sidewalks surrounding the hotel, hoping to get a glimpse of the "well known faces" of the Atlantic players. Many out-of-town fans, who had just arrived by train, headed for the Athletics' ball grounds early to procure a standing-room-only spot to watch the game. All the reserved seats were sold out days earlier, and on game day, according to the *Clipper*, "they could not be had for love or money."

Despite an early afternoon shower, 10,000 fans packed the Athletics' grounds to watch the contest.[6] The sky cleared somewhat by game time and the Atlantics took the field. To the delight of its fans, the Philadelphia club took an early 7–0 lead at the end of the first inning. After three innings the Atlantics had pulled to within five runs, but in the seventh inning, with rain clouds again darkening the sky, the Athletics scored five more runs to take a commanding nine run lead. In the eighth inning, rain began to fall again and the crowd, with their team safely ahead, began to call for a halt to the game. Although players and fans were drenched and the field had turned to mush, play continued. In the top of the ninth, the Atlantics rallied with four runs to pull within five. But, with a runner on second base the rain came down even harder and the umpire called the game. The score reverted to that of the previous inning; the Atlantics had lost 18–9.

The following week, the return match was played at Union Grounds. Despite the loss in Philadelphia, the oddsmakers favored the Atlantics to even the series. Swapping leads several times through the early innings, the Athletics led 9–8 at the end of five. Then, the disheartened Brooklyn fans watched the Athletics go on a tear. The *Daily Eagle* marveled at the Athletics' hitting display: "They hit here, they hit there, they hit everywhere except within the reach of their opponents. This inning was the finest display of batting that was ever witnessed on the Union Grounds."[7]

Before the inning was over, the Athletics had scored 14 runs, putting the game out of reach. Adding insult to injury, they scored an additional 14 runs over the next two innings, drubbing the Atlantics 37–13.

The Athletics and their fans who had made the trip north were jubilant. According to the *Daily Eagle*'s report:

> The Philadelphians are crazy. Intoxicated with joy, they embrace their players and would fairly eat them up in their extravagances. The Atlantics coolly pick up their bats and go to their dressing rooms, and to their credit be it said, they bore their defeat manfully and gentlemanly.

For the first time ever, the Athletics had beaten the Atlantics on the Brooklyn club's home grounds. To the delight of Philadelphians, the *Clipper* in its September 12 issue would immortalize the event with an unusual page one illustration of the game. Sounding a note of consolation, one of the Atlantics' officials told the *Daily Eagle*, "[the Athletics] had to import Reach and Fisler, their two best players, from Brooklyn to beat us ... Brooklyn has yet got the best players."[8] But hometown heroes were rapidly becoming a dying breed. In fact, Brooklyn players could be found on the rosters of clubs all over the country. Fox, Norton, Fletcher, and Forker were on the Washington Nationals; Flanly, Galvin, Swandell, and Devyr on the Mutuals of New York; Lennon and Treacy with the Athletics of Chicago; Reach with the Philadelphia Athletics; Reach on the Olympic of Washington; Rogers on the Lowell Club of Boston; Brainard with Cincinnati; and Pratt with Boston's Tri-Mountain Club. In a few short years, most of the Atlantic players would be lured away from Brooklyn.

Although reeling from two successive losses to the Athletics, the season was far from over for the Atlantics. Only a few days later, the Atlantics had the opportunity to take revenge on the Unions who captured the championship from them in 1867. The *Daily Eagle*, in its commentary before the first Union game, became the Atlantics' best cheerleader while taking a jab at the Atlantics' critics:

> There has been developed since Monday's game a number of base ballists, who always knew the Atlantics could not play ball; who always thought the Atlantics were an over rated club. But, for the most part these gentlemen are those, whose praise of the Atlantics a few days ago was the very loudest. There are others, however, who honestly think they have discovered signs of weakness in the nine and that they will have no chance with the Unions. For our own part we are just as confident that our pet club of Brooklyn will defeat the Unions as we are that the Athletics will defeat the same club, and we are just as confident that if the Atlantic and Athletics should meet again this season that the Athletics would be a defeated party. To-day the strongest club in the United States is the Atlantic Club... So

we think that on Thursday, the Atlantics will go into the game with a determination that will completely rout the Unions from the first. For the sake of your own names boys, have no mercy, but hammer from the start.[9]

On Thursday the customarily large crowd gathered at Union Grounds. The oddsmakers, lacking the *Daily Eagle*'s confidence, favored the Unions to win. In an evenly played match, the Atlantics held a 7–4 lead after five innings. In the sixth inning, the Unions rallied with three runs. In the inning, Union third baseman, Ed Shelley, hit a line drive off the forehead of Atlantic pitcher George Zettlein. The Atlantic players rushed to the pitching box, fearing that their star was lost for the game. But "The Charmer," amidst the applause of the Atlantic faithful, hung on to complete the inning and shut out the Unions the remainder of the game. In the seventh inning, reminiscent of the Athletics' batting the week before, the Atlantics unleashed an awesome hitting attack. In the words of the *Daily Eagle*:

> The batting of the Atlantics in this inning far exceeded that of the Athletics, both in safety and powerful strokes. They batted the balls long and they batted them short, they batted them left and they batted them right, in short, just where the Union fielders could not get at them. After awhile they changed the old woman, and put George Wright in, but it made no difference. They hit him away, and before they got done had scored fifteen runs.[10]

By the end of play, the Atlantics had come off with a convincing 31–7 victory. They would have to wait nearly a month for the rematch with the Unions in Morrisania.

With their confidence bolstered, on September 11 the Atlantics traveled to New Jersey for another revenge match against the Irvington Club. The two previous years the Atlantics had lost to the Irvingtons on the New Jersey club's home grounds. This time the Atlantics literally escaped with a 13–6 win when they were pursued by "drunken rowdies" following the game.[11] Fortunately, the locals were content to fight among themselves as the Atlantics quickly caught a horse car to Newark.

The Atlantics won another road game against the Haymakers in Troy before returning to the friendly confines of Union Grounds where they hosted the Cincinnati Red Stockings. A large crowd came out to watch the team which included a number of former New York and Brooklyn players, including Harry Wright of the old Knickerbockers, John Hatfield from the Mutuals, and the former Atlantic Asa Brainard.[12] The spectators also marveled at the new Cincinnati uniform of white flannels trimmed in red, red belts and stockings, and pants fastened at the knee.

Although Cincinnati was a year away from formulating its dominant nine, it was still one of the best clubs from the West. But, the Atlantics easily handled the team from "Porkopolis," defeating them 31–12.

On October 6 the Atlantics traveled across the East River to Morrisania to meet the Unions in their return match.[13] A large contingent of Brooklyn fans made the ferry trip to Mott Haven, but were too numerous to fit on but one horse car going to Morrisania. About half the crowd was forced to walk four miles to the ball grounds and missed the opening innings. The Brooklyn cranks who arrived late had to fight for viewing space amidst the largest crowd of the season at Union Park. Among the enthusiastic spectators, the *Clipper* noted the presence of "a bevy of Westchester's fairest daughters."[14]

Unfortunately for the Brooklyn cranks who arrived late, the game began on time at 3 o'clock. The Unions jumped to an early 5–0 lead at the end of two innings. But in the third inning, the Atlantic bats came alive, scoring three in that inning and 24 overall in the game. Meanwhile, Zettlein "skunked" the Unions in six of the final seven innings, holding them to a total of eight runs. Vindicated in its confidence, the *Daily Eagle* crowed that the game "was won by the Atlantics and the championship is again borne by them, as the *Eagle* has so often predicted it would."[15]

At 9 o'clock that evening, the Atlantics arrived back at the Fulton Ferry House. The *Daily Eagle* described the scene as the conquering heroes returned to Brooklyn:

> ...unusual excitement was observed at the Ferry; then the sounds of joyous and triumphant voices were heard. The astonished denizens rushed to their doors and windows and a strange sight greeted their eyes. In procession came three carriages, and in front of the first was elevated a broom, the pine handle of which was ornamented with gay colored ribbons; the occupants of the carriages appeared to be enjoying a happy state of feeling. Inquiry was made and the well-informed were heard to say that it was the Atlantic Club returning from Morrisania, after playing with the Union Club, and that the broom carried in front meant that having whipped the champions, it could now sweep everything out of its way. This was the truth; it meant that the Atlantics had regained the championship and that the Unions had lost it.[16]

How quickly the Atlantics' fortunes had changed. Only a month before they were soundly defeated twice by the Athletics. But, this was prior to the Atlantics' matches against the reigning champion Unions and thus had no bearing on the championship. Before the month was out, however, the Atlantics' fortunes would change yet again.

Less than a week following their triumph over the Unions, the

Atlantics raised their "whip pennant" on the flag pole at Union ground before their contest with the Mutuals of New York.[17] It appeared to be an easy match for the Atlantics. The Mutuals had suffered through a disappointing season, losing to the Athletics, the Keystones, the Haymakers, the Unions, the Actives, and Cincinnati. About five thousand fans, a relatively small crowd for a championship match, was on hand for the game. The Mutuals took a 7–2 lead at the end of two innings, but the Atlantics came back to tie the game at 9 at the end of four. The Mutuals regained the lead with a six run outburst in the sixth inning. The Atlantic fans remained confident; their team had often come from behind to win. But, at game's end they fell short by two, losing 25–23. The wagering fans that lost money complained that the Atlantics had thrown the game, figuring to win the series in the rubber match. The Atlantics did play terribly in the field, every player except Zettlein guilty of muffs. If the Atlantics were guilty of hippodroming, the pressure was on to take two consecutive games from the Mutuals.

The *Clipper* set the stage for the return match at Union Grounds:

> How anxiously the ball playing fraternity looked at the clouds on the morning of the 26th! How relieved they felt when they observed that the clouds were thin and light; that the wind was sending them from west to east, and that old Sol was peeping cheerfully out between them and that everything augured for a fine day! But why this anxious examining of the heavens? Why should the prospect of a fine day bring more delight than on any other day? Any member of the base ball world would answer these questions by saying, "The Mutuals and the Atlantics play the home and home game today, and everybody wants to see it."[18]

The fielding of both teams was sharp through the first three innings, with each team only managing one run. The hitting of both clubs picked up in the next two innings with the Mutuals taking an 8–7 lead. The Atlantic fans began to breath a sigh of relief when their team surged ahead, scoring five runs in the top of the sixth. But, the Mutuals countered with nine tallies in the bottom half of the inning, and then skunked the Atlantics in the top of the seventh. When the New York club added four more runs in the bottom of the seventh, the Atlantics and their fans were demoralized. This time the Brooklyn club had dug a hole from which it could not escape. The Atlantics lost the game and their short-lived championship to the Mutuals by a final score of 28–17. According to the *Daily Eagle*:

> The Atlantics went to their rooms and without a word changed their garments. They sadly pulled down the streamer they threw to the breeze so

proudly two weeks before, and laid by for another season ... Brooklyn last night was in sackcloth and ashes...[19]

The Mutuals, the club of Boss Tweed and Tammany Hall, after a decade of failed attempts had finally overtaken the Atlantics. The *Daily Eagle* proclaimed them "the champion ball players of the United States and consequently of the *World*." For the first time a New York club had gained the championship.

In this dramatic season of strange twists and turns there was yet one more scene to be played at Union Grounds. The Unions met the Mutuals in the rubber match of their series on October 28. Short two of their regular nine players, the Unions upset the third "championship" team of the year by a score of 27–21. The game was a show of muffin play. Ten runs scored by the Mutuals in the second inning resulted from six Union errors. Outdoing the Unions, the Mutuals committed 12 errors in the third inning, which led to 12 Union runs. "Fine play," quipped the *Daily Eagle*, "for two clubs occupying the position they do in the baseball world."[20] But, exactly what position did these clubs occupy? Although it appeared that the Unions had regained the throne that they relinquished to the Atlantics earlier in the season, the informal convention determining the championship had become quite muddled.

Before the beginning of the 1868 season, *New York Clipper* editor Frank Queen once again offered a Silver Ball trophy to the championship team for that year and individual trophies to the best players at each position. Late in the summer Queen was reluctant to award the trophy, arguing that the Philadelphia Athletics deserved the opportunity to play a final series for the championship.[21] But, as the season was drawing to a close, the Athletics were unwilling or unable to arrange a final series.[22] Queen awarded the all-star player trophies but held onto the Silver Ball for the best team.[23] It was anybody's guess who was the championship club. The press referred to the Mutuals as the top team, overlooking the fact that the Unions had won their series from the Mutuals after the Mutuals had assumed the title.

To further confuse the matter, the following year the *Clipper* arranged a series between the Mutuals and the Athletics to determine the championship of 1868. In September, the Athletics swept two games from the Mutuals.[24] Thus, near the end of the 1869 season, the championship team of 1868 was crowned. By this time the ambiguity of the title had reached a point where newspapers reports would refer to various teams as the "nominal" championship club. In the fall of 1868, the *Clipper* began reporting on various regional championships: the "gold ball championship of

Western and Central New York," the "championship of the Western Reserve" (Cleveland), the "silver ball championship of Maryland," the "gold ball championship of Wisconsin," the "championship of the West," and the "Championship of the Northwest."[25]

In an effort to develop a truly unified national game, after the 1868 season Henry Chadwick challenged the NABBP to draw up a code of rules governing the arrangement of matches and the determination of the championship.[26] Moreover, he called on the Association to recognize the de facto existence of professional clubs. In its winter meeting the NABBP failed to address the former issue, but it finally dealt, at least minimally, with the issue of professionalism. According to a new rule established: "All players who play base-ball for money, or who shall at any time receive compensation for their services as players, shall be considered *professional* players; and all others shall be regarded as *amateur* players."[27]

The gates were now open for baseball to be run openly as a business, and professional clubs scurried to hire the top players. The *Daily Eagle* reported rumors that George Wright and Charlie Sweasy of the Unions would be playing for Cincinnati the next year. In November, four different clubs (Unions, Cincinnati, Washington Nationals and the Mutuals) each claimed that Wright had promised to play for them.[28] Various rumors had Charley Bearman of the Mutuals jumping to six different clubs.[29] Revolving reached new heights as players offered their services on the players market.

In 1869, the first year of openly professional play, the Eckfords and the Atlantics would once again battle for the "nominal" championship. But a team from the West, Cincinnati's first "big red machine," the Red Stockings, would soon overshadow the local rivalry.

The Mutuals entered the season as the "nominal" champion, but the Eckfords challenged them early in the season. In a rain shortened game on June 5, the Eckfords defeated the Mutuals by a score of 6–1.[30] The Eckfords put on a fine display of fielding, committing not a single error. The return match was set for July 3. In the meantime, both teams, along with the Atlantics, awaited the arrival of the Red Stockings in Brooklyn.

The Red Stockings were a relatively new club, organized by Cincinnati lawyer Aaron Champion in 1867.[31] Intent from the start on creating a profitable business enterprise, Champion issued $11,000 in stock to renovate the Red Stockings Union Grounds. He also brought in Harry Wright, who played professionally for Champion's Union Cricket Club, as player-manager. In 1869, Champion sold an additional $15,000 in stock to buy the best players in the country. Although Champion's labor recruiters were unsuccessful in luring the winners of the *Clipper*'s Silver

Ball trophies, in effect the all-star team of 1868, Harry Wright was able to put together a stellar lineup for the 1869 season.

In the formidable Red Stockings roster, Andy Leonard—who had played with the Irvingtons of New Jersey—and Cal McVey from the Actives of Indianapolis joined Harry Wright, who had started playing with the New York Knickerbockers, in the outfield. The infield featured Freddie Waterman from the New York Mutuals; Harry's brother George, late of the Unions of Morissania and the Washington Nationals; Charley Sweasy from the Irvingtons of New Jersey; and Charley Gould, the only native of Cincinnati, who played with the Cincinnati Buckeyes. Doug Allison from the Geary Club of Philadelphia. Wright was the catcher. The former Excelsior, Asa Brainard, was the pitcher.

While in Brooklyn, Brainard had the misfortune of playing on a less than competitive team where his pitching was always compared to the Excelsiors' fallen hero Jim Creighton. On the powerful Red Stockings, he became a star pitcher. Now in the public eye, Cincinnati fans would call him "The Count" for his stylish dress and manners.[32] He would also earn the reputation of being one of baseball's first "oddball" pitchers. According to baseball historian David Voigt, Brainard was a hypochondriac who often complained of imaginary ailments.[33] Much to the consternation of Reds manager Harry Wright, he also skipped practices, missed trains, and enjoyed the nightlife. His behavior on the field at times bordered on the bizarre. When Brainard was pitching in one 1869 contest, a rabbit ran across the field. Unmindful of two runners on base at the time, Brainard threw the ball at the bounding bunny, allowing both runners to score.

Although the Red Stockings were not the first club with professional players, it was the first openly professional team comprised entirely of players under written contract to play the season. Salaries ranged from $600 to $1,200 for the season, which ran from March 15 through November 15. Harry Wright may have been paid as much as $2,000 to play and manage the team.

The Red Stockings became a model, not only for its financial organization, but also for its approach to playing the game. Under the tutelage of Harry Wright, the team was put through a rigorous regimen of training and practice, drilling on the finer points of play, and melding the individual talents into an efficient unit. Following the season, the *Clipper* would recognize the key to the Red Stockings' success:

> Their *forte* is in supporting one another... As individual players in fielding there is not one who is superior to others in the same position in rival clubs,

but their strength lies in their working in harmony: and as the enthusiastic "Porkites" assert, "Our boys work like a regular machine, no jarring of parts, but each part fits in and works without discord."[34]

On the evening of June 14 the Red Stockings arrived in New York from New Haven where their scheduled match with Yale had been rained out.[35] They had won all 17 of their matches in the early season, but in their next three games in Brooklyn they would be tested against three of the best teams in the country.

Rain fell throughout the morning of the 15th, but the sky cleared by mid-day for the opening match at Union Grounds against the Mutuals. The small crowd of only 1,500 people would witness what was arguably one of the best-played games in the young history of baseball. The Mutuals threatened in the opening frame, but stranded two runners on base without scoring. In the bottom of the first, Doug Allison drove in Cincinnati's first run with a "daisy cutter" between shortstop's legs. The Red Stockings added another run in the third to take a 2–0 lead. The score remained the same through the next four innings as each team exhibited exceptional defensive play. In the top of the eighth, Everett Mills brought the crowd to life when he drove in the Mutuals' first run with a line drive to right field. Cheers turned to groans, however, when Mills was cut down trying to stretch his hit into a double. In the bottom of the eighth the Red Stockings threatened to score, but Mutual center fielder Charley Hunt saved a run when he ran down a long drive to right center field. The Mutuals rallied in the ninth inning with three consecutive hits that tied the game. With two runners on base and none out, third baseman Fred Waterman intentionally dropped a pop fly on the infield, allowing him to start a third-to-second double play that stunned the crowd. In the words of the *Clipper*:

> All this happened in less time than it takes to relate it, and was performed so quickly as to take the spectators completely by surprise. When they realized the situation, cheer after cheer rent the air at the sharpness of the Western chaps, and even the partisans of the Mutuals could not help but admire the trick.

Allison, the catcher, then caught a foul pop-up for the third out, sending the game into the bottom of the ninth knotted at two.

After eight innings of brilliant fielding play by the Mutuals, matching the celebrated Red Stockings throughout the game, the New York club's defense collapsed in the bottom of the ninth. On a sharp grounder to third, Asa Brainard made it all the way to third on an errant throw by Marty Swandell, and then came home on a passed ball by the catcher.

Charlie Sweasy followed with a triple and scored on a wild pitch before the Mutuals could retire the side. The Red Stockings had survived with a 4–2 victory. The Mutuals' fielding was exceptional, but the Porkopolis team's play was flawless. In its evaluation of the game, the *Clipper*, often guilty of overzealous superlatives, this time was probably close to the mark:

> Without exception, the game never had its equal and probably never will have. From first to last, the exhibition of fielding was the best ever seen in this vicinity, and we doubt it like was ever witnessed anywhere. The "Red Stockings" exceeded all expectations formed of their fielding powers, and did not make an error during the game that gave the Mutuals a run.

The following day the Atlantics hosted the Red Stockings at Capitoline Grounds. The weather had cleared and now fans and ball players from all over the region had come out to see the notorious team from the West play the Bedford Boys. Three hours before the game, the *Daily Eagle* reporter observed the scene in downtown Brooklyn:

Souvenirs of Atlantic victories. (Spalding Collection, New York Public Library.)

As early as twelve o'clock the stream began to flow across Fulton Ferry, and every car that passed the *Eagle* office was black with people, who not only climbed to the top but hung on the sides. Market wagons, trucks, carts, and every other kind of vehicle that would go on wheels were to be seen full with ball players, anxious to get to the grounds as soon as possible.[36]

A half an hour before game time, 12,000 fans had packed into Capitoline while many more filled the embankments, houses and trees around the grounds.

Fans who were expecting a replay of the defensive battle of the day before were sorely disappointed. Hard hitting by Cincinnati and miserable fielding by the Atlantics resulted in 18 runs for the Red Stockings in the first three innings while the Atlantics were "whitewashed." The Atlantics finally managed to score a run in the fourth inning and ten overall for the game, but the Red Stockings countered with ten more runs of their own and easily won the game 23–10. The disappointed Atlantic fans audibly voiced their displeasure throughout the game as their favorites muffed one play after another. "Old Reliable" Joe Start, alone, made five errors in the match. "The Atlantics were out-played at every point," concluded the *Daily Eagle*. "They were out-batted and out-fielded. Never since the club has been a club, has it played such a poor game."

That evening at the Atlantics' new headquarters, Henry's Saloon, on Fulton Street near the courthouse, friends and fellow club members gathered to commiserate over their team's loss. Praise could be heard of the outstanding play of the "Western Champions" as well as laments over the contrasting "muffinism" of the Atlantic nine. A crowd had gathered at the trophy case, which displayed the numerous game balls won by the Atlantics. The *Daily Eagle* reporter on hand either overheard or created the comments of one Atlantic follower: "I tell ye what fellers, when these game balls were won, the Atlantics thought they had something to learn in base ball and they kept a practicin' to learn, not now-a-days, they think they know all there is to know about it, and they won't practice among themselves."

Whether fictionalized or not, the comment struck at the heart of the Atlantics' problem and indicated the changing nature of the game. The Atlantics were caught in the transition from amateur or semi-professional to a full-fledged professional game. Although many of their players had been compensated in one way or another and had shared the gate receipts in matches throughout the 1860s, most had other occupations and business interests that occupied a significant portion of their time. In contrast, the Red Stockings were full-time baseball players during the playing season who could devote all their time and energy to perfecting their game. They would travel coast to coast in the summer of 1869 while the Atlantics stayed close to home, playing the majority of their games in Brooklyn. In order to play in the "big league" teams would have to adopt the Red Stockings' model of strong financial backing and player dedication to training and practice. Over the next few seasons, the Atlantics would be ambivalent over which road to take.

On June 17 the Red Stockings went for a sweep of their series in Brooklyn when they took on the Eckfords at Union Grounds.[37] The growing reputation of the Cincinnati club brought out another large crowd to watch the contest. Like the day before, the Red Stockings took an early lead, scoring 13 runs in the first four innings while "skunking" the Eckfords. The fielding play of the Eckfords was considerably better than the Atlantics, but they could not match the heavy hitting and flawless play of Cincinnati. The Red Stockings held a commanding 24–4 lead at the end of seven innings. Normally with the victory out of reach for the home team, many of the fans would take an early leave in hopes of beating the postgame traffic. But on this day, most of the Brooklyn spectators stayed glued to their seats, marveling at the outstanding play of the western club until the final out of the game. The Eckfords managed to score one more run, but fell far short, losing the game 24–5.

Undaunted, the Eckfords in July took their best of three series from the Mutuals and regained the "championship" title.[38] They then embarked on an extensive western road trip, playing 11 games in 12 days in eight different cities. On August 9 and 10 in Oswego, New York, the Eckfords beat the Ontario Club 37–9 and the Central Citys of Syracuse 41–13. On the 11th, in Rochester they beat the Alerts 38–27. The following day they were in Cleveland where they defeated the Forest Citys 41–27. In Mansfield, Ohio, on the 13th they were victorious over the Independents by a 34–19 margin. On the 14th they traveled to Cincinnati and defeated the Buckeyes 37–16. Following a well-earned day's rest, on the 16th the Eckfords suffered their only defeat of the road trip to the hands of the Red Stockings by a score of 45–18. With little time to recover, the Brooklyn club then traveled to Detroit where they beat that city's club 43–12. Returning east, in Buffalo they continued to win, defeating the Niagaras 24–18 on August 19th and the Young Canadiens 29–16 the following day. For their final game, they stopped in Troy, New York, where they slipped by the Haymakers 20–17. The Eckfords had completed the longest road trip in their club's history, defeating every team except the Red Stockings. Back home in Brooklyn, their confidence was bolstered as they prepared for their series with their local rivals the Atlantics.

On September 6, the Eckfords and the Atlantics met in their first match for what the *Clipper* was now calling the "mythical white pennant."[39] The 8,000 fans at Capitoline would be treated to an outstanding display of hitting by both Brooklyn clubs. Going into the bottom of the fourth the Atlantics had built up a 16–6 lead. The Eckfords came back with 12 runs in the bottom of the inning to regain the lead. But, the Atlantics put together two back-to-back big innings of their own in the 6th and 7th and went on to cruise to a convincing 45–25 victory.

The second match of the series was played a month later at Union Grounds. The *Clipper* noted that "knowing ones" among the baseball fraternity speculated that the Atlantics would throw the game in order to set up a third match.[40] This may account for the relatively small crowd of 3,000 that showed up in Williamsburg. It may also account for the poor fielding, hitting and pitching of the Atlantics. The Eckfords came away with an easy 25–9 win.

On a cold and blustery day in early November, the two Brooklyn clubs met to decide the championship at Union Grounds.[41] The carnival-like atmosphere and massive crowds which had attended many championship matches in the past at Cammayer's ball park was no longer evident. Whether it was the late fall chill or diminishing interest, only 1,200–1,500 fans showed up for the match. Despite the cold, both teams fought a close battle throughout. After the Atlantics took an early lead, the Eckfords went ahead with six runs in the fifth inning. The rally was cut short, however, when Ed Pinkham was tagged out trying to steal third base. The Atlantics regained the lead in the sixth inning and held a five run margin when the Eckfords came to bat in the bottom of the ninth. The temperature had dropped throughout the afternoon and the wind had increased. By this time, according to the *Clipper*, everyone was nearly frozen. In their last time at bat the Eckfords pushed one run across, but once again their rally was killed when Pinkham was cut down at home plate on a sharp throw from Pearce to Ferguson. The Atlantics had regained the "championship," but few fans remained to celebrate.

Following their victory, the Atlantics challenged the Red Stockings to a return match to determine the "absolute championship." But Cincinnati declined the offer, saying that it had closed its season and that its players' contracts had expired.[42] When the *Clipper* claimed that the Atlantics made the challenge knowing that the Red Stockings would be unwilling to play, the *Daily Eagle* defended its local team and attacked the *Clipper* for making false accusations. In defending the Atlantics, the *Daily Eagle* made a prescient observation about the Red Stockings that had the ring of boosterism at the time but would be vindicated in the following season:

New York Fashions—From an 1870 color lithograph possibly issued by the Peck & Snyder sporting goods company. Ballplayers are modeling the latest fashions in baseball uniforms at Union Grounds in Brooklyn. (Brooklyn Public Library, Brooklyn Collection.)

> The position of the Atlantic club is too high for the Cincinnati Club to touch. The "Red Stockings" may be the better club to-day. But its popularity is of the ephemeral kind, that lives to-day and dies tomorrow. The history of the Atlantic Club is such as the "Red Stockings" never can reach. When those men in Cincinnati are tired of spending their money to support such an expensive club, the "Red Stockings" will melt away like dew before the morning sun. The excitement of having a first-class club may be very well now, but the first defeat of the "Red Stockings" will make it a thing of the past.[43]

Regardless of what the future held, at the end of the memorable baseball season of 1869, the Cincinnati Red Stockings were by all accounts, even the *Daily Eagle*'s, the best team in baseball.[44] They had traveled nearly 12,000 miles from coast to coast, winning 57 games with professional teams without suffering a defeat. Not since the Atlantics' championship club in the mid–1860s had a team appeared so invincible.

When the 1870 season opened, the baseball fraternity had high expectations for an even more exciting year. The "experiment" in professional play the year before appeared to be a success. The Red Stockings had shown what a professional team run as a business could do in raising the standards of play. Going into the new season, the Atlantics' management announced that its players had freed themselves of outside commitments to dedicate themselves to the game. The much-improved Eckfords strengthened their roster by acquiring Ed Duffy from the Mutuals. The White Stockings of Chicago and the Forest Citys of Rockford threatened to shift the balance of baseball dominance from the Northeast to the West.

Although the professional game proved successful on the field, beneath the surface the picture was less rosy. The Cincinnati investors who staked the best team money could buy in 1869 were disappointed when the club barely turned a profit.[45] Relatively large salaries and travel expenses required sizeable income from gate receipts. In large market areas like Brooklyn, the team was financially successful. In smaller cities, however, gate receipts would not cover expenses. Barnstorming would prove to be a fatal flaw in the business model developed by the Red Stockings.

Hoping to maximize profits where they could, Cincinnati demanded that the Atlantics raise their admission fee for the Reds games at Capitoline from 25 to 50 cents and demanded a 40 percent share of the gate receipts.[46] Since the Atlantics had to share their cut with the Capitoline owners, this would have significantly affected their income. Sensing an unfavorable response from Brooklyn fans, the Atlantics initially refused and made the Red Stocking demands public. But, when Cincinnati visited Brooklyn in June, the Atlantics had acceded at least to the demand for increased admission: Brooklyn fans faced a 100 percent increase in the price of admission to watch their team play the Reds.

In the early part of the season, the Reds continued their winning streak, reeling off 27 consecutive victories. They then made their much-anticipated trip to Brooklyn. On June 13, a crowd of 10,000 fans gathered at Union Grounds.[47] In an unusually low scoring defensive battle the year before, Cincinnati edged out a 4–2 victory over the Mutuals. This time, however, the Red Stockings decisively beat the Mutuals 16–3. The following day the team from "Porkopolis" moved to Capitoline Grounds to face the Atlantics. The village of Bedford, the site of many rancorous and hotly contested battles, would once again host one of the most dramatic matches in baseball's early history. On June 14 the Atlantics would enjoy perhaps their finest hour.

A crowd of 9,000 spectators paid the 50-cent admission fee to watch the match.[48] Their spirits were dampened early when the Red Stockings jumped to a 3–0 lead after three innings. But surprisingly, Cincinnati

Monumental game between the Cincinnati Red Stockings and the Brooklyn Atlantics on June 20, 1870, at Capitoline Grounds, Brooklyn. (From *Harper's Weekly*, July 2, 1870).

errors led to two Atlantic runs in the fourth and sixth innings, giving the home team a 4–3 lead. "The crowd," according to the *Clipper*, "yelled themselves hoarse, as they began to think victory for the Brooklynites as among the possibilities."[49] The Reds quieted the crowd when they regained the lead, scoring two runs in the seventh. In the bottom of the eighth, Charley Smith hit a towering drive over the left fielder's head for a triple. Joe Start followed with a single to drive in the tying run. The teams entered the final frame tied at five. The Red Stockings threatened again in the top of the ninth, but George Wright hit into an inning ending double play.

With the game knotted at the end of regulation play, it appeared that the Atlantics were satisfied with a tie. When they gathered their bats and headed for the clubhouse, fans rushed out onto the field. Confusion reigned as Aaron Champion and Harry Wright lobbied the umpire, Charley Mills from the Mutual Club, for the game to continue. Unsure of what to do, Mills consulted with Henry Chadwick who was covering the game as a reporter, but was also a member of the Association's Rules Committee. Chadwick ruled that the game should be continued. Meanwhile, with the Bedford cranks sharing the field with the Red Stocking players, the Atlantics were in their clubhouse changing out of their uniforms. Mills went to the Atlantics' clubhouse and ordered Atlantics captain Bob Ferguson to get his team back on the field or they would forfeit the game. When the Atlantics finally returned to the field, the Atlantic fans met them, according to the *Clipper*, with an "icy silence."

In the 10th inning, two players known for their "headwork" showed why they had justly earned their reputations. With one out and a runner on first, the Atlantics' Dickey Pearce hit one of his trademark "fair-foul" hits, dropping the ball down the third base line so that it rolled foul, out of the reach of the third baseman. Until the rule was changed in 1877, a ball hit fair on the infield did not have to pass first or third base before rolling foul. Pearce's strategic place hits were arguably the first "bunt" hits in baseball. With runners now on first and second and one out, Cincinnati shortstop George Wright made a defensive play that he had become known for. He intentionally dropped a pop fly on the infield, threw to third, forcing the runner from second. The third baseman, Waterman, then returned the throw to second to complete an inning ending double play. Until the "infield fly rule" was implemented, Wright and other "scientific" infielders would employ this strategy to effectively deceive base runners.

The game moved to the 11th inning. Among the spectators, according to the *Clipper*, the "degree of excitement was unprecedented; the suspense was at times painful." But the Atlantics' fans were soon disappointed when the Red Stocking scored two runs. With their backs to the wall, the Atlantics came to bat in the bottom of the 11th. With a runner on third, Joe Start hit a towering drive to right field that landed at the edge of the crowd. When the right fielder, Cal McVey ran to retrieve the ball, a zealous fan jumped on his back. McVey wrestled free, and returned the ball to the infield, too late to prevent Start from reaching third base. The fan was promptly arrested, but luckily for the Atlantics, the umpire did not call interference. Next at bat was switch-hitting Bob Ferguson. Batting left-handed, he pulled a ball to right field, driving in Start to tie the game. The crowd erupted and "for a minute nothing could be heard for the yells and cheering which resounded from the crowd." George Zettlein then came to the plate and hit a line drive that was muffed by the second baseman Sweasy, allowing Ferguson to score all the way from first base with the winning run. According to the *Daily Eagle*:

> Hats, coats, sticks and crutches even, darkened the air, thrown up by the enthusiastic attendants on the ball field. The crowd broke from their confines, and rushed upon the Atlantic players, most of whom were elevated upon their shoulders and carried to the club-house. As the face or uniform of an Atlantic was discovered struggling through the crowd, he was immensely cheered, and as they drew near to the house, the ladies occupying the windows waved their handkerchiefs, and sent up their shrill voices in behalf of the "Brooklyn" boys. One enthusiastic individual mounted a shed and began ringing a large bell he found there, much to the delight of the crowd.

During the afternoon, a large crowd had gathered at the Atlantics' headquarters to await the results of the game. The *Daily Eagle* described the scene when reports came in of the Atlantics' victory:

…an immense crowd gathered on the sidewalks in front of the building and filled the bar room, and when the glorious news came down that the Atlantics had won the game, such a shout went up as startled all the neighborhood round, the crowd rapidly increased, so that it was almost impossible to reach the door. The Atlantic nine, as they returned from the ground, received a perfect ovation and were petted the entire evening. As it grew dark, the windows of the Club room were illuminated, and the members and their friends congregated to hold a jubilation meeting. The Hon. John C. Jacobs was captured in the vicinity of the Club House by some enthusiastic members, and hurried into the room of the Atlantic Club to make a speech, which he did, amid the enthusiastic plaudits of the assemblage. In other places, in fact all over town, the great topic of conversation was the glorious victory of the Atlantic Club.

The following day the *Daily Eagle* could not contain its civic pride in heralding the Atlantics' victory: "It was the greatest game ever played between the greatest clubs that ever played, and as usual, when Brooklyn is pitted against the universe, the universe is number two."[50] In contrast to the Cincinnati team, which was comprised almost entirely of players from the Northeast, this was "a Brooklyn victory won by Brooklyn boys."

The *Daily Eagle*'s description of the public's response would sound strikingly similar to the Brooklyn faithful's celebration following their beloved Dodgers' World Series victory in 1955:

The deep chord which the victory vibrated in the city's heart, more than anything we know of, demonstrated the depth and keenness of the sentiment of local pride, of pride in Brooklyn, which is so distinguishing a characteristic of this people. The staidest stockholder, and the doughiest directors broke bottle over the battle of the gods. The Rink was, as to all its very audience, marked by little conversation other than such as related to the game. The Park Theatre, Hooley's, and the Olympian braves were suffused with a like excitement. Even casual Christians in occasional prayer-meetings acknowledged the unction of victory, and exorted the ungodly to make a home run for glory at once.

One Atlantic fan was inspired to hail the Bedford conquerors in verse:

> Well done, Atlantics, one and all.
>   You've nobly won the fight;
> You've vanquished those who vanquished all.
>   Though trying all their might.
>
> Right proud is Brooklyn of her nine!
> Atlantics never tire,
> There is no other Nine
> Can stand their raking fire!

> Long may the pennon wave,
>> With your banner in the sky;
> Loud cheers shall meet the brave.
> Atlantics, never die!
>
> Then fill your glasses high—
>> We'll "flip a cork" for wine—
> May they never lose a game,
>> The old Atlantic Nine!

Word spread rapidly throughout the country of the Atlantic's victory over the Red Stockings. The Cincinnati newspapers were subdued in their responses and tried to minimize the Red Stockings' loss.[51] The *Commercial* and the *Inquirer* each referred to the loss as a "slight reversal" of fortune. The *Gazetteer* claimed that if the Cincinnati team had not been "fagged out" from their long road trip they would have "made the nine victorious Atlantics feel like beaten Pacifics."

In Chicago, where the White Stockings had become the Reds' top western rival, baseball fans were jubilant. A *Chicago Tribune* sportswriter, reporting from Cincinnati, could not contain his mockery of the Porkopolis faithful:

> The news of the defeat of the Red Stockings by the Atlantics, fell upon the inhabitants of this town like a thunderclap out of a sunny sky. The death of Dickens did not create anything like as profound sensation, because Dickens was known only to a few newspaper men and others, while the boys with the red hose were known and beloved everywhere from the Ohio to the railroad depot, and from the depot back again to the Ohio. [Charles Dickens had died only the week before in England.] ... strong men were seen to drop tears on the sidewalk, women rushed frantically into mourning stores to procure somber apparel, and little boys and girls went home sobbing, and at this moment they are sitting in sackcloth and ashes... MID-NIGHT—Nobody in bed yet. Several babies cut their teeth prematurely, owing to the excitement, two have been attacked suddenly by measles, and seven two-year olds have been sent to the Insane Asylum. The saloons are in full blast, everybody getting drunk to drown his misery, and everything is going to smash...

For Cincinnati fans and investors, the situation would only get worse. Although the Red Stockings rebounded the next two days with convincing wins over the Unions and the Eckfords, they would lose four more games during the season, including a match with the Chicago White Stockings and a second game with the Atlantics. Attendance at home and on the road declined. Manager Harry Wright, praised for his strict discipline of his players, both on and off the field, appeared to be losing control when newspapers reported incidents of public intoxication and quarreling among Reds teammates.[52] Sensing the end was in sight, Reds president Aaron Champion, along with the club's vice president and secretary, resigned. In November, the club went out of business.[53]

The Atlantics fared even worse for the remainder of the season. As exhibited in the Cincinnati games they could play extremely well. But, at other times they played like a muffin team.[54] Although they took their series against the Red Stockings, Eckfords, and Unions, they came up short in their series against the Athletics, Mutuals, White Stockings, and Haymakers of Troy. On October 8, they lost for the first time in their history to the amateur Stars from Brooklyn by a score of 31–24. By the end of the season, the Atlantics' record against professional teams stood at 21 wins and 16 losses. The slumping Eckfords ended the season with a losing record of 12–16. Only two of the Eckfords' victories were against professional teams.

In November, the *Daily Eagle* reported that the Atlantic nine had broken up and that the club would be reorganized as an amateur team in 1871.[55] The Chicago White Stockings were rumored to be bidding for the services of Ferguson, Start, and Pearce. Chapman and Hall were likely to be heading for Indianapolis. Zettlein was "on the fence, and open for cash terms for any leading organization."

Throughout organized baseball's first decade, the Atlantics either reigned as champion or contended for the throne. Formed as a largely Irish working class club funded by the local political machine, the Atlantics would be throughout its history a local team of players mostly born and raised in Brooklyn. The names of such Brooklyn natives as Pearce, Chapman, Ferguson and Zettlein would become legendary.

Dickey Pearce, one of the original members of the club, would play 17 years for the Atlantics.[56] A veritable cannonball, at five foot seven and 161 pounds, Pearce was arguably the best offensive and defensive shortstop in baseball during the 1860s. He perfected "place hitting" techniques such as "fair-foul hitting" and bunting long before another Brooklyn native, Willie Keeler, would become more famous for "hitting them where they ain't." After his playing days were over, Pearce fell on hard times. On July 29, 1881, a benefit match in his honor was played at the Polo Grounds between the Mets and a picked nine of professional players. From the proceeds, Pearce was able to open what today would be called a "sports bar" in downtown Brooklyn.[57]

Outfielder John Chapman played nine years for the Atlantics before embarking on a managerial career with various professional clubs.[58] Known for his quiet and courteous demeanor, Chapman was universally respected by fans and players alike. After Chapman retired from baseball he became a successful businessman in Brooklyn until his death in 1916.

In contrast to Chapman, Bob "Death to Flying Things" Ferguson could be short-tempered and tactless, but was also an intelligent and authoritative player and manager.[59] During his baseball career, Ferguson played many roles: player, captain, umpire, manager and president of the NABBP from 1872 to 1875. As a player, he was an outstanding defensive player behind the plate and at various positions on the infield. Ferguson was also creditable on offense as a switch-hitting batter and expert baserunner.

George "The Charmer" Zettlein began playing in Brooklyn with the Eckfords in 1865, but gained his fame as a member of the Atlantics in the late 1860s. His nickname, incidentally, came not from his effect on the ladies, but from "George the Charmer," a character in Hooley's minstrel show.[60] Zettlein became the star hurler for the Atlantics and was the winning pitcher in the Atlantics' upset victory over Cincinnati in 1870. But, according to the *New York Clipper*, because of his Teutonic heritage he lacked the "headword" to be a great pitcher in the line of Jim Creighton.[61] In the 1870s, Zettlein had varied success pitching for several professional clubs. Following his retirement from the game in 1876, he returned to Brooklyn to work in the district attorney's office for several years.

Pearce, Chapman, Ferguson, and Zettlein—Brooklyn lads one and all—would play together for the last time in 1870. The Atlantic Club would continue to sponsor a baseball team for several years, but the terrain of competition had irrevocably changed. Baseball in Brooklyn would never be the same.

In November 1870, the delegates at the NABBP's annual convention clashed over the issue of professionalism.[62] Led by the Knickerbockers and the Excelsiors, the amateur clubs introduced a resolution that condemned professional play. In support of the resolution, Frank Pigeon of the original Eckford nine argued that professionalism gave unfair advantage to wealthier clubs and decreased the level of competition. But, the governing body, now controlled by delegates from professional clubs, rejected the resolution. After the vote, the defeated amateur delegates walked out of the hall. The NABBP convention adjourned, never to be reconvened.

CHAPTER FIVE

For the Love of the Game

In the 1860s the "grand championship matches" engaged in by prominent teams such as the Excelsiors, Eckfords and Atlantics were serious
affairs. In addition to the pride of club members and local communities,
the financial interests of professional gamblers as well as players were at
stake. But baseball in Brooklyn had its lighter side. At the same time that
baseball experts such as Henry Chadwick were analyzing the "scientific"
approach of the upper echelon of clubs and players, amateur players and
fans enjoyed the game for sheer pleasure rather than profit.

Muffin matches played by the least skilled club members were one
source of amusement for players and fans alike. A modern day infielder
who "muffs" a grounder probably does not realize that the term is derived
from the general quality of play of muffin teams in the 1860s. But, the
ineptness of the nineteenth century muffins did not diminish their joy of
playing. An announcement of a forthcoming game sent by the Excelsiors
to the *Daily Union* in 1864 reflected the muffin attitude and parodied the
customs of championship matches.[1] Referring to themselves as the "great
American players of the Excelsior Club" they notified the public that
prizes at the game would be awarded at the end of the game. The best
hitter would be awarded a bat, "a brick bat," and the best fielder a ball, "a
fish ball." Moreover, "The umpire will sing the new song sung by C. Carroll Sawyer, entitled 'A Swinging in the Lane.'"

Newspaper accounts of muffin games would often reflect a less than
serious attitude toward the matches. Contrast, for example, the tone of
the following account in the *Daily Union* of a muffin match in 1865
between the Excelsiors and the Enterprise with a typical account of a
championship first nine contest.

The great American nine of the Excelsior Club sustained defeat for the first time this season—it was their first match to be known—on Saturday 1st on the Capitoline grounds, at the hands of "ye muffs of ye Enterprise Club" … the score of the latter being 56 to 45 on the part of the Great Americans … We expected to receive a score of the match from the Americans, but when we heard of their defeat we did not longer expect the documents, and as the Enterprise muffs were too magnanimous—or too lazy—to have their victory recorded in full, we are obliged to confine ourselves to the mere totals of the game.[2]

In 1868, reporters from the *Daily Eagle*, led by their star pitcher Henry Chadwick, challenged the "Great American Nine" to a contest. In its announcement of the game, the *Daily Eagle* not only set the tone of the match, but also managed to slight its rival *Herald Tribune*:

In order that the citizens of Brooklyn may not be unnecessarily alarmed tomorrow, by the unusual stir of one half of the population of Brooklyn and not be led to think that it is one of the *Tribune's* Ku Klux Klan outrages, it becomes the duty of the *Eagle* to advise them that it will only be the excitement attendant on the match between the reporters of Brooklyn and the Great American nine of the Excelsior Club. President Pierson will take all the cars off the other roads and place them on the Fulton avenue line, running to the Capitoline. Fifteen doctors and twenty-five surgeons will be in attendance at the ground to attend to the wounded combatants.[3]

Following the momentous visit of the Cincinnati Red Stockings to Brooklyn in 1869, the *Clipper* described a "Grand Muffin Match" between the Blue Stockings and Green Stockings at Union Grounds that parodied the matches of America's elite clubs. According to the *Clipper*:

Great preparations were made for the encounter. Costumes of the most elaborate description were procured for the players. The Greens were attired in white shirts and pants, green stockings, red belts, and green caps with white fronts. The Blues were capped, shirted, pantalooned and stockinged in blue, and wore red belts.[4]

Like the Reds, the two teams traveled to the ball grounds in a procession of coaches "and as they traveled through the streets attracted considerable attention." A large crowd of spectators greeted the clubs as they arrived at Union Grounds, which was decorated with streamers befitting a championship match.

The *Clipper* characterized the match:

There was fun … lots of fun. It stuck out everywhere. With one or two exceptions, the players were prime muffs, and their antics in stopping and throwing the ball were worth seeing. When a real "green" player was found on either side he was allowed to run the bases twice if he wanted to, and other tricks were played on him... Everybody was captain, and everybody gave orders. The din at times was like the cry of a pack of hounds in full chase. In the neighborhood of the reporters' desk all the "quondams" were congregated and their opinions of the players, and their merits and demerits were ludicrous in the extreme... Taken altogether, the game was novelty in the way of muffin matches. The costumes were picturesque and handsome and in pretty contrast. The only drawback to the day's sport was the refusal of the proprietor to "whack up" on the gate money, which, as the players allege, he had agreed to do.

Although the Blues-Greens match was perhaps not typical, it does illustrate the purpose of muffin games, which was to have fun and not take oneself too seriously. Muffin matches also reaffirmed the elite status of professional players. Although anyone could play baseball, participants and spectators at muffin matches realized first hand that few players could achieve the level of skill of the professionals.

In addition to organized clubs, Brooklyn ball players would employ various criteria for matching up against one another. As noted in Chapter One, occupation or workplace were popular bases for competition. A sampling of reports from the *Daily Eagle*, the *Daily Union* and the *New York Clipper* reveal the range of the matchups: the "Current" vs. the "Uncurrent" departments at the Metropolitan Bank; the Machinists vs. the Sailmakers and the Carpenters vs. the Joiners at the Brooklyn Navy Yard; the Controller's Office vs. the Water Department of Brooklyn; employees of the Fulton, Catherine and Wall Street ferries vs. the Atlantic and Hamilton Avenue ferries; the New York Post Office vs. the Brooklyn Post Office; and, Bryant's Minstrels vs. Hooley's Minstrels.

Marital status and weight were two of the more unusual criteria for establishing contestants. Clubs and workplace teams would often play intrasquad matches of the "singles" against the "married" men. Surely a more interesting spectacle for fans were matches between "heavy weights" and "light weights," players over or under 200 pounds. Ball players over 200 pounds were certainly a novelty. In contrast to modern day professional athletes, most of the elite players in the 1860s were well under six feet tall, and weighed less than 160 pounds.

By far the most unusual expression of the national pastime combined baseball with the equally popular winter sport of ice skating. While baseball fever had infected the male population of Brooklyn from early spring to late fall, during the cold winter months both women and men were overcome by a mania for ice skating. Just as every vacant lot was utilized for ball playing, Brooklynites took to the ice on any available frozen pond throughout the environs of the city. Throughout the 1860s and 1870s, the two sports would converge. Entrepreneurs, quick to capitalize on the popularity of both sports, constructed facilities which would be flooded during the winter for ice skating, and drained in the spring for baseball.

Oscar F. Oatman opened the first outdoor rink, Washington Pond (also referred to as Oatman's Pond and Litchfield Pond), in 1860 at Fifth Avenue and Third Street, on land leased from Edwin Litchfield, land speculator and railway official.[5] Litchfield had purchased the property in 1852 from the Cortelyou family, the last residents of the old stone house that was originally constructed in 1699.[6] The house was the site of a bloody confrontation during the Battle of Brooklyn in 1776 when nearly 300 American soldiers died while holding off the British advance on New York. The old stone house was also a prominent location in Brooklyn baseball history. In 1855 the Excelsiors first began playing on the meadow below the house. In 1883, the same hallowed grounds would become the home of the baseball team that would become the Dodgers.

In order to insure an adequate return on his investment, and to control his clientele, Oatman organized Washington Pond as a private club which people could join by paying a seasonal membership fee. Oatman offered attractive package deals. For $5 a gentleman and two ladies could purchase a membership. An extra lady could be added for $1.50. The fee for boys under 18 was $2. Requiring a membership fee, which became the norm for all private skating ponds, was also a way of screening the clientele. Appealing to a middle class audience, an advertisement for Union Skating Pond emphasized the restrictive and exclusive nature of membership:

> Greater efforts that [sic] heretofore will be put forth to render the company upon the Pond select in every particular as tickets will be sold to parties of the highest respectability. Strangers purchasing tickets will be required to give references, and the right to cancel any ticket that may have been obtained through misrepresentation, is reserved by the proprietor. Holders of tickets must conform to the Rules and Regulations under penalty of a forfeiture of membership.[7]

Oatman's venture was an immediate success. Following his model, other sports entrepreneurs constructed skating ponds in Brooklyn in the 1860s. Chichester's Pond in Bushwick, Union and Satellite Ponds in Williamsburgh, and Capitoline Pond in Bedford each were equipped with dressing rooms and refreshment stands, and featured colored gas lamps and live music for evening skating. In addition to open skating, each rink hosted elaborate costume balls, carnivals, performances by professional skaters and drill teams, and fireworks.[8] The local newspapers promoted skating as a healthful entertainment which, unlike baseball, could be enjoyed by the whole family.[9] The *Clipper* described skating's particular appeal to a middle class audience:

> …a fashionable skating pond affords all facilities for conversation, exercise, amusement, flirting, fun and frolic, that is combined in the several occupations that engage the attentions of the fashionable portion of the community during the whole winter's season.[10]

Skating lessons were available for the uninitiated or novice skater. An advertisement in the *Daily Times* for "parlour skating lessons" made its pitch specifically to women: "it is now considered just as necessary for a young lady to know how to skate, as to know how to play the piano."[11]

It was not long before adventurous Brooklyn skaters realized that sporting events conducted on land and water could also be performed on ice. Racing on skates and in ice sailboats became popular events. Skating pond proprietors promoted every imaginable novelty sport on ice, including backward racing, racing blindfolded, hurdles and wheelbarrow racing.[12] Perhaps the most novel sport was baseball on ice.

Although Brooklyn baseball players took to the diamond for nine months out of the year, from the earliest spring thaw of March to winter's onset at Thanksgiving, the thirst for the game could seemingly not be quenched. "Winter ball" in the 1860s well into the 1880s had a decidedly different meaning than today. When the skating ponds opened in December or January, ballplayers laced up their skates and took to the ice with their bat and ball.

The rules of the game on ice were basically the same as on land with some necessary accommodations. The ball was softer than that of regulation play and colored red to make it more visible. Bases, three-foot squares, were drawn on the ice and base runners allowed to "overskate" the bases as they normally would at first base. Teams were comprised of ten players and the game length set at five innings.[13] Although one-bound catches constituted an out, as in the early days of the game, difficult fielding conditions generally resulted in high scoring matches.

The Union, Satellite, and Capitoline Ponds were all venues for baseball games on ice. When the Prospect Park Pond opened in 1868, it also became a prominent location for the slippery sport. The first recorded baseball game on ice was played on February 4, 1861, on Washington Pond between the Atlantics and the Charter Oaks of Brooklyn.[14] According to the *Clipper*, 12,000 fans—1,500 of whom were ladies—turned out to watch the novel sport. Spectators stood in lines three deep on the embankment

BASE-BALL ON SKATES, WASHINGTON PARK, BROOKLYN.—Drawn by C. J. Taylor.—[See Page 63.]

Base Ball on Ice, Washington Park, Brooklyn. (From *Harper's Weekly*, January 26, 1884.)

surrounding the pond. Other fans watched from their carriages parked along the streets surrounding the arena. At game time, a mob of fans had to be cleared off the ice to make room for play.

The Atlantics, champions of baseball on solid ground, were just as adept on ice. They easily beat the Charter Oaks by a score of 36 to 27. According to the *Clipper*, the "Bedford Boys" were the best skaters as well as the best ball players and were "about as hard to beat on the ice as on *terra firma*." The newspaper particularly singled out Dickey Pearce who was "as good a short stop on the ice as he is on a summer day."

Unlike the summer game, however, ballplayers on ice competed for rink time with the general skating public. An 1865 editorial in the *Daily Eagle* called for an end to the winter game:

> We hope we shall have no more ball games on ice. The ballplayers have their season, and a long one; playing on skates is more tom foolery; it inter-feres with the rights of the ticket holders and creates dissatisfaction... If any of the ball clubs want to make fools of themselves, let them go down to Coney Island and play a game on stilts.[15]

Despite the *Eagle* commentary, baseball on ice continued to be a popular sport and was played each winter well into the 1880s. Because of the unique skills required to play the game, few baseball clubs had enough players who could perform on the ice. It was not, therefore, unusual for a team to draw players from different baseball clubs. For example, in 1868, the New York Skating Club was comprised of such players as Harry Wright and John Hatfield from the Cincinnati Reds, and Charley Bearman from the Mutuals.[16] The Atlantics, Eckfords, and Fultons of Brooklyn were fortunate to have ball players who were also adept on ice. In 1868, seven of the nine Atlantic regular players played in the winter games.

In 1884 *Harper's Weekly* reported a series of matches played at Washington Pond, which that summer would become home to Brooklyn's first major league baseball club.[17] A team of professional ballplayers led by Baltimore manager Bill Barnie faced off against students from Adelphi and Polytechnic Institutes, coached by Henry Chadwick. In contrast to the seriousness of the summer game, the magazine portrayed the winter spectacle as an amusing entertainment for both the players and spectators.

> Where a grand hit would have elicited applause, perchance a sudden subsidence in the act of hitting may have evoked audible signs of merriment, and the insecurity of steel-shod feet is a fertile source of such balked ambition, and consequent amusement to the on-lookers. And it is safe to let loose one's laughter on such an occasion, for even the most enthusiastic of professionals—even he whose daily bread depends upon the game—feels that he is in a position in which he can trifle with the game because of the abnormal conditions under which it is being played. The spectators who gather around the field of ice are entertained; and if the game is, after all, but a travesty of its proper self, at least it proves its exuberant vitality in that it can flourish when other sports, less hardy and less ingrained in the national character, are "frozen out."

At the time of the *Harper's Weekly* report, the popularity of baseball on ice was reaching its peak. Accounts of games no longer appeared in the *Clipper* or in the Brooklyn newspapers. The private outdoor skating ponds, the major venues for baseball matches, were disappearing. In the late 1880s, when professional baseball clubs began to routinely travel south for spring training, the professional players lost interest in playing on ice. For two decades, though, players and spectators in Brooklyn enjoyed the novel game of baseball on ice.

CHAPTER SIX

The Professional Leagues

In March of 1871, the professional and amateur clubs formally went their separate ways. On St. Patrick's Day, ten professional clubs met in at Colliers Rooms, a saloon at the corner of 13th Street and Broadway in New York to found the National Association of Professional Base Ball Players (NAPBBP).[1] The charter members included the Philadelphia Athletics, Washington Olympics, Washington Nationals, New York Mutuals, Unions of Troy, Boston Red Stockings, Forest Citys of Rockford, Forest Citys of Cleveland, Chicago White Stockings, and Kekiongas of Fort Wayne. During the 1871 inaugural season, the Fort Wayne club folded in August and was replaced by the Brooklyn Eckfords.

Other than openly proclaiming itself professional, the new league was quite similar to the amateur NABBP. The NAPBBP was a loose confederation of clubs with the same structural flaws of its amateur predecessor that would lead to its undoing. The nominal league entry fee of $10 made it easy for less competitive clubs to join. Like the NABBP, the new professional league did not establish a fixed schedule; each club had to arrange a five game series with every other team. The club that won the most series would be the champion. Lacking a mechanism of disciplining players, clubs faced the same problems of player revolving, gambling and hippodroming. The nascent league's prospects were further dampened in 1873 when the country entered an economic depression.

The new professional league struggled through five seasons, a revolving door of various clubs that tried to remain financially solvent. The wide discrepancy in the quality of club entries soon became apparent. The strongest teams, organized as joint stock companies, were better able to pay for the best players and withstand the financial pressures. The weaker clubs, referred to as "cooperative nines," relied on gate receipts and were less able to pay for higher quality players or withstand financial losses. In

1874 only eight teams completed the season. At the end of the 1875 season, the league was in disarray. Only six of the 13 teams that began the season finished their schedules.

On March 16, 1871, at the invitation of the Brooklyn Excelsiors, amateur clubs from New York, Brooklyn, Philadelphia, Baltimore and other northeastern cities met and established the National Association of Amateur Baseball Clubs.[2] The delegates basically adopted the rules of the NABBP which forbid professionalism. But, like its predecessor, the new association could not come to terms with distinction between amateurs and professionals. At the convention, disputes erupted over the issue of clubs sharing gate receipts. Like the NABBP, the Amateur Association chose to avoid the issue, thereby opening itself up to the same problems of player revolving and lack of parity among clubs. By September amateur rule violations had reached such a point that the *Daily Eagle* asked:

> What are rules to your gate money nines? They infringe them with impunity when it suits their purpose. The way revolving has been encouraged by the Star, Athletic [Brooklyn], and Atlantic club nines this season, and especially by the junior fraternity, is enough to destroy all interest in their contests.[3]

In reality, among the "amateurs" there were still two classes of teams. Clubs like the Excelsiors were truly amateurs, taking no compensation whatsoever for their play. Many clubs, however, were "cooperative nines" that relied upon gate receipts to finance their expenses and recruit better players. The *Daily Eagle* saw little difference between these clubs and the professional teams.

> They all compensate their players in one way or another, and share gate money receipts, and differ from professionals only to the extent that they do not pay their players regular salaries, are not corporated stock companies, and are not enrolled in the Professional Association.[4]

The real distinction in the quality of teams was between the professional joint stock company clubs that could afford to hire the best players and finance a lengthy season of road trips, and the cooperative nines (professional and "amateur") that could only support a semi-professional team.

As the *Daily Eagle* predicted at the end of the 1870 season, most of the Atlantic players jumped to other professional clubs. Joe Start, Bob Ferguson, and Charley Smith all joined the rival New York Mutuals. Lip Pike went to the Troy Haymakers and George Zettlein signed with the Chicago White Stockings.

With its roster deconstructed, the Atlantic Club met in January 1871 and reorganized the team to play as amateurs. Only three members of the old Atlantics decided to forgo professional play: John Chapman, Dan McDonald, and George Hall.[5] But when the 1871 season began, Hall also decided to join the professional ranks and signed with the Washington Olympics.

On May 2, sporting flashy new uniforms, the Atlantics took the field at Capitoline Grounds in their first amateur game against the Tony Pastor Club of Brooklyn (Tony Pastor was a well known New York theater manager and sponsor of a vaudeville touring company). Clad in red checked stockings, blue knickerbocker pantaloons, and white shirts and caps, the Atlantics won easily, 26–3.[6] The *Daily Eagle* noted that, among the crowd, the Atlantic veterans now playing for the Mutuals avidly watched the reorganized Bedford nine. Ironically, former Atlantic star Bob Ferguson umpired the contest. The *Daily Eagle*, longtime booster as well as critic of the Atlantics, urged on the "resuscitated" club: "Go in, boys, and show those who have left the club that the Atlantics are still living, and ready to fight as plucky as ever."[7]

Though plucky they might have been, the Atlantics had a lackluster season. In what the *Daily Eagle* referred to as the "State Championship," the Atlantics were surpassed by the Brooklyn Athletics.[8] Fan interest had declined precipitously. Before a sparse crowd at the Atlantics' deciding match against the Athletics on September 7, the *Daily Eagle* lamented "such little patronage" at a championship match.

In the professional ranks, when the Ft. Wayne Kekiongas folded in August, the Eckfords finished out their season. Although until then they were considered an amateur team, they had played against professional clubs throughout the season, winning 11 of 25 contests up to September. On September 7, at Union Grounds the Eckfords defeated the pennant contending Chicago White Stockings for the second time during the season.[9] But only 1,000 fans turned out to watch the local team battle the "coming champions" from the West. Because of such poor attendance, the Eckfords cut their admission prices at Union Grounds in half, from 50 to 25 cents, for their remaining games.[10]

Despite its loss to the Eckfords, the White Stockings were in a close battle with the Philadelphia Athletics for the first NAPBBP championship. The Chicago club had become a powerhouse in its inaugural season, often vanquishing its opponents by enormous margins. Sportswriters began using the expression "to Chicago" to mean that a team overwhelmingly beat its opponent. Reflecting the club's optimism, the White Stockings resigned its players for the next season at salaries ranging from $1,500 to

$2,500.[11] But, tragedy struck on the night of October 8 when the great Chicago fire leveled the city. The White Stockings lost not only their new lakefront stadium, but the team and players lost all their possessions. According to team captain, former Eckford Jimmy Wood, "all the players now in the Club were burnt out, except two, and … not one has a dollar left."[12] The club itself announced that it was bankrupt and would release its players from contract at the end of the season. In order to finish the season, the White Stockings arranged to complete their schedule on the road.[13] Railroad lines offered them free passes to travel and various baseball clubs and well wishers made contributions to help cover the team's expenses. The deciding game for the pennant would be played in Brooklyn.

On October 30, Chicago faced the Philadelphia Athletics at Union Grounds to determine the first championship of the professional league. It would seem like a homecoming for the Brooklyn fans who turned out for the match. Six of the White Stocking players had played at one time for the local Eckfords. Having lost their uniforms in the fire, the Chicago nine took field sporting the colors of local teams. The *New York Herald* described the unusual sight:

> …the appearance [the White Stockings] made yesterday in their suits of various hues and make was ludicrous in the extreme. Pinkham wore a Mutual shirt, a pair of Mutual pants and a pair of red stockings. Bannock wore a complete Mutual uniform with the exception of the belt, which belonged to one of the Eckfords. Foley wore an Eckford suit out and out. Zettlein—"him of the big feet"—wore a huge shirt with a mammoth A on the bosom, and Duffy appeared as a Fly Awayer. Some wore black hats, some wore caps, and a few had regular ball hats, while others again played bare headed. Whether this had anything to do with their play or not is still open to question, but certain it is they have not appeared as weak at the bat this season.[14]

The Athletics defeated the White Stockings 4–1 to win the first NAPBBP championship. Forty-year-old Nate Berkenstock, who had not played for the Athletics since 1866, made the final putout of the game. Demoralized, the White Stockings finished their season by losing two more games at Union Grounds. The final game against the Haymakers of Troy drew a crowd of less than than one hundred.

In January 1872, the Atlantics announced that they were joining the professional league.[15] Bob Ferguson returned to lead his old team which prided itself as being a "cooperative nine" of all Brooklyn players. But the Atlantics, whose roster was virtually the same as the previous year, were clearly outclassed by the professional teams. They finished the season with a record of 9 wins and 28 losses, 25 games out of first place.

During the season, the Atlantics tragically lost their 22-year-old left fielder, Al Thake. In September, Thake, one of the Atlantics' best hitters, drowned while fishing off Fort Hamilton in New York Harbor.[16] Ferguson organized a benefit game in Thake's honor that reunited the players from the 1869 Atlantics and Cincinnati Red Stockings. On October 23, Brooklyn fans would once again see the old Atlantics' Pearce, Start, Chapman, Zettlein, Mills and McDonald meet the Reds' Gould, Leonard, Sweasy, McVey and George and Harry Wright.[17] Al Spalding pitched for the Reds in place of the absent Asa Brainard. Once again the Atlantics came away with the ball in a 12–10 victory. Unfortunately, threatening weather kept down attendance and only $200 was raised for the benefit of Al Thake's mother. For the Brooklyn fans who braved the weather, the benefit match may well have been the high point of the season.

In a year of disappointment and tragedy, the hitting of Tommy Barlow stood out as one of the few positives for the Atlantics. Barlow led the team in batting average, hits, and runs scored. Following in the footsteps of Dickey Pearce, bunting, or "baby hits" as opposing infielders called them, became a regular part of Barlow's hitting repertoire. Although there is some controversy over whether Pearce or Barlow invented the bunt, it appears that the honor should go to Pearce.[18] Barlow, however, became a master of the technique. In an 1873 contest, Barlow remarkably made six bunt base hits against Baltimore. The *Daily Eagle* described how Barlow eluded Baltimore third baseman John Radcliff:

> All Barlow had to do to secure his base safely with Radcliffe playing his position as he did, was to allow the ball to fall dead from his bat to the left of the base, so as to touch the ground fair. This he did, and as Radcliffe had to run and field the ball from third base, the result was Barlow reached first base ahead of the ball. This style of hitting annoys a field exceedingly, beside which it corners a pitcher. As for sneering at it and calling it baby hitting, that is absurd ... the batsman ... earns his base by skillful, scientific batting.[19]

The Eckfords continued to play in the NAPBBP during the 1872 season, but the team was in shambles. According to baseball historian William Ryczek, "the Eckfords signed virtually every malcontent in the New York area."[20] Frustrated after a string of losses at the beginning of the season, the players began to openly bicker among themselves on the field. As losses mounted, crowd attendance declined. Since the Eckfords, as a cooperative nine, relied upon gate receipts for income, a number of players left the team in search of steady income.

The Eckford roster, in flux throughout the season, included 26 different players. The low point of the season came in a game against Cleveland on July 6 at Union Grounds. Although Cleveland was able to field only eight players, the Eckfords lost by a score of 24–5 before a crowd of not more than 200 people.[21] The Eckfords could manage only three wins in the 29 games they played, two of these at the expense of the Atlantics. Finishing 10th, 27 games behind Boston, the once proud artisans of Williamsburg dropped out of the league.

Each year throughout organized baseball's first decade, the Eckfords were consistently among the game's better teams. In 1862 and 1863, they were the "champions of baseball," featuring such outstanding players as Al Reach and Jimmy Wood. Reach, only 5 foot 6 and 155 pounds, was a journeyman fielder for the championship Eckford squads, playing outfield, shortstop, third base and first base.[22] He is perhaps better known for his post–Eckford career.[23] In 1865, he moved to the Philadelphia Athletics where he played for 12 seasons. In 1871, the *New York Clipper* selected Reach the best second baseman in the NAPBBP. While in Philadelphia, he established a sporting goods business that became one of the largest suppliers in the country of baseball equipment. After his playing career ended, the talented and now wealthy Reach edited a popular annual guide to the American Association of Base Ball and was part-owner of the Philadelphia Phillies from 1883 to 1903.

Jimmy Wood played for the Eckfords for nine years (1860–1869).[24] As diminutive as Reach (5 feet 8 and 150 pounds), Wood was both an outstanding infielder and batter. In 1863, he led the NABBP in runs scored. In 1870, Wood became manager of the Chicago White Stockings and was leader of the club during the tragic 1871 season when the Chicago Fire destroyed not only the team's possessions and ball park but also its chances for a pennant.

The champion Eckfords featured other great players such as shortstop Tom Devyr, third baseman Ed Duffy, and pitcher Joe Sprague. But for the Eckfords, success would be their downfall. The stars of the craftsmen Eckfords would succumb to the lure of greener pastures. As baseball increasingly professionalized, the Eckford Club continued to field teams comprised of local Brooklyn talent. But, at the end of the 1872 season it was obvious that the cooperative nine Eckfords were out of their league. The Eckfords abandoned the ball fields, but they continued as a men's social club well into the twentieth century with their headquarters as 95 Broadway in Williamsburg.[25]

In 1873, the Atlantics moved from Capitoline to Union Grounds, but fared little better, placing sixth out of seven teams that finished the season. Only one player, Charlie Pabor, batted over .300. The Atlantics' unfortunate season was highlighted by accusations of hippodroming by Brooklyn players in mid season. Following a July 22 loss to Baltimore, the *Daily Eagle* remarked that it was quite "singular" that this was the third consecutive Atlantic match where the opposition gained their victories by heavy scoring in one or two innings.[26] In each case the fault lay with the "easy chances" allowed by the Atlantic pitcher. Suspicions of "fraud" or game fixing had surfaced earlier after the Atlantics' July 4 match with the Mutuals.

Following the Baltimore contest, it became known that at the start of the match gamblers were setting odds on the score at the end of the first two innings. When captain Bob Ferguson learned of this, in the words of the *Daily Eagle,* he became "the maddest of all madmen who ever got mad."[27] He hurriedly changed into his street clothes and confronted the gamblers. According to the *Daily Eagle,*

> ...he gave them such a verbal castigation as it has not been our fortune to hear in many a day. Language strong enough to express his meaning failed the captain. "I've marked you, you infernal (we draw the adjective mild, for fear of offending polite ears) thieves and robbers, I'll bust you yet, and drive you out of here, you contemptible scoundrels, thieves and blackguards. I'll teach you to buy up my men, you low-lived loofers—every one of you. There ain't one of you who wouldn't steal a penny from your dead mother's eyes, and kick the corpse because it wasn't a quarter. Come out here, if you want to, any one of you who don't like it, or whom the coat fits, and I'll warm the ground with your miserable carcass till you won't want to buy up my men again."

Ferguson did not identify them, but said that three Atlantic players were involved in the scheme. Although the names were not published, pitcher Jim Britt was likely one of the suspects. Britt disappeared from professional baseball at the end of the season. One of the other suspects was possibly the Atlantics' popular catcher Tommy Barlow. After the season, the *Clipper* reported that Barlow had been "under a cloud," but had been cleared following an investigation of unspecified charges.[28] Barlow moved to the Hartford Club the following season.

Ferguson's temper erupted again two days after the Atlantics-Baltimore game while he was umpiring in a match between Baltimore and the Mutuals. As the teams were changing sides in the middle of the ninth inning, the Mutuals' John Hatfield and Nat Hicks engaged in "chin music," each charging the other with "selling the game." Overhearing the argument, Ferguson offered his opinion that Hicks was playing like he wanted the Mutuals to lose. Hicks responded by calling Ferguson "a d—n liar." According to the *Daily Eagle*:

Just then Ferguson, on the impulse of the moment, picked up a bat near by and struck quickly at Hicks, but had not Hicks put out his arm the bat would not have reached him. As it was, the end of the bat simply bruised the skin, causing blood to flow and gave the appearance of an ugly wound.[29]

At the conclusion of the match, the crowd rushed onto the field toward Ferguson. The police "surrounded the umpire, and one of them handed Ferguson a club to protect himself." Ferguson made his way to the clubhouse where he and Hicks exchanged apologies and, according to the *Daily Eagle*, the "whole affair was finally settled amicably." The newspaper's gloss of the incident did not reveal that Hicks had sustained a multiple fracture, sidelining him for nearly two months of the season.[30]

The Atlantics' best season was 1974, although they still finished sixth with a 22–33 record, 22½ games out of first place. Led by 18-year-old rookie pitcher Tommy Bond, the Atlantics gave hope to the Brooklyn faithful as they finished the season strong. By October, the Atlantics had beaten the Boston Red Stockings in three of their five meetings.[31] On a rainy October 7 afternoon at Union Grounds, Brooklyn held their own against the champions from Boston, settling for a tie when the game was called after 11 innings. The following week, the Atlantics defeated the heavily favored second place Mutuals by a score of 9 to 2. The *Clipper* observed that Brooklyn batted like the Atlantic nine of their glory days in the 1860s.[32]

The second game in their series with the Mutuals on October 20 would rank as one of the finest games in the Atlantics' illustrious history.[33] Three Mutual errors in the first inning allowed two Atlantic runners to cross the plate. Brooklyn would add three more runs in the game to "Chicago" the Mutuals 5–0. But the real drama of the match was taking place in the inning-by-inning performance of Tommy Bond. Through eight and two-thirds innings, Bond had not allowed a single hit. But with two out in the ninth inning, former Atlantic star Joe Start doubled to left field to spoil Bond's no-hitter. Carey followed with a single, sending Start to third base. With Bond's no-hitter ended and a shutout in jeopardy, John Hatfield then hit a towering drive to right field. John Chapman dashed toward the ball and made a fine running catch to end the game, preserving Bond's two hit shutout. The Mutuals, who had trailed Boston by only two and a half games in the first week of October, were knocked out of the pennant race.

Although the Atlantics were far out of contention for the championship, Brooklyn had reason to be optimistic about its chances the next year. But Brooklyn fans, who would become known for their "wait 'til next year" attitude, would be deprived of a contending professional team for nearly a decade. Over the winter, Bob Ferguson and his star pitcher Tommy Bond both signed with Hartford. For Brooklyn, the 1875 season would be a disaster.

In what would be the league's final season, the former champions of baseball would set the record for incompetence. With the team in disarray, the Atlantics would employ a record 35 different players, 14 of whom played only one game. At a time when only one or two pitchers were the norm, the Atlantics went through eight different hurlers. After recording their second victory of the season on May 26, the Atlantics would proceed to lose their next 31 games.[34] By September, crowds of less than 100 turned out at Union Grounds to watch the patchwork lineup of Atlantic players. By the end of the season, the Atlantics had managed only two victories against 42 defeats, buried at a staggering 51½ games behind the league leader. Only the team from Keokuk, Iowa, finished behind them, but they had folded early in the season with one win in their 14 contests.

Following the 1875 season, Chicago White Stockings director William L. Hulbert led a movement to overcome the weakness of the NAPBBP by creating a professional league directed by club owners, not players. Hulbert garnered the support of the best professional teams and brought them together for a meeting in New York in February 1876. In the country's centennial year, representatives of clubs from St. Louis, Louisville, Cincinnati, New York, Philadelphia, Boston, and Hartford met at the Grand Central Hotel, located at 673 Broadway, the current site of a New York University apartment complex, to found the National League of Professional Baseball Clubs (the National League).[35] The League's intent was to bring order to professional baseball and help insure solvency to individual clubs. Of greater long-term significance, professional baseball was to be run as a business, the interests of which were the profits of club owners. Players, although of a unique kind, were conceptualized as employees subject to contractual obligations to club owners.

According to the National Leagues rules, member clubs were required to be joint stock companies that would pay annual dues of $100. Eight charter clubs, organized in Eastern and Western divisions, were granted territorial monopolies, and agreed to play a fixed schedule. New clubs would be admitted only by the approval of the existing clubs. To appeal to a middle class consumer audience, the league set admission fees at 50 cents, banned gambling, the sale of liquor and Sunday games at league parks.

In order to overcome the problem of "revolving," clubs were required to have players sign binding contracts that the league would enforce. Over the next several years, the National League would more finely tune what would become known as the "reserve clause," which would bind players to particular teams unless their contracts were sold to other clubs.

With the National Association of Professional Base Ball Players in collapse, the National League would hold a monopoly on baseball for five years. In its inaugural season, the Mutuals were granted the sole franchise for the New York Metropolitan area and were thus the only game in town. Although nominally a New York team, the Mutuals, now managed by Union Grounds proprietor William Cammayer, continued to play their home games at Cammayer's park. But Brooklyn fans were neither happy about the 100 percent increase in admission nor particularly impressed with the quality of the Mutuals' play. The team's batting was abysmal. "Old Reliable" Joe Start would lead the team in hitting with only a .277 average.[36] Financially strapped, the club did not make its late season western road trip. The Mutuals finished the season in sixth place, with a record of 21–35. In its winter meeting in December, the National League expelled the Mutuals for failing to complete its schedule.[37] The turbulent history of the old Tammany Hall club came to an inglorious end.

In 1877, Brooklyn was given another opportunity to support a major league team when the Hartford Dark Blues surprisingly moved to Union Grounds.[38] Although the Blues had a respectable season in 1876, finishing third in the league with a 47–21 record, the team sought greener financial pastures in Brooklyn. Curiously, the former Connecticut team continued to call themselves the "Hartfords," and thus the record books give no clear indication of their Brooklyn residence. Brooklyn baseball fans also seem not to have noticed their migration. Unfortunately for the Hartfords, the locals were as unwilling to pay 50 cents to see them play as they were to watch the Mutuals.

At an April 26 game at Union Grounds against the Philadelphia Athletics, the *Clipper* noted that over 1,000 fans had showed up at the Williamsburg grounds before game time.[39] But, when they learned that the price of admission was still 50 cents, only 200 to 300 purchased tickets. The *Clipper* presciently observed:

> This will probably be the course pursued by the patrons of the game in this vicinity right through the season, and the result will be the loss of hundred of dollars at each game where the charge of half a dollar admission is made... People cannot afford it.

At the end of season, the Hartfords again finished third, with a record of 31–27, ten games back of Boston. But, having suffered financial losses with a winning team for the second straight year, the Hartfords disbanded.[40]

The "City of Baseball" would wait five years before it had its own professional league team.

Lacking a professional franchise, however, did not mean that baseball's popularity in the city waned. Amateur baseball thrived during the period. Capitoline Grounds continued to be a prominent venue throughout the early 1870s. When the Atlantics moved to Union Grounds in 1873, Capitoline was divided into two fields to accommodate more amateur games. The Brooklyn *Eagle* called it "the finest, most extensive, and complete ball grounds in the country."[41] It was particularly noted for its prohibition of betting, intoxicating liquors, and its efforts made "to induce the patronage of the fair sex."

Rivaling Capitoline Grounds was the newly developed Prospect Park Parade Grounds designed by the renowned architects Olmstead and Vaux. Although the official inauguration of Prospect Park did not occur until 1874, the *Eagle* reported a May 25, 1869, game at the Parade Grounds between two amateur teams: the Eagle of Flatbush and the Powhattan.[42] The report indicated that the Parade ground had been leveled, rolled, and the grass cut, but a regular field was yet to be laid out. By 1872, 20 ball fields had been laid out and a clubhouse built near Coney Island Avenue. By the mid–1870s, the Parade Grounds had become the prominent location for amateur baseball, with at least a dozen games in progress at one time on a Saturday afternoon.[43]

In addition to amateur league matches, the Parade Grounds would be the site of an increasing number of games among "commercial nines," representing particular occupations or workplaces. For Henry Chadwick, these matches, engaged in for the sheer pleasure of the game, recalled "the palmy days of amateur play." In Chadwick's words:

> ...one nine is ambitious of winning the championship of the drygoods houses; another, that of the paper or hardware establishments, and others again, of the insurance and banking firms and houses.[44]

With the evils of revolving, gambling and hippodroming permeating the professional game, Chadwick rejoiced in the spirit of amateurism and healthful exercise to be found at the Parade Grounds:

> It is questionable whether in any part of the world such real enjoyment in the way of outdoor recreative exercise is to be seen to the square acre as the great family recreation ground at Prospect Park provides on every Saturday afternoon from April to November of each year. It is a glorious sight to see the hundreds of young men and boys enjoying themselves to their hearts' content as they do on the Prospect Park Parade Ground every fine afternoon during the summer.[45]

Yet, Chadwick's romantic portrayal of amateur sports at the Flatbush ball fields did not always correspond to reality. In an 1872 editorial, for example, the *Daily Eagle* portrayed a strikingly different scene at the Parade Grounds:

> People frequently talk about the evils of professional ball playing, but there are evils connected with the amateur class fully as degrading to the frater-nity as those of the professional system. One of these is drunkenness, with its consequent rowdiness, indulged in by extemporized base ball clubs who visit the Prospect Park Parade Grounds on occasional Saturday afternoons, a striking example of which was afforded on Saturday last by a party of ball players connected with a well known commercial house of New York, who visited the Park to play a match with the employees of another house, and afterward made beasts of themselves with beer and spirits. This party at about half-past eight o'clock on Saturday evening, tumbled into Car 81 of the Flatbush route, and jostled the passengers, indulged in spreeing, indifferent to the presence of ladies in the car, and though attired in the habiliments of gentlemen, conducted themselves like regular blackguards.[46]

Action on the field did not always follow Chadwick's notion of "great family recreation." In its report of an amateur match between the Name-less and the Borromeos, the *Daily Eagle* observed that the crowd contin-ually encroached upon the field, interrupting play.[47] According to the report, the Borromeo players and their "rather rough crowd of followers" indulged in profanity throughout the contest and derided the umpire to such an extent that he quit in mid-game.

The *Daily Eagle* reporter also noticed at the Parade Grounds "a num-ber of young thieves prowling around ready to steal balls, bats, coats, or anything they could lay their hands on." Noting the total lack of police supervision, the newspaper called for regular police patrols at the grounds on game days to curb the excesses of drunkenness, rowdiness, and thiev-ery.

Although Brooklyn did not have a professional league team, the city was home to many players who played in the professional league. From 1877 through the mid–1880s, in March these players along with other New York professionals would play a series of "picked nine" Saturday games at the Parade Grounds as a sort of spring training before the play-ers would join their respective teams for the season. Chadwick notes a March 30, 1878, game that there was "a large crowd of spectators present" to watch the professional play, while a dozen amateur games were in progress on other diamonds.[48]

In the spring of 1879, player-manager Bill Barnie tried to resurrect the Atlantics to play as a cooperative nine.[49] Barnie, a Brooklyn native, first played ball for the amateur Nassau Club of Brooklyn and joined the Atlantic squad for the 1873 season. From 1874 to 1879 he played for a succession of clubs including Hartford and the Mutuals.[50] Barnie's Atlantics began practicing as the Parade Grounds but played only a few games before disbanding.[51] Barnie moved to San Francisco where he played for the Knickerbockers of that city through the 1980 season.

In 1881, Barnie returned to Brooklyn with grander plans for the Atlantics. On April 12, he met in New York with representatives of the Washington Nationals, the New York Metropolitans, and the Jersey City Club to form the Eastern Championship Association (ECA), a professional minor league.[52] When the season began, seven clubs had joined the ECA: the Atlantics, the Philadelphia Athletics, the Albanys of Albany, and three New York teams: the Metropolitans, New Yorks, and Quicksteps.[53]

The ECA was plagued by the same problems as the NAPBBP.[54] It had no fixed schedule, was comprised of financially weak clubs, and it could not control the revolving of players to other teams. National League clubs regularly creamed off the better players, leaving the ECA teams with a less marketable product.

The Atlantics started the season with a solid lineup that included Dennis "Big Dan" Brouthers, John "Candy" Nelson, and Lipman "Lip" Pike. All three, however, were lured away to National League clubs during the season. Brouthers, who pitched and played outfield, played in only seven games before signing with the Buffalo club.[55] "Big Dan" would enjoy a 19-year career in the major leagues and become one of the game's dominant power hitters. Shortstop Candy Nelson, a Brooklyn native, played for the Eckfords from 1867 through 1869 and again in 1871.[56] Nelson played 30 games for the Atlantics in 1881 before joining Worcester. Particularly remembered as a great leadoff hitter, Nelson would lead the American Association in bases on balls in both 1884 and 1885 while playing for the Mets. Left-handed infielder Lip Pike was possibly organized baseball's first Jewish player.[57] He was a member of Atlantics during the 1869 and 1870 seasons, and played second base in the memorable Atlantic victory over the Cincinnati Red Stockings in 1870. Pike moved with Candy Nelson to Worcester during the 1881 season.

With their stars having jumped ship, the Atlantics had a disappointing season. At one point in late summer, they lost 11 out of 12 games. Hoping to reinvigorate the team, the Atlantics coaxed its former star pitcher, Tommy Bond, out of retirement. Earlier in the season with the Worcester Club, he had hung up his cleats after losing his first three games.[58] But, with the minor league Atlantics Bond was no better. On

August 20 at the Polo Grounds, Bond gave up 16 runs in a loss to the Mets.[59]

By August, the New Yorks and the Quicksteps had dropped out of the league.[60] Relying upon gate receipts for income, the remaining clubs scheduled as many games as possible with ECA and other clubs. The Mets played over 100 games before the season ended. Because the Mets-Atlantics matches usually drew good crowds, the two teams played at least 15 times during the season, all but one at the Polo Grounds in New York.

With little fanfare, the Mets won the first and only ECA championship with a 32–13 record in league play.[61] The Atlantics finished the season with a losing record and looked ahead to an uncertain future.

Following the 1881 season, the officials of several baseball clubs mounted a challenge to the major league monopoly held by the National League. On November 2, William Barnie of the Atlantics joined representatives from Cincinnati, Louisville, Pittsburgh, and New York in Cincinnati to plan the formation of what would become the American Association.[62] Because the new league was dominated by several brewery and distillery interests, it would also come to be referred to as the "Beer and Whiskey Circuit."[63] In contrast to the restrictive National League, the American Association clubs agreed to play on Sundays, charge an admission fee of only 25 cents, and sell beer at their ball parks. The new American Association thus appealed to a larger, especially working class, audience.

Interviewed by the *Clipper* in January, Barnie expressed uncertainty over whether the Atlantics would join the American Association or the League Alliance, an association of minor league clubs affiliated with the National League.[64] An advantage to League Alliance membership would be protection from the problem of players revolving, since Alliance clubs were bound to the reserve clause restrictions of the senior circuit.

By April, Barnie had secured Union Grounds for Atlantic home games and announced the team's roster for the 1882 season. Barnie told the *Clipper*:

> I have very carefully selected these players as to their habits, etc., and intend to improve wherever necessary. I will not keep one man that does not live up to the League Alliance rules, to which association I have made application for membership.[65]

Barnie's questionable decision-making proved costly to Brooklyn. When the 1882 season opened, the Atlantics had not been accepted into the League Alliance and had lost its opportunity to become a charter member of the American Association. By June, the Atlantics' season was beginning to look, as Yogi Berra would have put it, "like déjà vu all over again." Five players from the starting nine had revolved to major league clubs.[66] John Cassidy returned to Troy where he had played the year before. O'Leary and Clinton joined the Worcester club. Smith and Schenck moved to clubs in the new American Association. The *Clipper* observed, "Hard luck seems to follow Manager Barnie's Atlantic team."[67] The Atlantics only managed five wins out their first 26 games.

The Atlantics were now only a semi-professional team of novice players trying to break into professional ball. Lacking a regular schedule, they pieced together a limited barnstorming tour that extended not far beyond the New York metropolitan area. Their itinerary in July included the Actives of Reading, Pennsylvania; the Foote Club of Philadelphia; and the Houstons of Chester, Pennsylvania.[68] Perhaps sensing he was at the helm of a sinking ship, sometime in July Barnie left the club to assume management of the Philadelphia Athletics.

In August, reports of the Atlantics disappeared from the pages of the *Brooklyn Daily Eagle* and the *New York Clipper*, the newspapers of record for Brooklyn baseball. The typical newspaper articles that would appear in November or December summarizing a team's season and looking ahead to the promise of the coming year were absent. Neither did the scribes of the sports world pause to pay tribute to the glorious history of Brooklyn's greatest team. The Atlantics simply died in silence. Yet, there was probably very little to write about. After all, Bill Barnie's team was really the "Atlantics" in name only. They bore no relation to the old Atlantic Club of Bedford that was the "championship team of the world" in the 1860s. The old Atlantics ceased to exist upon the collapse of the National Association in 1875. One might argue that they began the slow process of dying in the late 1860s. Regardless, neither the old Atlantics nor its reincarnations could adapt to the competitive business environment of "modern" professional baseball.

In a few short months, a small consortium of business men with financial backing would form, for the first time in Brooklyn, a baseball company, the Brooklyn Base Ball Association. The company would eventually be known as the Brooklyn Dodgers, and for many of the Dodger faithful, 1883 would mark the beginning of baseball history.

Balanced here between the passing of one era and the coming of the new, it is worth pausing to revisit this story. The chronicle of baseball in Brooklyn told thus far is a narrative of and by the white male baseball fraternity. The "voices" of Henry Chadwick and his contemporaries, full of boosterism and manly virtue, described baseball as a microcosm of society, moving steadily yet inexorably toward the modern, the scientific, the capitalist world. Noticeably absent from the story are the voices of women and people of color. Before turning to the final scene in this story, the hidden history within the "white man's game" is worth examining.

CHAPTER SEVEN

The White Man's Game

The ideology which supported separate spheres of life for men and women in the nineteenth century included recreational and athletic activities.[1] Middle class women went horseback riding, played "ten pins" and croquet in the warmer months and were avid ice skaters in the winter. Baseball, rooted in associations of "gentlemen," artisans and politicos, was clearly defined as a male endeavor. In her excellent history of women in baseball, however, sociologist Gai Inham Berlage shows that women have played baseball from the game's early days.[2] As early as 1867, a black women's professional team, the Dolly Vardens, was organized in Philadelphia. In the same year, students at Vassar College also began playing baseball. A decade later their organized team, the Resolutes, was playing squads from other women's colleges in the Northeast.

Beginning in the mid–1870s, professional women's teams were barnstorming throughout the Midwest and East. Although many of the players exhibited skill at playing the game, promoters capitalized on the novelty of women playing the man's game. Their performances were more farce than competitive sport. The Blondes and the Brunettes (so named for obvious reasons) formed an early pair of barnstorming teams that played one another. Similar to the uniforms worn by male ballplayers, the Blondes sported blue suits trimmed in white, while the Brunettes wore suits of white trimmed in blue.[3] In contrast to the men, the women players wore light leather gloves, used a somewhat lighter ball, and played on a field with bases set at fifty feet apart.

In their first match played in Springfield, Illinois, on September 11, 1875, the Blondes defeated the Brunettes by a score of 42–38. Two days later in Decatur, Illinois, the Brunettes won 41–21. In September 1875 the *Clipper* and the *Daily Eagle* published announcements of an impending match between the two women's teams to be played later in the month at Union Grounds in Brooklyn. The *Daily Eagle* report included the rosters of "The Lady Base Ball Combination:"

Blondes	Positions	Brunettes
Estella Brown	Catcher	Maud Levi
Jane Wyman	Pitcher	Mary Broden
Nettlie Glidden	First Base	Ellan Burgan
Eva Sheppard	Second Base	Charlotte Clark
Eliza Sheppard	Third Base	Annie Wilson
Lydia Lambert	Short Stop	Magy Young
Mary Foster	Left Field	Josephine Spencer
Emma Staeckling	Centre Field	Louisa Chaffner
Kate Tinsley	Right Field	Georgiana Avery
Carrie Reupe	Substitute	Amy Bell

In less than subtle play on words, the *Daily Eagle* pitched its announcement to the male baseball fraternity:

> What a crowd there will be to see the match, and with such a susceptible set of fellows as our Brooklyn boys are, what a number of catches the fair ball tossers will make, especially the brunettes, who are famous for that sort of thing.[4]

Unfortunately, no report exists indicating that the match took place. Four years later, however, the *Clipper* reported a match between the Blondes and the Brunettes on May 10, 1879, on ball grounds at Madison Avenue and 59th Street in New York.[5] Only one player listed in the roster above, Blonde third basewoman Eliza Sheppard, appeared in the box score of the 1879 match. The Blondes won the contest by a score of 45 to 31. Although the fate of the Blondes and Brunettes is unclear, other women's teams performed burlesque matches throughout the 1880s. By the end of the century, barnstorming "Bloomer Girl" teams were exhibiting considerably more skill and often defeated local male teams.

Despite the fact that women could and did play baseball, often with exceptional skill, gender ideology largely proscribed female incursion into the male bastion of the baseball fraternity. There is no documentary evidence that women participated in any organized baseball in Brooklyn during the time period of this chronicle. But there is some indication that there may have been some interest in organizing a women's team. The following item appeared in the September 10, 1868, issue of the *Daily Eagle*.

FEMALE CLUB IN BROOKLYN—An exchange has the following: Following in the example of the "Gushing Girls" of Peterboro, a movement is on foot in Brooklyn to organize a Club of female base ball players. They are to discard hoops and skirts utterly, and appear in a genuine Arab rig. Most of them are undergoing physical discipline, and all of them are making preparations for a match.

If the story be true, and we doubt it, the first appearance of the Club, will be a grand success. Where will they play? On the Capitoline or the Union?

There is no evidence that such a team did materialize. Although the *Daily Eagle* questioned the veracity of the "exchange" sent to the newspaper, the Peterboro team referred to did exist. Peterboro happened to be the home of Elizabeth Smith Miller, daughter of abolitionist and women's rights advocate Garrit Smith, and relative of Elizabeth Cady Stanton.[6] Miller is credited in the early 1850s with modifying Turkish pantaloons, or the "Arab rig," into what became known as bloomers. With Peterboro in the geographical center of the women's rights movement, the women players may well have been making a political statement in playing the male-dominated game.

According to the *New York Clipper*, from a total membership of 50 members, the Peterboro club fielded both a senior nine and a junior nine.[7] In August 1868 the Seniors played a match with the Juniors before a large and appreciative crowd in Peterboro. Their outfits, which the *Clipper* judged to be "at once neat, easy and exceeding beautiful," consisted of "short blue and white tunics, reaching to the knees, straw caps, jauntily trimmed, white stockings and gaiter shoes." In the match, the Seniors took command early and easily defeated the younger team by a score of 29–2. According to the *Clipper*, "the Seniors acquitted themselves well, and nearly every member showed some particular points of fine play."[8] In the tradition of the male baseball fraternity, the players and their friends enjoyed a postgame dinner, followed by singing and speeches.

Although women did not appear on the playing field in Brooklyn, baseball promoters and sports reporters encouraged them to attend games as spectators. As noted earlier, the attendance of the "fairer sex" was thought to have a civilizing effect on crowd behavior at games. In 1867, the *Ball Player's Chronicle* defined women's contribution to the manly sport:

> If there is one effort that clubs ought to make more than another to promote the popularity of our game and to encourage its respectability, it is the one to encourage the patronage of the fairer sex... The presence of an assemblage of ladies purifies the moral atmosphere of a base ball gathering, repressing, as it does, all outbursts of intemperate language which the

excitement of a contest so frequently induces... We all know that in their presence we always strive our best to excel; besides which better order will always be observed in our assemblage in which the fair sex form a part than when they are not to be found.[9]

The proprietors of Capitoline and Union grounds provided special seating accommodations for women, and newspaper accounts of games routinely commented on the number of ladies in attendance. While reporters often moralized on the evils of drinking and gambling at games, they would also condemn the ungentlemanly conduct of male cranks. For example, reporting on the July 20, 1865, match between the Atlantics and the team from Lowell, Massachusetts, at Capitoline, the *Daily Union* strongly criticized the less than chivalric behavior of several male fans.

> We passed the platforms of seats reserved—or rather they should be reserved—for the lady visitors, and to the discredit of the city we have to state that the boorish occupants of the seats remained in them until actually forced by the police to retire, even while a dozen ladies were standing in the sun right in front of them. We trust never to see such selfish rudeness displayed on a ball ground. Afterwards, through the extertions of the officers of the Atlantic Club, prominent among them Mr. Babcock, aided by the police, the well-dressed roughs of the crowd who thus disgraced the name of men were obliged to vacate their places and give them up to those who were entitled to them. Some more efficient arrangement is required than was made yesterday before we can expect to enjoy the patronage of the fair sex at our matches.[10]

This brief diatribe by the *Daily Union* revealed not only the image of women as passive, fragile creatures to be placed on a pedestal (in this case, benches protected from the sun) but also reinforced the male baseball fraternity's attitude toward women's role in the sport. Women were described as "visitors" to "our matches." With notable exceptions, throughout its history baseball would remain outside the sphere of women's activities.

If the white male baseball fraternity clearly defined the role of women in baseball, it virtually ignored the existence of African-American baseball clubs and players. Although documentation is sparse, there is evidence that African-American clubs existed in Brooklyn at least as early as 1859. The December 10, 1859, issue of the *Anglo-American* reported a November 15 match in which the Henson Base Ball Club of Jamaica defeated the Unknown of Weeksville by a score of 54–43.[11] Since the brief article refers to the game as "another victory for the Henson," it is likely that African-American teams had been in existence for some time. Weeksville, home of the Unknown ball club, was an African-American community founded in the 1830s in Bedford.

The *Daily Eagle* published a rare report of a match between African-American clubs in its October 17, 1862, issue. The game's coverage, which only occurred by chance, illustrates the racial attitudes of the anti-abolitionist Brooklyn newspaper.

A NEW SENSATION IN BASE BALL CIRCLES—
SAMBO AS A BALL PLAYER, AND DINAH AS AN EMULATOR
UNKNOWN OF WEEKSVILLE VS. MONITOR OF BROOKLYN

The return match between the Atlantic and Harlem Clubs did not take place as appointed yesterday afternoon, but was postponed on account of the unfit conditions of the grounds for playing. Among the large crowd that visited the ground was our reporter, who, on learning that the match would not be played, went on a perambulating tour through the precincts of Bedford, waiting for something to "turn up." He had not proceeded far when he discovered a crowd assembled on the grounds in the vicinity of the Yukaton Skating Pond, and on repairing to the locality, found a match in progress between the Unknown and Monitor Clubs—both of African descent. Quite a large assemblage encircled the contestants, who were every one as black as the ace of spades. Among the assemblage we noticed a number of old and well known players, who seemed to enjoy the game more heartily than if they had been the players themselves. The dusky contestants enjoyed the game hugely, and to use a common phrase, they "did the thing genteely." Dinah, all eyes, was there to applaud, and the game passed off most satisfactorily. All appeared to have had a very jolly time, and the little piccaninnies laughed with the rest. It would have done Beecher, Greely, or any other of the luminaries of the radical wing of the Republican party good to have been present. The playing was quite spirited, and the fates decreed a victory for the Unknown. The occaision was the first of a series. We append the score:

Unknown	HL	R	Monitor	HL	R
Pole, 3d	5	2	Dudley, 1st b	3	2
V. Thompson, l.f.	2	7	W. Cook, r.f.	2	2
Wright, 2s b	5	3	Willimas, s.s.	2	1
J. Thompson, p	5	1	Marshal, 3d b	4	1
Smith, c.f.	0	9	G. Abrams, p	3	2
Johnson, c	7	2	Brown, c	3	3
A. Thompson, 1st b	5	4	Cook, l.f.	4	1
Durant, r.f.	4	5	Orater, 2d b	3	2
Harvey, s.s.	3	4	J. Abrams, c.f.	3	1
		41			15

Runs Made in Each Inning

	1	2	3	4	5	6	7	8	9
Unknown	3	4	3	7	14	1	7	2	0—41
Monitor	3	3	0	0	2	1	1	5	0—15

Umpire—C. Ophate, of the Hamilton of Newark
Scorers—Baker, Unknown; Jones, Monitor

This is the first match to our knowledge that has been played in this city between players of African descent.[12]

Even though the *Daily Eagle* did not regularly report on matches of African-American clubs, it is curious that the newspaper appeared not to even be aware of their existence. It is likely that there were a number of clubs in existence in the metropolitan area by 1862. But, just as mid-nineteenth century ideology defined women's sphere, the mindset of whites treated blacks, at best, as "invisible men." At worst, an ideology supporting racism would lead to violence, destruction, and death.

The development of racist ideology was long and complex, but a significant element was the whites' notions about economic interests.[13] Although many Brooklynites supported the Union and abolitionist cause, the disruption of commerce with the Southern states was perceived by a significant proportion of businessmen in Brooklyn as an economic threat to their livelihoods. The large Irish working class in Brooklyn viewed blacks as competitors for their jobs. Brooklynites would respond to these interests in the political arena and in the streets.

Abraham Lincoln lost the election of 1860 in Brooklyn. Moreover, a Negro suffrage amendment on the New York State ballot that year, which would have abolished property ownership as a qualification for voting by blacks, was overwhelming turned down by Brooklyn voters by a 4 to 1 margin.[14] Arguing against the amendment, Brooklyn state assemblyman Theophilus Collicot expressed a common sentiment among many Brooklyn citizens: "the proposition to put Negroes on a footing of equal political equality with the white man is repugnant to the sense of the American people."[15] In Collicot's words, the American people would never agree to "share the proud title of 'American Citizen' with an inferior and abject race."

Throughout the 1860s, the *Daily Eagle*, the voice of Democratic Party opinion, would reinforce these racial attitudes. The following item, which appeared in the July 10, 1862, issue of the *Daily Eagle*, is typical of the newspaper's portrayal of blacks, even those with professional status:

THE NEGRO AMONG THE DOCTORS—At a meeting of the Kings County Medical Society held the other evening, the question of admitting a colored physician name Rae, came up for consideration. It appeared that the doctor was recommended by the "censors" of the society as a person competent to become a member. A good deal of opposition was offered to admission, partly on technical grounds and partly physical. The learned body finally, after solemn discussion, resolved to refer the question of Dr. Rae's admissibility to a special committee of three for thorough ventilation. Sambo appears to be ubiquitous. He is in the army—in the church—the Sabbath school—the Bar, etc., and now he turns up among the Doctors. Where next? Well that is hard to determine, probably in grand Opera.

During the Civil War, racial animosity would turn to violence. In August 1862 mobs of Irish workers marched on several tobacco factories in South Brooklyn where they attacked black workers and tried to set fire to the buildings.[16] The following summer, the New York City draft riots spread to Brooklyn where rioters sacked nearly every African-American home near the East River waterfront.[17] Many of the blacks who were unable to escape were beaten and some were killed.

Although open hostilities diminished following the Civil War, racial integration and some semblance of equality in American institutions, including baseball, would be long in coming. In 1867, however, an African-American team from Philadelphia would challenge the "color line."

In 1866, two African-American clubs, the Excelsiors and the Pythians, were formed in Philadelphia, which had the largest black population of any northern U.S. city. The records of the Pythian Base Ball Club of Philadelphia, uncovered in the archives of the Historical Society of Pennsylvania by baseball historian Harold Seymour, provide insights into the early African-American clubs.[18] The Pythians were organized by the Philadelphia chapter of the Knights of Pythias, a middle class African-American fraternal organization. The conventions of the club closely paralleled those of the early white gentlemen's baseball clubs. The Pythians enforced a strict moral code on club members, prohibiting "spirituous liquors," card playing, gambling and wagering on ball games. They arranged matches with other clubs through written invitations. And, the club would host postgame banquets. They maintained friendly relations with the Athletics, obtaining the use of their ball grounds and having an Athletics club member serve as umpire in Pythian matches. Like the white clubs, the Pythians engaged in the practice of revolving. In one instance, prior to an important match, they tried to aquire the services of two players, Clark and Wilson, from the Philadelphia Excelsiors. In addition to playing other area black baseball teams, they were known to have played informal matches with white ball clubs.

In his study of the demographics of baseball players in Philadelphia, sports historian George B. Kirsch finds similarities between white and African-American players.[19] Players from both races were largely artisans, petty proprietors, and clerks. This corresponds to Adelman's findings related to white baseball players in New York and Brooklyn.[20]

In 1867 the Pythians and the Excelsiors were playing black clubs from other cities. The Pythians hosted the Mutuals of Washington, D.C., a team of black federal government employees. After the match they provided their guests with a sumptuous feast of wine, meat, cheese, ice cream and cigars. In October 1867, the Excelsiors had sufficient resources to make a road trip to play African-American teams in Brooklyn and Albany.

The Excelsiors' visit to Brooklyn drew the attention of the *Daily Union* and the *Ball Player's Chronicle*. On September 30, the *Daily Union* announced the upcoming matches between the Excelsiors and the Unique and Monitor clubs of Brooklyn, scheduled for Satellite Grounds on October 3 and 4. The newspaper referred to the visitors as the "celebrated champion Excelsior club of Philadelphia." In contrast to the *Daily Eagle*, the pro–Republican Party *Daily Union* showed more respect for the black clubs. According to the *Daily Union*, all three clubs were "comprised of very respectable colored people well-to-do in the world, and the several nines of the three clubs include many first class players." The *Daily Union* article also notes that white fans in attendance at African-American games were known to harass the black players:

> The visitors will receive all due attention from their colored brethren of Brooklyn, and we trust, for the good name of the fraternity, that none of the "white trash" who disgrace white clubs, by following and bawling for them will be allowed to mar the pleasure of these social colored gatherings.[21]

But, there is also some evidence that there were positive relationships between black and white clubs in Brooklyn. In its announcement of the upcoming matches, the *Ball Player's Chronicle* noted that J. Grum, a well-known member of the all-white Eckfords, had volunteered his services as umpire for the contests.[22]

On October 3, before the largest crowd of the season at Satellite Grounds, half of which was white, the Unique Club of Brooklyn's Eastern District hosted the Excelsiors. A large contingent of fans and the club's band accompanied the Philadelphia team. The Excelsiors also brought with them, according to the *Ball Player's Chronicle*, "a reputation as skillful experts on a par with the Athletic Club."[23]

From the very beginning discord among the clubs and fans marred the contest. Before the first pitch, a dispute arose over the choice of an umpire. The Excelsiors refused to accept an official from Brooklyn and insisted upon a ball player from Albany. Both the *Daily Union* and the *Ball Player's Chronicle* commented upon the chosen umpire's incompetence which led to disputes in every inning. Moreover, crowd disturbances erupted thoughout the game; in one instance a Philadelphia fan was arrested for "insulting" the *Daily Union* reporter.[24]

The Excelsiors dominated the game throughout and held a commanding 42–37 lead at the end of six innings. In the seventh inning the Uniques staged a rally and appeared on the verge of catching the Excelsiors when the Philadelphia club refused to play further on account of darkness. A row ensued, and in the confusion the *Daily Union* reporter was unsure of the final outcome of the game. The *Ball Player's Chronicle*, however, later reported that the match had indeed been called on account of darkness and the score thus reverted to the tally at the end of six innings. The Excelsiors had come away with the ball. According to the *Ball Player's Chronicle*, "The proceeding terminated in a rather unsatisfactory manner."[25] But, the tenor of the match, rife with discord among fans and players, was not atypical of matches among white clubs in the 1860s.

Following the game, the Excelsiors traveled to Albany, then returned to Brooklyn to take on the Monitors. Although no details of this match were published, the *Ball Player's Chronicle* reported that the Monitors avenged their brethren, the Uniques, by a handsome victory over the Philadelphians.[26]

On October 25, the Uniques and the Monitors met on Satellite Grounds for what the *Ball Player's Chronicle* called "the contest for the championship of colored clubs."[27] The early innings were closely contested as "the play exhibited on each side was very creditable." But, in the later innings, the Monitors pulled away thanks to their batting, which "they did in terrific style." The Monitors incredibly scored 15 runs in the seventh inning and 17 in the eighth to gain a 49–17 victory over the Uniques. Two weeks after the long championship reign of the Atlantics of the NABBP came to an end, the Monitors of Brooklyn could lay claim to the championship of "colored" teams.

The coverage in October 1867 of African-American baseball matches by the *Daily Union* and the *Ball Player's Chronicle* provided publicity and a degree of legitimacy to the black ball clubs. But the emergence of black baseball clubs that exhibited a quality of play comparable to white clubs proved to be a threat to the white baseball fraternity. Before the year had ended, the NABBP would ban black players from membership in any of its member clubs.

A week before the match between the Uniques and Monitors, the Pythian Club applied for membership in the Pennsylvania chapter of the NABBP. Although several NABBP club delegates were sympathetic to the Pythians, the association refused to accept the black club's application.

Two months later, at its annual convention in Philadelphia, the NABBP formally banned "colored" players from league clubs. The *Ball Player's Chronicle* published the significant clause in the report of the NABBP Nominating Committee:

> It is not presumed by your committee that any club who have applied are composed of persons of color, or any portion of them; and the recommendations of your committee in this report are based upon this view, and they unanimously report against the admission of any club which may be composed of one or more colored persons.[28]

African-American baseball clubs continued to play in the New York area, although they received very little publicity. Like their white counterparts, in the 1870s they were playing for gate receipts. The *Daily Times'* September 27, 1871, issue announced an upcoming match of two black teams, the Keystones from Troy and the Amicables of New York, to be played at Union Grounds with an admission of 25 cents to be charged. This was not a singular event since the article refers to previous matches "between clubs of a similar description ... still fresh in the memory of those who were fortunate enough to witness them." The newspaper promoted the contest as a novelty game. In a follow-up announcement the next day, the *Daily Times* described the Amicables' pitcher as one who could "pitch with either hand, and throw a ball with his teeth to the bases with great precision. There will be fun, you bet."[29]

The Keystones defeated the Amicables 41–23 in the game played on September 29. The performance apparently did not fulfill the expectations built by the promotional hype. According to the *Daily Times*:

> The white "trash" who paid their quarter to have some fun, as they supposed, were greatly disappointed in the tameness of the affair, and after shivering for a while in cold expectation to see something exciting, took a farewell look at the "mokes," and wended their way outside the enclosure.[30]

In the 1880s white minor league professional teams began recruiting black players. According to Sol White, an African-American player who was also baseball's first black historian of the game, "twenty colored ball players were playing in various professional leagues throughout the country."[31] Although the National League enforced a "gentlemen's agreement" which banned players of color, the minor leagues were apparently more interested in talent than skin color.

Bud Fowler, born ironically in Cooperstown in 1858, was one of the first outstanding black players to play on predominately white professional teams.[32] Among his early exploits, in an exhibition game in 1878 he defeated the Boston Red Stockings and the former Atlantic pitcher Tommy Bond. Fowler played for 14 teams in nine leagues before ending his career barnstorming with all black clubs.

Another early black baseball star, Moses Fleetwood "Fleet" Walker, would be a landmark figure in the history of baseball. Walker's early life was strikingly similar to that of Jackie Robinson.[33] He grew up in a middle class family in Ohio. He entered Oberlin College in 1877 where he starred in baseball for three years. In the spring of 1882, Walker enrolled as a law student in the University of Michigan and continued to display his baseball talents for the Wolverines. But, the following year he decided to forgo the promise of a law career and signed as a catcher with the Toledo baseball club of the newly formed Northwestern League.

In 1884, Toledo and Brooklyn became new members of the American Association, a major league rival of the National League. As a member of the Toledo team, Fleet Walker would have the honor of being the first African-American to play major league baseball. As a catcher, with little padding or protection, Walker suffered the physical abuse that only a fellow "receiver" would understand. The Toledo batboy would later recall, "I have seen him with his fingers split open and bleeding, but he would go right on catching. He had more nerve and grit than anybody I have ever seen."[34] Like Jackie Robinson, he would also face the racial animosity of players, fans, and the press, especially when Toledo played in the southern cities of St. Louis, Louisville, and Richmond.

On June 15, Toledo arrived in Brooklyn to play a three game series at Washington Park. On that day the *Daily Eagle* eulogized the longtime great Eckford player Frank Pigeon who had recently died. In the next few days, in its reports of the Toledo-Brooklyn matches, the newspaper known for its racial epithets curiously made no mention of Fleet Walker's presence. Walker did not play in the first match on June 16, won by Toledo, 6–4. But, the following day Fleet Walker became the first African-American to play a major league baseball game in Brooklyn. He had one hit in four times at bat in Toledo's 6–4 loss. The *New York Sun* singled out Walker, not because of his skin color, but for his outstanding play on the field: "Walker's fine play behind the bat was the feature of the Toledo's work in the field, his throwing being very swift and accurate."[35] In the final game of the series, Walker went one-for-five in another Toledo loss to Brooklyn. Not until 1947, when Jackie Robinson appeared for the first time at Ebbets Field, would an African-American play in a major league game in Brooklyn. When Walker was released by Toledo at the end of the season, he would in fact be the last black player to play in any major league game until Robinson.

Washington Park, Brooklyn, 1887. (Transcendental Graphics.)

By the late 1880s, just as Jim Crow laws in the South legally segregated blacks and whites, by "gentlemen's agreement" the white professional baseball fraternity enforced the color line in the country's national pastime.[36] Black professional teams such as the Cuban Giants, initially comprised of waiters at the Argyle Resort Hotel in Babylon, Long Island, in 1885, and the Brooklyn Royal Giants, formed in 1905 by John Conners, a black businessman and propriartor of the Royal Café in Brooklyn, would play as independents against other black clubs.

In the twentieth century, black baseball clubs formed their own professional leagues, providing opportunities for some of the best baseball players in the country. Segregated baseball finally came to an end when Jackie Robinson signed with the Brooklyn Dodgers in 1947. Although he was not the first black to play in a major league game, Robinson broke the color line in baseball, and by his example helped to crack the barriers of segregation in American.[37]

CHAPTER EIGHT

The Birth of the Dodgers

In 1882 professional baseball was experiencing a resurgence of interest with the newly formed American Association joining the National League, but with the demise of the Atlantics the "city of baseball" was without a professional team. In the winter of 1882, George Taylor, an editor at the *New York Herald*, made plans for establishing a new baseball franchise. According to the *Clipper*'s account, Taylor located a Wall Street financier to back the project.[1] When Taylor's supporter realized how expensive the effort would be, however, he tried to back out of the deal. Taylor hired a lawyer, John Brine, to help him in the legal matter. Coincidently, Charles Byrne, a realtor who rented desk space in Brine's office, learned of the project and saw it as a financial opportunity. To the delight of Taylor, Byrne secured financial backing from his brother-in-law, Joseph Doyle, who ran a gambling casino on Ann Street in New York.[2] Brine drew up the papers of co-partnership establishing Taylor, Byrne, and Doyle as owners of the new Brooklyn Base Ball Association. They hired a young Brooklyn printer, Charles Ebbets, as a jack-of-all-trades to print score cards, sell tickets and do the bookkeeping. Although the initial idea for the team was Taylor's, Byrne became the guiding force of the new franchise. By 1905, Ebbets would gain controlling interest in the club and begin making plans for the stadium in Flatbush that would bear his name.

While the club was still being planned, controversies erupted over the team's financing. Rumors circulated that baseball mogul John Day, who controlled both the New York Club of the National League and the New York Metropolitans of the new American Association, was a financial backer of the Brooklyn Club.[3] More troublesome were the reports of a con artist who, presenting himself as a representative of the Brooklyn

Club, fleeced a number of people through the sale of fraudulent stock in the team. Although the club was yet to have a roster of players, a league to play in, or a home ballpark, it was at least getting media attention.

The first order of business was to find a home field. For the site of their ballpark, the entrepreneurs selected a parcel of land which they leased from Edwin Litchfield near the Gowanus Canal. Bordered by 3rd and 5th streets, and 4th and 5th avenues, the locale was known at the time to Brooklynites as the popular Washington skating pond. Located in a predominately Irish neighborhood, the park was easily accessible by way of horse-car lines which ran along 3rd and 5th avenues. Just over a century earlier these historically significant grounds was the scene of a major conflict in the Battle of Brooklyn in 1776. On August 27, nearly 300 American troops were killed near the Vechte-Cortelyou Dutch farmhouse ("old stone house at Gowanus") while successfully holding back the British advance. In what today is Byrne Park, a replica of the house, rebuilt from the original stones, operates as an historical interpretive center to commemorate the battle. Ironically, today's Byrne Park is also the site of the first ball grounds of Brooklyn's first baseball club, the Excelsiors.

After quickly spending $12,000 to grade and prepare the property, Doyle turned to Ferdinand Abell, a fellow gambling hall operator in Naragansett, Rhode Island, for additional funding.[4] The club spent a total of $30,000 to construct a ballpark on the site. Despite inclement weather, work began in January 1883. A wooden "L" shaped grandstand was built along 5th Avenue, where the main entrance was located, and along 5th Street.[5] Dressing rooms for the visiting teams and a bar were constructed under the 5th Street stands. The "old stone house" was renovated and used as a clubhouse.[6]

The Club began accepting formal applications from prospective players in January. It appears that the club owners were closely examining the résumés for evidence of outstanding personal character as much as playing skill. The *Clipper* reported that:

> The Brooklyn management will under no circumstances employ any player whose integrity of character is not a feature of his recommendations, nor any one who has not a clear record for temperate habits. They want men of intelligence, and not corner-lot roughs who may happen to possess some skill as players, but whose habits and ways unfit them for thorough teamwork, and such players need not trouble themselves to apply for positions on the new Brooklyn Club's team.[7]

Of the 40 applications received, by the end of January 16 "honest, intelligent and earnest players" made the first cut.[8]

The Brooklyn Club applied for admission to the newly formed Inter-state Association, a professional minor league. On March 31, only one month before the opening of the season, Brooklyn was accepted into the ranks of teams from what were clearly less than major league cities: the Active of Reading, the Anthracite of Pottsville, the Harrisburgh Club, the Merritt of Camden, the Quickstep of Wilmington, and the Trenton Club.[9]

In mid–April the club announced its initial roster for the coming season. Three sets of battery mates included Eagan and Dugan, Doyle and Farrow, and Creden and Murphy. On the infield were Walker, Manning, Schenck, and Geer. Luff, Dolan and a "change pitcher" would play the outfield. The goodly number of Irish names must surely have been attractive to the Gowanus fans. As construction continued on Washington Park, the team began a daily regimen of practice at the Parade Grounds.

As the playing season approached, the Brooklyn Club had much to compete with for the public's attention. The Barnum Circus, "the Greatest Show on Earth," was in town. The traditional "moving day" in Brooklyn when renters' leases expired was nearing. And, most significantly the city was abuzz over the inauguration of the recently completed Brooklyn Bridge. In late April, people lined up to obtain passes for a pre-inaugural walk across the "eighth wonder of the world."[10] Newspaper coverage of sporting events was squeezed as the dailies filled their pages with stories of the bridge's construction and inaugural events. Less heralded was the opening game of the Brooklyn Club in Wilmington on May 1. The Quickstep defeated Brooklyn 9–6.[11]

Brooklyn was to have opened its home season at Washington Park on May 9 against Harrisburgh. But, since the ballpark was not yet ready for play, the club planned to move the game to Newark. Unfortunately, due to a mix-up in arrangements, a circus was occupying the ballgrounds. Faced with the prospect of forfeiting the game, the Brooklyn Club, with little public notice, moved the game to the unenclosed Parade Grounds. Thus, on May 9, a surprisingly large crowd of about 1,000 fans witnessed free of charge the first home game of the baseball team that would evolve into the Brooklyn Dodgers.[12] Brooklyn pitcher Eagan struck out seven men and held the opponents to only one run, while the Brooklyn hitting, combined with six Harrisburgh errors, led to a 7–1 home team victory. Ever watchful of ungentlemanly conduct, the *Clipper* report of the match noted that the Harrisburgh players were continually "kicking," disputing the umpire's decisions throughout the entire game. In an interview following the game, Harrisburgh shortstop Myers told the *Clipper* that "all the clubs did the same thing out of town or away from home." The *Clipper* responded, "If they do, then the clubs ought to promptly reform the abuse."

On May 12, before a crowd of 6,000 fans, the Brooklyn team played its inaugural game at Washington Park against Trenton. The grandstand and bleachers were packed, and according to the *Daily Eagle*, "Campstools and chairs on the grounds were used in every available spot, while many spectators were standing near the boundary fence which surrounded the field."[13] The *Daily Eagle* noted that many of the spectators had not attended a baseball game in several years. According to the observant *Clipper*, "never before in the history of the game in that city have so many ladies been present as were seen on the grandstand."[14]

For an hour before game time, the Twenty-Third Regiment Band entertained the fans as they filed in to find their seats. Each team, as they entered the field for pregame practice, drew a round of applause from the appreciative crowd. The Trentons sported grey uniforms, trimmed in red with red stockings. The Brooklyn team was also clad in grey suits, but with blue trim and blue stockings. Brooklyn would acquire the nickname "Grays," a variant of the color of their uniform, although this did not distinguish them from most other clubs who were similarly attired.

Under a clear sky, the game commenced on time at 4 p.m. Trenton went to bat first and scored three runs in the opening inning. The visitors were aided by several fielding errors which the *Daily Eagle* attributed to nervousness exhibited by the home club. Brooklyn quickly responded in their half of the first inning, scoring two runs. After the shaky first inning, the Brooklyn fielders settled down and exhibited outstanding defensive play throughout the remainder of the game. Eagan, the Brooklyn hurler, only allowed Trenton three additional runs in the contest. Meanwhile, timely hitting by the home club resulted in 13 runs. In its inaugural game at Washington Park, the Brooklyn team awarded its appreciative fans with a decisive 13–6 win.

In the month of May 1883, Brooklyn was symbolically at a fulcrum point. The inauguration of the Brooklyn Bridge on May 24 was emblematic of the tranformation of America to the modern world.[15] The inauguration of Washington Park by Brooklyn's new baseball franchise likewise represented the beginning of a new era in baseball history. At this point of transformation, the staid *New York Times*, America's newspaper of record, published an announcement which brought closure to an earlier era of Brooklyn baseball:

> The most famous base-ball grounds in the country will soon be blotted out and overrun by streets and buildings. Heyward-street is to be extended from

Marcy-avenue to Harrison-avenue through the old Union Grounds in Brooklyn, Eastern District, so well known to every base-ball enthusiast in the palmy days of the national game. Twenty years ago these were the grounds of the old Eckford Club, that held the championship for seven successive seasons [sic]. Then came the Atlantics of Brooklyn and the Mutuals of New York, whose memorable contests on the diamond field gave pleasure to thousands of spectators. The approach of the day when these grounds must disappear and be buried under brick and mortar recalls to the memory of the old base-ball players a host of events connected with the growth of the game and the fortunes of noted batsmen, pitchers, and fielders. Many of the base-ball giants are dead and gone, but a few survive, and some of these still tread the base lines. The feats of MILLS and HATFIELD, of ZETLEIN [sic], START, and FERGUSON, of the old short stops and slow pitchers, of PIKE and PEARCE and the WRIGHTS, and the many great players who met the Atlantics and Mutuals upon this old field are still fresh in the minds of those who followed the fortunes of the nines as closely as a Wall-street "slave of the tape" watches the variations in the price of this favorite stock. For many years the history of the Union Grounds was the history of the game, but at last betting and pool-selling gave the place a bad name, and its glory departed never to return. Now the scene is to be shifted. The green field, the old lines, the buildings, and the pagoda from which rises the rod once bent by a ball struck from the home-plate by "LIP" PIKE, are going, and the busy hum of trade and travel will drown the dying echoes of the umpire's voice and the cheers that once shook the grand stand.[16]

With the passing of the era of "cooperative nine" baseball, Brooklyn fans looked ahead to the promise of their new corporate team. Throughout the first half of the season, although not sensational, the Grays played competently. By early August, they were in third place, but their fortunes would improve when the league-leading Merrits of Camden disbanded. Charles Byrne shrewdly picked up five of the top players from the Merrits: infielders Bill Greenwood, Charlie Householder, and Frank Fenelly; pitcher Sam Kimber; and catcher John Corcoran.[17] Byrne also signed William "Adonis" Terry, a 19-year-old pitcher who had been playing for the semi-pro Rosedale Club of Bridgeport, Connecticut.[18] Terry became a stalwart hurler for Brooklyn, playing with the team for nine seasons, accumulating nearly two hundred victories in his professional career. Terry also was one of Brooklyn's most popular players in the 1880s, particularly among the lady fans.

Revitalized by the infusion of new players, the Grays steadily improved their record. In mid–September, they passed Harrisburgh to take over first place.[19] From Brooklyn's first match with Harrisburgh at the Parade Grounds in May, the contests between the two teams would be rancorous affairs. While continually assailing the umpire's decisions, the Alleghenies would bend the rules to their advantage. Schappert, one of the Harrisburgh pitchers, achieved exceptional velocity by throwing what bordered on a then-illegal overhand pitch. According to the *Clipper*, the Alleghenies had so intimidated the umpires that they were afraid to enforce the pitching rule.[20] Schappert would also intimidate batters with what would later be called the "bean-ball pitch." In its inimitable fashion, the *Clipper* described Schappert's strategy:

> Schappert in his delivery of the ball to the bat has adopted a line of conduct which is hardly worthy a manly player, and one which is in direct violation of the American rules of the game; and that is his intimidation of batsmen by sending the ball to them so as to either hit them or oblige them to look more to avoiding a dangerous blow than to hitting the ball.[21]

Apparently the Alleghenies' fans were as vitriolic as the players, if not more so. In an August 4 contest in Harrisburgh, Brooklyn came from behind in the bottom of the ninth to capture a narrow 2–1 win. The Brooklyn players and the umpire had to be escorted from the grounds by police to protect them from being stoned by the incensed Harrisburgh crowd.[22]

In the last month of the season the two teams battled for first place, neither being able to pull away. The deciding match to determine the Interstate championship was played on the final day of the season on September 29 at Washington Park. The day before, Schappert had pitched Harrisburgh to an 8–5 win over Brooklyn, setting up the dramatic showdown.[23]

Brooklyn took a commanding 7–1 lead after the first three innings. But, Harrisburgh rallied with five runs in the fifth and sixth innings. In the sixth, with the tying run on third base, Terry struck out Allegheny first baseman Shetzline for the third time to end the inning. The Grays scored four more times in the game, while Terry blanked Harrisburgh the rest of the way. The Brooklyn Grays had won the pennant, bringing Brooklyn its first baseball championship since the glory years of the Atlantics.

In 1884, the Grays joined the American Association; Brooklyn was now in the major leagues. Charlie Byrne's baseball team would survive many illustrious, and some not so illustrious, years. It would be known by a succession of names: Grays, Bridegrooms, Hanlon's Superbas, Trolley Dodgers, Robins, Brooks, Dodgers, and Bums. The team would call home a series of ballparks: the Parade Grounds; Washington Park I (1883–1890); Eastern Park in Brownsville (1891–1887); Washington Park II, between

1st and 3rd streets, and 3rd and 4th avenues (1898–1913); and Ebbets Field (1912–1957). In 1958, the Dodgers left Brooklyn for the sunny climes of Los Angeles, inaugurating the postmodern era of baseball. For many Brooklyn baseball fans, however, 1958 marked the end of baseball history.

CHAPTER NINE

Brooklyn's Early Stars

(Note: The information for these biographical sketches has been accumulated from various sources: local newspapers; the *New York Clipper*; the *Sporting News*; the Spaulding Collection, New York Public Library; Robert L. Tiemann and Mark Rucker, eds., *Nineteenth Century Stars* [Cleveland: Society for American Baseball Research, 1989]; and Frederick Ivor-Campbell, Robert L. Tiemann and Mark Rucker, eds., *Baseball's First Stars* [Cleveland: Society for American Baseball Research, 1996]. Team records and individuals statistics are compiled from John Thorn and Peter Palmer, *Total Baseball* [New York: Warner Books, 1989]; Marshall D. Wright, *The National Association of Base Ball Players, 1857–1870* [Jefferson, N.C.: McFarland & Company, 2000]; *Nineteenth Century Stars*; and *Baseball's First Stars*.)

When the National Baseball Hall of Fame opened in Cooperstown, New York, in 1939, two baseball figures from Brooklyn—Henry Chadwick and Candy Cummings—were among the first inductees enshrined for their contributions to the game. To this day, no other pre–Dodger era baseballist has been so honored. Although their credentials perhaps do not merit baseball sainthood, many Brooklyn players from the game's early era are owed a debt of gratitude for helping to establish baseball as the country's national pastime. In their time, they were among the very best. This final chapter pays tribute to some of the star players from the city of baseball.

Asa "The Count" Brainard
Born: 1841 Albany, NY
Died: December 29, 1888 Denver, CO
5'8" 150 lb.

Over the years Brooklyn has known its share of unusual characters, but Asa Brainard surely ranks among the more interesting players who have donned a Brooklyn uniform. As a pitcher, Brainard threw the ball exceptionally hard, but he also lived life hard and became known for his quirkiness both on the field and off.

Brainard began playing second base and in the outfield for the famous Excelsior Club of 1860. After a year's hiatus, when the Excelsiors returned to competition in 1862, Brainard continued to play largely in the outfield. But, following Jim Creighton's death in October, Asa was called upon to replace the Excelsiors' star hurler. It is interesting to speculate on what Brainard's playing career might have been had Creighton not died. But, until his retirement from the game, Brainard would be a pitcher. Through the completion of the 1866 season with the Excelsiors, he would pitch in the shadow of Creighton on less than competitive teams.

In 1867, Brainard escaped to the Nationals of Washington. The Nationals that year, led by George Wright, captured America's attention by embarking on the first trans-Allegheny road trip, posting a 29-7 record for the season. Brainard only played in six games for the Nationals, but he must have impressed George Wright's brother, Harry, who was building a professional squad in Cincinnati. The Red Stockings recruited Asa to play in Cincinnati in 1868. The following year, Brainard was the "iron man" pitcher for the dominant big red machine.

When Brainard first moved to Cincinnati he found lodging in the home of widowed Elizabeth Truman and her daughter Mary.* Elizabeth, the wife of William T. Truman, publisher of the McGuffey Readers series, had fallen on hard times after her husband's death and found it necessary to take in boarders to help ends meet. Brainard would prove not to be a typical boarder. Shortly after his arrival he contracted smallpox. While Mary Truman helped to nurse Asa back to health, a love affair developed and the two were soon married at the Truman home.

Although now a family man, when the Red Stockings were on the

---

*Information on Asa Brainard's personal life is reported by Stephen D. Guschov, The Red Stockings of Cincinnati: Base Ball's First All-Professional Team and Its Historic 1869 and 1870 Seasons (Jefferson, N.C.: McFarland, 2000).

road (and that was most of the season) Brainard enjoyed the night life and often caroused until the wee hours of the morning. If the team had a game the next day, it was not unusual for him to be absent or late, or complain of illness. Cincinnati captain Harry Wright, a strict disciplinarian, often threatened to dock Brainard's pay to get him to play. More troublesome still, Brainard was suspected of accepting $200 to fix an 1869 match against the Unions of Lansingburgh.

Brainard was apparently as quirky on the field as off. His base running techniques reportedly bordered on the vaudevillian. The often-told story of Brainard throwing a ball at a wayward rabbit running across the field while a game was in progress perhaps best exemplifies Asa's particular brand of "headwork." As teammate George Wright said of Brainard, "he gets odd notions."

In 1870 the bubble burst on the Red Stockings. Brainard was the losing pitcher when the Atlantics upset Cincinnati at Capitoline Grounds in June. The team lost six more games and collapsed at the end of the season. Brainard moved on to the Washington Olympics in the newly formed National Association in 1871. Brainard ingloriously finished his career with a 24–56 record playing for the Olympics, Mansfield, and Baltimore. He retired from the game at the end of the 1874 season.

Brainard fell on hard times after his playing days. He tried to enlist Harry Wright's assistance in procuring an umpiring position but to no avail. He abandoned his wife and infant son. In the early 1880s he secured a job managing an archery range on Staten Island, but ill fortune continued to plague the Count. The *New York Clipper* reported in 1882 that, in a freak accident, Brainard was severely injured when a stray arrow pierced his hand. Asa later moved to Denver where he operated a billiard parlor until he died on December 29, 1888.

John Joseph "Black Jack" Burdock

Born: April 1852 Brooklyn, NY
Died: November 27, 1931 Brooklyn, NY
5'9½" 158 lb.

Jack Burdock began playing with the amateur Atlantics as a catcher in 1871. When the club joined the professional ranks in 1872, Burdock continued to play for the hapless Atlantics behind the plate and at third base.

In 1874, Burdock moved to the Mutuals and in 1875 began a three-year stint with Hartford where he switched to second base, the position

John Burdock (*New York Clipper*).

he would command for the rest of his career. From 1876 through 1884 Burdock was arguably the best fielding second baseman in the game. From 1876 through 1880, Burdock led the National League in putouts by second basemen; between 1877 and 1884, he was the leader in fielding percentage five times.

In 1878 Burdock joined the Boston Red Caps (formerly, Red Stockings) where he played for 11 seasons. His playing career and possibly his life were nearly cut short in a freak accident on April 8, 1881. En route to a game at Boston's South End Grounds, the horse car he was riding jolted when it struck a rock on the track, throwing Burdock from the car's platform. The back of his head hit the pavement, causing a severe concussion. The *New York Clipper* reported that he was taken to his home where he was comatose and in critical condition. The *Clipper* predicted that it would be a long time before he returned to play again. But, Burdock miraculously recovered and played in 73 of the team's 83 games.

Although not known as a great batter, in 1883 Burdock had a career season at the plate. As Boston (now called the Beaneaters) battled Chicago for the pennant into the last week of the season, Burdock's hitting rallied Boston past the White Stockings to win the championship. Burdock finished the season with a .330 batting average and 88 RBIs. He remained solid in the field with a .921 fielding percentage.

In the later years of his career, Burdock suffered numerous injuries and developed a drinking problem. According to baseball historian Mark Sternman, before the 1888 season, Burdock with charged with intoxication and assaulting a woman. Rooming with fellow alcoholic "King" Kelly, the "Babe Ruth of the 19th century," surely exacerbated Burdock's problems.

During the 1888 season, Burdock's alcoholism led to his release by the Beaneaters. He was picked up by Brooklyn where he finished the season with a dismal .142 batting average. Over the next few years he played for minor league clubs in New Haven, Jersey City and Salem. In 1891 Burdock returned to his hometown where he played the final three games of his career with the Superbas. He retired after playing 16 seasons in the major leagues and 21 years overall. During his long major league career he recorded an amazing .996 fielding average.

Despite his numerous injuries and many years of alcohol abuse, Burdock outlived many of his contemporaries. He died in Brooklyn on November 27, 1931, at the age of 79.

Henry "Father" or "Chad" Chadwick
Born: October 5, 1824 Exeter, Devon, England
Died: April 20, 1908 Brooklyn, NY

Henry Chadwick, more than any other individual, is responsible for promoting and shaping the contours of the game of baseball in the nineteenth century. Born in England in 1824, he moved with his family to Brooklyn at the age of 13. Three decades after watching a baseball match between the Eagle and Gotham Clubs at Elysian Fields in Hoboken, Chadwick reflected on the 1856 experience, describing it as an epiphany:

> The game was being sharply played on both sides and I watched it with deeper interest than any match of the kind I had seen. It was not long before I was struck with the idea that base ball was just the game for a national sport for America, and reflecting on this subject on my return home I came to the conclusion that from this game of ball a powerful lever might be made, by means of which our people could be lifted into a position of more devotion to physical exercise and healthful outdoor recreation than they had hitherto been noted for.

Chadwick began reporting on baseball matches for the *New York Times*, and would over the years write for most of the major dailies in New York and Brooklyn. As longtime baseball editor for the *New York Clipper*, the premier sports weekly, Chadwick reached a nationwide audience, promoting as much a reporting on the game.

A man of his time, Chadwick believed in the power of reason to guide the progress of mankind. In baseball, he championed "scientific" play and the "head game" over brute strength, and forever railed against the irrational evils of gambling, drinking and unmanly "kicking."

Chadwick promoted the development of a truly "national" pastime, governed by uniform game rules, a standard method of scoring, and the compilation of statistics to measure performance and chart the game's

Henry Chadwick, c. 1900. (Transcendental Graphics.)

progress. More than a mere reporter, he was actively involved in implementing his vision. Chadwick served on the National Association's rules committee He introduced the box score and the line-score as regular features of game reports. In 1872, his *New York Clipper* first introduced the modern-day batting average, which would eventually become the major standard for evaluating hitting prowess.

Through his capacity as editor of the annual *Beadle's Dime Base Ball Player* (1860–1881) and annual *Spalding Base Ball Guide* (1881–1908) Chadwick was indeed the voice of baseball in the nineteenth century. An expert on "scientific" techniques of play, he published how-to books on pitching and fielding, batting and base running, and umpiring. Combined with his reports, commentaries and instructional writing in various newspapers, magazines and books, he provided the language and shaped the mental framework for understanding the game. As Jules Tygiel succinctly puts it, "Henry Chadwick invented the baseball experience."

Chadwick was not unaware of his importance to the game. At times he even referred to himself as "Father Chadwick." It is unclear whether he was alluding to himself as the "father of baseball" or the high priest of the game whose homilies guided the baseball fraternity toward the path of righteousness. In its June 8, 1907, issue, *Harper's Weekly* published an interview with Chadwick just one year before his death. Unabashedly, Chadwick describes his role in saving baseball from the evil of gambling:

In the early history of professional baseball, especially during the decade of the seventies, when that curse of all field sports, pool gambling, nearly gave a death-blow to the whole professional business of the game, I had to battle with the evil in question until I drove every "crook" of the period out of the professional fraternity, and then it was that the baseball business began to earn the splendid reputation it now possesses of being the most honorably conducted sport or game there is in vogue.

Chadwick was truly a Renaissance man. He was interested and knowledgeable about many sports and games, and published handbooks and guides on pedestrianism (track and field), skating, curling, ice boating, baseball on ice, cricket, football, rugby, yachting and rowing, lawn bowling, and chess. Chadwick was also interested in billiards, music and drama. In the cold winter months in Brooklyn he was as likely to be seen in his box at the Brooklyn Academy of Music as in his ice boat gliding across the frozen pond in Prospect Park.

On a cold and blustery afternoon, April 14, 1908, at Brooklyn's home opener at Washington Park, Chadwick caught a severe cold which developed into pneumonia. On April 20, at the age of 83, Henry Chadwick died at his home at 840 Halsey Street. Chadwick received tributes from all the major newspapers and sports weeklies, and flags flew at half-staff at ballparks across the country. Following a memorial service attended by numerous baseball dignitaries, including National League President Harry Pulliam, Brooklyn Club owner Charley Ebbets, and longtime friend Al Spalding, Chadwick was buried in Greenwood Cemetery in a plot donated by Spalding. Patrick Powers, president of the National Association of Minor Leagues, initiated a fundraising drive that provided for an elaborate monument erected on Chadwick's grave. In 1939, the "Father of Baseball" was honored as one of the original inductees into the National Baseball Hall of Fame.

Henry Chadwick continues, long after his death, to contribute to the game he loved. After his death, Chadwick's wife gave to Al Spalding all of Henry's scrapbooks, diaries and other materials related to baseball which he had saved over his lifetime. Spalding used these materials to write his 1911 history of baseball, *America's National Game*. After Spalding's death the collection was given to the New York Public Library where baseball historians today continue to examine one of the richest troves of information about baseball's early history.

John Curtis Chapman

Born: May 8, 1843 Brooklyn, NY
Died: June 10, 1916 Brooklyn, NY
5'11" 170 lb.

The baseball career of lifelong Brooklynite Jack Chapman spanned the game's development from an amateur pursuit to a professional spectator sport. After playing for the Putnam and Enterprise clubs of Brooklyn in 1860 and 1861, Chapman joined the Atlantics in 1862. Except for the 1867 season, when he played for the Quaker City Club of Philadelphia, Chapman was the right fielder for the Bedford Boys during their glory years until 1870. A solid hitter, he made his reputation as an outstanding defensive player, known for spectacular long running catches in the outfield.

In the 1871 inaugural season of the National Association of Professional Base Ball Players, Chapman played for the rival Eckford Club. In 1874, he returned to play for a final year with the Atlantics. Reunited with his former teammates Dickey Pearce and Bob Ferguson, Chapman led the club with total bases (78) and tied Pearce with RBIs (25). The following year, Chapman served as player-manager of the Louisville Club in the newly formed National League. At age 33, the overweight outfielder had lost his ability to track down drives to the outfield. But, he continued his career as a manager for Milwaukee, Worcester, Detroit and Buffalo. In 1889 Chapman returned to manage the Louisville Club in the American Association and led them to a championship in 1890.

CHAPMAN.

Jack Chapman (*Harper's Weekly,***
November 25, 1865).**

Following his baseball career, Chapman became a successful liquor salesman and a prominent member of the Elks Club and the Society of Old Brooklynites. He maintained his interest in baseball, however, and was known for recounting to receptive audiences stories of the glory days of the old Atlantics. One episode which he described to the *Brooklyn Daily Eagle* involved a near fatal mishap of the Atlantics on their 1868 western road trip:

We were playing in Louisville and had planned to take the steamer Patrick Rogers to Cincinnati that night. The tourists were induced to stop over for a banquet, which was done. We took the morning train for Cincinnati where we learned that the steamer had burned to the water's edge during the night and many lives had been lost. We were congratulated on our lucky escape by Manager Harry Wright of the Cincinnati Red Stockings. We beat that famous team.

On the morning of June 10, 1916, Chapman suffered a heart attack and died at his home at 192 Lexington Avenue in Brooklyn. Following a memorial service attended by such baseball notables as Charles Ebbets, Chapman was buried in Greenwood Cemetery.

James Creighton
Born: April 15, 1841 New York, NY
Died: October 18, 1862 Brooklyn, NY

Although Jim Creighton played in fewer than 30 league games, he is remembered as baseball's first star player and tragic hero. Creighton began his playing career at the age of 16 in 1857 and quickly rose through the ranks of junior clubs to the premier club, the Brooklyn Stars, in 1859. He was recruited, and reputedly paid to play, by the pennant contending Brooklyn Excelsiors in 1860.

It is often said that "timing is everything" in baseball. Creighton is perhaps the exemplar of this adage, both in his style of play and in his brief career. He came upon the scene just as baseball was becoming known as the "National Pastime." In 1860, the Excelsiors made the first road trip of any club in baseball's early days, drubbing every "country team" they faced in upstate New York. Creighton's hitting prowess, but more especially his pitching form, amazed the locals. They had never seen anything like it. At a time when pitchers offered the ball to the plate in the style of slow-pitch softball, Creighton hurled the ball with great velocity, baffling the opposing batters. Newspapers and sports weeklies made Creighton a household name among followers of the game. The young hurler was just what the game needed, a star player.

Creighton truly revolutionized the art of pitching. According to Henry Chadwick, Creighton's great speed was enough to baffle "country club" hitters. But, against experienced hitters such as the formidable Atlantic batsmen, Creighton used "head work" to outwit his opponents. He changed speeds and moved the ball around the plate to entice hitters to chase bad pitches. This, according to Chadwick, he learned as a bowler in cricket.

The often-told story of Creighton's untimely death at the age of 21 is the stuff of baseball legend. Although the exact circumstances are unclear, the popular version has Creighton fatally injuring himself in a home run swing in a game on October 14, 1862. Creighton was taken to his father's home on Henry Street in Brooklyn where he died two days later. Creighton, baseball's first star player, was now the game's first tragic hero.

For many years, Creighton was the point of comparison for other pitchers. In 1867, Henry Chadwick wrote, "Creighton ranked as the pitcher *par excellence* in base ball and there has been no one to equal him since." When teams from other cities played in Brooklyn they often made a pilgrimage to Creighton's grave in Greenwood Cemetery. The Norfolk, Virginia, baseball club made perhaps the ultimate tribute to the Brooklyn pitcher when it named its team the "Creightons."

William Arthur "Candy" Cummings
Born: October 18, 1848 Ware, MA
Died: May 16, 1924 Toledo, OH
5'9" 120 lb.

Although he had an outstanding pitching career, it was largely Candy Cummings' reputation for inventing the curve ball that earned him a place in the National Baseball Hall of Fame. He is the only pre–Dodger era Brooklyn player to be enshrined in Cooperstown.

Born in Ware, Massachusetts, in 1848, Cummings moved to Brooklyn at an early age. In 1908, Cummings recalled that he got the idea for throwing a curve when, at the age of 15, he and some other boys were throwing clam shells and watching them curve through the air. According to Cummings' often repeated account, he spent nearly every spare moment of his teenage life trying to perfect the same technique with a baseball.

In 1865 or 1866, Cummings joined the junior Star Club of Brooklyn and during the 1866 season was recruited to play for the Excelsiors. That year he played in only six games as a reserve shortstop and backup pitcher to Asa Brainard. When Brainard revolved to the Washington Nationals in 1867, Cummings became the Excelsiors' regular pitcher. Pitching in every game that season, Cummings led the Excelsiors to an 11–5 record, their best since 1860.

The Excelsiors' revival was short-lived. In 1868, all but one of the team's starting lineup left the club. Cummings was recruited by the Stars first nine where in his four years with the club he became the premier pitcher in amateur baseball. Before the end of the 1871, he was actively recruited by several professional clubs. The curve-baller reportedly signed contracts to play for three different clubs: Philadelphia, Troy, and the Mutuals. When the National Association finally resolved the matter, Cummings was in uniform for the Mutuals in 1872.

In his National Association career, Cummings pitched for a different club each year, revolving to Baltimore in 1873, Philadelphia in 1874, and Hartford in 1875. He compiled a respectable 124–72 record in the four years and posted an ERA of less than 2 in 1874 and 1875. With the Hartford Dark Blues in 1875, Cummings had a remarkable 35–12 record and an ERA of only 1.60. But, when the Dark Blues joined the National League in its inaugural season in 1876, Cummings was relegated to a secondary pitching role behind the young Tommy Bond. He still finished the season with an excellent 16–8 record and 1.67 ERA, but the strain of pitching curve balls had taken its toll on Cummings' arm.

In 1877, Cummings became the president of the newly formed International Association, which was possibly baseball's first minor league. Like his former Hartford manager, Bob Ferguson, Cummings also continued to play while performing his presidential duties. During the season, he signed with Cincinnati in the National League, but his attempt at a comeback was futile. In his last major league season, he compiled a dismal 5–14 record with an ERA of 4.34.

Cummings played one more season of minor league and semipro ball before returning to his native Massachusetts home in Ware. According to baseball historian Joseph Overfield, Cummings became successful in the home decorating trade in mid-northern Massachusetts before retiring to Toledo where he lived with his son Arthur.

Although Cummings was an outstanding pitcher throughout his career, his credentials for inclusion in the Hall of Fame are somewhat questionable. Contemporary pitchers, such as Dick McBride of the Athletics and Tommy Bond of Hartford and Boston, had better statistical records. But, his reputation for inventing the curve ball, a feat for which Cummings took great pride, would ensure his enshrinement in Cooperstown. In 1908, Cummings wrote, "I get a great deal of pleasure now in my old age out of going to games and watching the curves, thinking that it was through my blind efforts that all this was made possible."

Candy Cummings died on May 16, 1924, at the age of 75, in Toledo.

Robert V. "Death to Flying Things" Ferguson
Born: January 31, 1845 Brooklyn, NY
Died: May 3, 1894 Brooklyn, NY

Bob Ferguson began his playing career inauspiciously in 1865 with the Enterprise Club of Brooklyn, a team than won only one of its 11 games that year. The following year, he joined the champion Atlantics where he became the premier third baseman in baseball throughout the late 1860s, earning the nickname "Death to Flying Things."

The switch-hitting Ferguson was also an effective batsman and base runner. In 1869 he led the league in runs scored and was third in total hits. Ferguson moved behind the plate to catch for the old Atlantics in their final season in 1870. In their famous match with the Cincinnati Red Stockings in June, Ferguson scored the winning run in the 11th inning to the end the Red Stockings 84 game winning streak.

Following the breakup of the Atlantics, Ferguson and his teammates, Joe Start and Dickey Pearce, moved to the Mutuals of New York in 1871. The following year, Ferguson returned to Brooklyn to reorganize a new Atlantic Club to play in the National Association. As player-captain, he led his team through three dismal losing seasons. In 1875, Ferguson and his star pitcher, Tommy Bond, moved to the more competitive Hartford Club for the National Association's final season.

Throughout the National Association's five-year history, Ferguson wore many hats. In addition to being a player and captain, he umpired numerous league games. And, strangely enough, Ferguson also served as the league president from 1872 to 1875. It was surely Ferguson's personality and temperament which enabled him to serve in these various and potentially

Bob Ferguson (Transcendental Graphics.)

conflicting roles. He was known to be straitlaced; he neither smoked nor drank nor gambled. He was strict and rule-bound. He was intelligent and authoritative, but could also be authoritarian and temperamental. According to the *Sporting News*, Ferguson was "honest to a fault ... in all the years he devoted to the game his honesty was never once questioned." But, the *Sporting News* continues, "Ferguson had few friends among the players. He was a man of too blunt ways to cultivate friendships of many and he courted the ill rather than the good will of his fellow men." Ferguson's temper was evident in 1873 when as the Atlantic captain he confronted and verbally castigated gamblers following a game, and while umpiring, attacked a player with a bat in the midst of an argument.

From 1876 through 1884, Ferguson captained and played for teams in Hartford, Chicago, Springfield, Troy, Philadelphia and Pittsburgh. In 1885 he hung up his spikes but served as manager of the New York Mets in the American Association for two losing seasons. Ferguson completed his baseball career as an umpire, a position in which he garnered the most respect from players. He officiated games in the American Association from 1886 to 1889 and in 1891. He also umpired in the short-lived Players League in 1890.

On May 3, 1894, Bob Ferguson died suddenly at his home at 687 Greene Avenue in Brooklyn. At his funeral service, according to the *Brooklyn Daily Eagle*, "The parlors were not large enough to accommodate the crowd of people who came. The front stoop was crowded and a few turned away when they found it was impossible to gain admission." Among the mourners were many of Ferguson's former teammates, including Dickey Pearce, John "Candy" Nelson, and George Zettlein. Henry Chadwick was also in attendance, and Jack Chapman, who was managing the Buffalo club, sent his condolences. Following the service, Ferguson was buried in Cypress Hill Cemetery.

Joseph Bowne Leggett
Born: January 14, 1828 Saratoga, NY
Died: July 25, 1894 Galveston, TX

Joe Leggett began playing with the Wayne Club of Brooklyn in 1856, but became an Excelsior when the teams merged the following year. Although his playing career was short and marred by injuries, he was recognized as the best catcher in the early years of baseball. Leggett was behind the plate for Brooklyn in the first Brooklyn–New York all-star match at the Fashion Race Course in 1858. During his career with the Excelsiors he had the good fortune of being the battery mate for three of the best pitchers in the amateur era: Jim Creighton, Asa Brainard, and Candy Cummings.

In addition to his defensive prowess, Leggett was a skilled batsman. He led the National Association in runs scored in 1859, and in both runs scored and batting average in 1860.

Although he was a staunch competitor on the playing field, Leggett was an exemplar of the gentleman's code of behavior in the early years of the game. He was the team's captain in 1860 when the Excelsiors challenged the Atlantics for the championship. In the decisive game of the championship series played at the Atlantics' home grounds, following several innings of derision and verbal abuse from the Bedford cranks, Leggett pulled his team off the field. The Excelsiors forfeited the game and lost the opportunity to win the championship. Because of the animosity engendered by the game, the Excelsiors never again played the Atlantics.

The Excelsiors, arguably the best team in baseball in 1860, were never again a serious challenger for the championship. Because of the Civil War the club did not play in 1861. When the Excelsiors resumed play in 1862, Leggett was already past his prime. At age 34, the rigors of catching had taken its toll on the Excelsiors' captain. After catching several innings of the speedy pitches of Jim Creighton in an 1862 match against the Charter Oaks, Leggett was forced to leave the game. According to the *Brooklyn Daily Eagle*, "His hands, from want of practice, were too soft for such hard usage, and soon became puffed up and exceedingly painful, and a lame arm prevented his throwing to bases." Leggett played sparingly over the next few years. In 1866, Leggett returned to play in 14 games for the Excelsiors and caught a promising young pitcher who would be elected a charter member of the National Baseball Hall of Fame, Candy Cummings.

Although his career was brief, Leggett had a major impact on the game of baseball. In the early days of the game, he set the standard of play for catching. Moreover, along with his teammate Henry Polhemus, he helped establish the first baseball club in Baltimore. Leggett was widely respected by the baseball fraternity for his leadership, integrity and "pluck." He was paid perhaps the highest tribute by the newly formed baseball club of Cohoes, New York, when they named their team the "Leggetts."

Little is known about Leggett's life after baseball. According to baseball historian Robert Tiemann, in the mid–1870s Leggett was reported to have been in ill health after his business interests had failed. According to a genealogical record, Leggett died in Galveston, Texas, in 1894.

John W. "Candy" Nelson
Born: 1849 Brooklyn, NY
Died: September 4, 1910 Brooklyn, NY
5'6" 145 lb.

Jack Nelson began playing in 1867 with the Eckfords in what was one of the worst seasons ever for the Brooklyn club. The Eckfords only managed six victories in 23 games. The following year, Nelson, along with second baseman Jimmy Wood and pitcher Phoney Martin, led a reversal of fortune for the Williamsburg club. In July, the Eckfords defeated the Mutuals to briefly regain the championship title. They then embarked on the longest road trip in the club's history, winning 10 of 11 games from Western teams. Their only loss came at the hands of the Cincinnati Red Stockings. Nelson led the club in runs scored with 111 as the Eckfords posted a 23–11 record for the season.

As baseball became an openly professional sport, Nelson's career exemplified the tendency for players to revolve from club to club. He concluded the 1869 season with the Eckfords before moving to the Mutuals in 1870. He was back with the Eckfords in 1871. Nelson began the 1872 season with Troy, but returned to the Eckfords when the Haymakers folded in mid-season. In 1873 he returned to the Mutuals where he played for three seasons. Nelson hit .327 for the Mutuals in 1873, by far his best batting season.

From 1876 through 1881, Candy played for ten different clubs. He was briefly back in Brooklyn in 1881, playing 30

John Nelson (*New York Clipper*).

games for Bill Barnie's Atlantic club. Nelson finally achieved some stability in his career beginning in 1882 when he anchored the middle infield for six consecutive years for the New York Mets in the American Association. Nelson ended his playing career in 1890 in typical form, playing for three different clubs: Wilmington, Brooklyn (AA) and Albany.

Throughout his career Nelson was a steady left-handed batter who occasionally showed signs of brilliance. But, it was his outstanding play at shortstop that earned him the nickname "Candy." Although he was overshadowed by such stars as Dickey Pearce and George Wright, the *New York Clipper* described Nelson as "one of the best and most effective infielders." His lifetime fielding average in the major leagues was .865.

Nelson died from a heart attack at his Brooklyn home on September 4, 1910.

Lipman Emanuel Pike

Born: May 25, 1845 New York, NY
Died: October 10, 1893 Brooklyn, NY
5'8" 158 lb.

Reputed to be organized baseball's first Jewish player and manager, Lip Pike began playing with junior clubs in Brooklyn in the early 1860s. In 1866, he joined the Philadelphia Athletics where he quickly became one the league's leading hitters. Pike returned to New York the following year and played two seasons for the Mutuals. The Tammany Hall connections he made with the Mutuals would pay off for Pike in his later years.

In 1869 Pike joined the Atlantics where for two seasons he played second base in all 106 Atlantic contests. In 1869 he was the team's second leading hitter behind first baseman Joe Start. Pike was an outstanding fielder

Lip Pike (*New York Clipper.*)

and base-runner, but he was particularly known as a dead-pull left-handed power hitter. In its 1893 tribute to Pike, the *Sporting News* described his hitting prowess: "in his day he could hit the ball as hard as any man in the business ... during his career [he] had sent the ball over the right field fence of nearly every park in which he had played." According to the *New York Times*, Pike once hit a towering drive that struck and bent the flagpole high atop the pagoda in the outfield at Union Grounds in Brooklyn.

From 1871 through 1875, Pike played for a succession of National Association clubs: Troy, Baltimore, Hartford and St. Louis. He batted .321 for the five seasons, and doubled as player-manager for Troy in 1871 and Hartford in 1874. Pike continued his outstanding hitting, batting .323 for St. Louis when they joined the National League in 1876. In 1877, he moved to Cincinnati where he batted .298. Pike completed his final full season in 1878, batting .311 for Cincinnati and Worcester.

Pike played in several games for Bill Barnie's minor league Atlantics in 1881 and played in a few matches for Worcester. In 1887, he played one final game with the New York Mets of the American Association, going hitless in four times at bat. Pike turned to umpiring, officiating in American Association games in 1887 and 1889, and in the National League in 1890. With his playing days at an end, Pike also worked for the Tammany Hall political machine, and according to the *Sporting News* operated a "sporting resort" near the Brooklyn Bridge.

In the early morning hours of October 10, 1893, Lip Pike died at the age of 48 at his home at 106 North Oxford Street in Brooklyn. According to the *Brooklyn Daily Eagle*, "Many wealthy Hebrews and men high in political and old time base ball circles attended the funeral service." Pike was buried in Cypress Hill Cemetery.

Richard J. (Dickey) Pearce

Born: February 29, 1836 Brooklyn, NY
Died: September 18, 1908 Wareham, MA
5'3½" 161 lb.

One of the original members of the Brooklyn Atlantics in 1855, Dickey Pearce spent most of his adult life on the baseball field. For nearly three decades he covered the ground between second and third base as no other player in his time. Short, stout and slow of foot, Pearce did not look like a star athlete. But he made up for his physical limitations with what Henry Chadwick called "head work." He virtually invented the position of shortstop. A skillful fielder with an accurate and strong throwing arm, Pearce positioned himself on the infield according to the proclivities of the opposing batters and in anticipation of plays. He perfected the deceptive infield fly double play which became a standard defensive ploy until the infield fly rule was implemented. His knowledge of the game, judgment and competitive spirit more than made up for his size and lack of speed.

Pearce was equally innovative at the plate, becoming the prototypical leadoff hitter. Lacking power, he was an effective contact hitter who had a knack for getting on base ahead his

Dickey Pearce (*Harper's Weekly*, November 25, 1865).

power-hitting Atlantic teammates. He took advantage of the existing rules by developing the "fair-foul" hit, an early variant of the drag bunt. Pearce was among the league leaders in runs scored in the early 1860s and had the third best batting average in 1868.

Pearce played 16 consecutive seasons for the Atlantics before the team broke up after the 1870 campaign. In 1871, Pearce and teammates Bob Ferguson and Joe Start moved to the New York Mutuals in the newly formed National Association of Professional Base Ball Players. He returned to the reconstituted Atlantics for the 1873 and 1874 seasons and played in every game. In 1874, Pearce led the team in batting average, on base percentage, runs, hits, and RBIs. Pearce joined with his former teammate Lip Pike to play for the St. Louis Browns in 1875 and 1876. In 1877, he played for Providence for most of the season, returning to St. Louis to complete his big league career.

Age did not diminish Pearce's enthusiasm for the game. Unwilling to hang up his spikes, he continued to play for local teams in the St. Louis area and later for various minor league clubs. With the spring thaw in March, back in Brooklyn Pearce could be seen playing with younger New York area professional players in preseason practice games at the Parade Grounds. But Pearce was no longer able to financially support himself and his family as a player. To honor Dickey's contribution to the game, in 1881 the New York Mets played a benefit match with a picked nine of veteran players captained by Pearce. The proceeds from the game allowed Pearce to open a "wine saloon" at 7 Boerum Street near the court house in downtown Brooklyn. The establishment became a sort of sports bar, decorated with mementoes of Pearce's playing days and stocked with the latest sports weeklies.

Not content with a sedentary life, Pearce was forever drawn back to the diamond. On May 10, 1883, at the newly formed Brooklyn Base Ball Club's inaugural game at Washington Park, a *New York Clipper* reporter noticed Pearce among the crowd of spectators. According to the *Clipper*, Pearce was in trim shape and looking for an opportunity to captain and play infield for an Interstate League team. The following year, at age 48, Pearce did return to the playing field as the player-captain of the Quincy, Illinois, baseball club in the Northwestern League.

Although an injury in 1884 finally brought an end to Pearce's playing career, he had one final contribution to make to the game. With the formation of the short-lived Players League in 1890, Pearce was hired to help design and maintain the ballpark for the New York franchise. Constructed in 1890 at the northern end of Coogan's Hollow in 1891, the New York club's ball grounds would be renamed the Polo Grounds, the third and final incarnation of the park that would be home to the New York Giants. Pearce continued to work as a groundskeeper at the Polo Grounds for several years.

Upon his retirement, Pearce moved to Boston and later Cape Cod. He was somewhat of a local celebrity, appearing in numerous Old Timers Games. According to Christopher Price of the *Barnestable Patriot* (Cape Cod, Mass.), Pearce caught the flu while playing in a 1908 Old Timers Game in Boston. He returned to his Wareham, Massachusetts, home on Cape Cod where he died on September 18.

Alfred James Reach
Born: May 25, 1840 London, England
Died: January 14, 1928 Atlantic City, NJ
5′6″ 155 lb.

Born in London, Al Reach came to the United States as an infant and grew up in Brooklyn. As baseball historian Joseph Overfield notes, Reach's life was truly a Horatio Alger tale. Following an impoverished childhood, Reach would attain fame and wealth. Like many later athletes, baseball would be Reach's ticket to success.

Reach began his playing career with the Eckfords in 1861. He played four seasons for the Williamsburg club, helping them win championships in 1862 and 1863. Following the loss of four of their starting nine, in 1864 the Eckfords played only five matches. In the short season Reach led the club in runs scored. A versatile defensive player, in his career with the Eckfords Reach played in the outfield and every infield position except shortstop.

When Reach began playing in 1861, he also started a trade that would eventually lead to enormous financial success: He began making baseballs by hand. Reach made game-quality baseballs, including the ball used in the all-star match that year between Brooklyn and New York. The trophy awarded to the victorious Brooklyn team, crowned by the game ball, is inscribed "Ball from the Grand Match of 1861—Brooklyn-v-New York—Handmade by Alfred J. Reach-of-Eckford BBC."

In 1865, Reach was paid by the Athletics to play in Philadelphia. He was thus, along with Jim Creighton, one of the earliest known professional players. Reach established roots in the City of Brotherly Love, playing 12 seasons for the Athletics and establishing a lucrative sporting goods business.

At the plate Reach was an outstanding on-base man, leading the league in runs scored with 134 in 1866 and 270 in 1867. In the newly formed professional National Association in 1871, Reach had by far his best batting season, hitting .353 and leading the Athletics to the league's first championship. The following year, he played in only about half of the Athletics' games and his batting average plummeted to .195. He played only sparingly the next three seasons before retiring from the field. By now his time was fully occupied by his expanding business.

Soon after his arrival in Philadelphia, Reach established a baseball equipment store at 404 Chestnut Street. Capitalizing on his name recognition, he called his business the A.J. Reach's Base Ball Depot. By 1870, the store had moved to larger quarters at No. 6 South Eighth Street and was renamed the Philadelphia Base Ball Emporium. In the early 1870s Reach began to manufacture sporting goods while continuing to operate the wholesale and retail operation. In 1892 Reach's company merged with its major competitor, A.G. Spalding & Bros., to form the largest sporting goods operation in the country.

Reach kept actively involved in baseball as a publisher and team owner. Beginning in 1883 he produced annual guides for the American Association and later the American League, counterparts to the Spalding Guides for the National League. Also in 1883, with Philadelphia lawyer and politician Colonel John Rogers, Reach gained controlling interest in the Philadelphia Phillies and briefly managed the team in 1890. He was co-owner of the club for 20 years before selling out his interest.

Al Reach died on January 14, 1928, at the age of 87. Through his entrepreneurial spirit and baseball connections, Reach overcame a hard-knock childhood to die a wealthy man. He was buried in West Laurel Hill Cemetery in Bala Cynwyd, Pennsylvania, near Philadelphia.

Joseph "Old Reliable" Start
Born: October 14, 1842 New York, NY
Died: March 27, 1927 Providence, RI
5'9" 165 lb.

Beginning in 1860, Joe Start and his longtime teammate Jack Chapman both played their first two seasons of baseball with the Enterprise Club of Brooklyn. Both players were recruited by the Atlantics in 1862 and both became major contributors to the championship clubs of Bedford throughout the 1860s.

With the Atlantics, the sure-handed Start became the premier first baseman in the game and earned the nickname "Old Reliable." Start was also a great hitter who seemed to improve with age. He led the amateur National Association in runs scored in 1865 and in batting average and total hits in 1868. Start is perhaps best remembered for driving in the winning run in the 11th inning of the June 1870 Atlantic victory that ended the two-year winning streak of the Cincinnati Red Stockings.

When the old Atlantics disbanded following the 1870 season, Start joined his teammates Dickey Pearce, Bob Ferguson, and Charley Smith with the New York Mutuals. Start played six seasons with the Mutuals before the team was expelled from the National

Joe Start (*Harper's Weekly*, November 25, 1865).

League for failing to complete its league schedule. Start batted .332 with the Hartford club in 1877 and increased his average to .351 and led the league in hits the following year with Chicago.

In 1879, Start moved to Providence and helped the Grays win the National League pennant that year. As player-captain in 1884, he led the Grays to baseball's first World Series Championship over the New York Mets. Start played seven seasons for Providence before ending his career with Washington in 1886.

In his ten full major league seasons, Start batted over .300 five times, while his fielding percentage at the game's most active defensive position never dropped below .957. In addition to the quality of play, however, Start earned his nickname for his reputation for honesty and integrity. According to Henry Chadwick, Joe Start "was honored and esteemed by the [baseball] fraternity" because he could "always be relied upon for honest and faithful service."

After his playing days were over, Start returned to Rhode Island and successfully operated the Lakewood Inn in Warwick for several years. He retired to Pawtuxet Village (now Cranston/Warwick) in 1919 and returned to Providence in 1922 where he and his wife lived their final years at 50 Haskins Street. Joseph Start died on March 27, 1927, one month after the death of his wife Angeline.

James Leon Wood
Born: July 18, 1844 Brooklyn, NY
Died: November 30, 1886 (?)
5'8" 150 lb.

In baseball's first decade and a half, Jimmy Wood was one of the game's best hitting and fielding second basemen. Beginning in 1860, the Brooklyn native played for the Eckfords for nine seasons, leading the club to championships in 1862 and 1863. The team's leading hitter, Wood led the league in runs scored in 1862 and in scoring average in 1863.

Wood (unusually, he did not have a nickname) missed the 1865 season entirely and played only sparingly for the Eckfords the remainder of the decade. Baseball historian Robert Tiemann suggests that Wood's employer may have been unwilling to allow him time off to play.

In 1870, the newly formed Chicago White Stockings offered Wood the position of player-captain. He not only accepted the job but brought along with him three other Eckford starters: outfielder Fred Treacy, catcher Charley Hodes, and pitcher Ed Pinkham. Now able to concentrate solely on baseball, Wood proved to be an outstanding hitter and team leader. Batting .417, he led his team to a 22–7 record in professional matches and a 65–8 overall record.

In the hard-hitting Chicago starting lineup, four players in 1870 batted over .400 and only one less than .300. Especially against amateur clubs, the White Stockings routinely defeated their opponents by enormous margins; for example, against Bluff City (TN) 157–1, Grove City (IL) 111–5, Active (IA) 96–7, and Ontario (NY) 108–12. The press coined the verb "to Chicago" which meant to shut out or drub an opponent.

Wood nearly led his team to a pennant in 1871, but the disastrous Chicago fire extinguished their chances. When the Chicago club disbanded for two seasons, Wood had brief stints with Troy, the Eckfords and Philadelphia. Before the 1874 season, the reorganized White Stockings rehired Wood as player-captain. But, in a freak accident, he severely cut his right leg, eventually requiring its amputation. Wood's playing days were over, but by late in the season he was able to bench-manage the club. He continued to manage one more unsuccessful season before club president William Hulbert brought in Al Spalding from Boston as the new manager.

There is conflicting information about Wood's later years. In 1885 Wood was operating a sporting goods company on State Street in Chicago. An advertisement in the *New York Clipper* clearly played upon Wood's reputation:

> With MR. WOOD'S practical experience as a BALLPLAYER, thoroughly understanding the various wants of the game, we guarantee to supply DEALERS and PLAYERS with a superior and improved class of goods, of which we have several new specialties, consisting of BALLS, BATS, BASE FASTENERS, and WOOD'S IMPROVED STEEL TOE AND HEEL PLATES. Patent applied for, the best and only steel plates made. SEND FOR PRICE LIST, CAPT. JAS. WOOD.

Total Baseball's player register indicates that Wood died in 1886. But, according to Robert Tiemann, Wood was involved in the management of the Memphis minor league club in 1887 and was later the proprietor of a successful saloon in Chicago.

George "The Charmer" Zettlein

Born: July 18, 1844 Brooklyn, NY
Died: May 23, 1905 Patchogue, NY
5'9" 162 lb.

Among Brooklyn's early baseball stars, George Zettlein had perhaps the most checkered career. He was criticized by the sporting press for his lack of "head work"; the *New York Clipper* attributed this to his "Teutonic heritage." He was nicknamed "The Charmer" after "George the Charmer," a big-footed buffoonish character in Hooley's Minstrels in Brooklyn. He was suspected of throwing games while playing for Chicago in 1874, and in 1875 left the club following a dispute with his manager (and former Eckford teammate) Jimmy Wood. Playing in Philadelphia, he again was plagued by accusations of throwing games. He finished his career ingloriously in 1876 with a 4–20 pitching record for the Athletics.

In his five seasons with the Atlantics (1866–1870), however, the Charmer was a serviceable pitcher, posting a 74–33 record. Zettlein, who fought in both the Union Army and Navy during the Civil War, began playing for the Eckfords in 1865 and moved to the Atlantics the following year. Although he was noted for his lack of "head work," Zettlein did have the proclivity for stopping line drives with his head and body rather than his hands. In an 1867 match with the Unions, for example, Zettlein was felled with a line shot off his forehead. In typical fashion, he completed the inning and finished the game with a victory.

In 1870 Zettlein was the winning pitcher in the Atlantics' upset victory over the Cincinnati Red Stockings. His contribution at the plate in the game, however, is often overlooked. After Bob Ferguson drove in Joe Start for the tying run in the 11th inning, Zettlein kept the inning alive by hitting a line drive that was muffed by the Red Stocking fielders, allowing Ferguson all the way from first base.

Following the breakup of the Atlantics at the end of the 1870 season, Zettlein was recruited by Chicago. Behind his steady pitching, the White Stockings led the league for most of the season. But following the great Chicago fire in early October, the demoralized White Stockings collapsed. Wearing an oversized borrowed Atlantic jersey, Zettlein lost the deciding game of the season to Philadelphia at Brooklyn's Union Grounds. The Charmer changed teams five times over the next five years, ending with Philadelphia in 1876.

Zettlein worked in the Brooklyn district attorney's office for several years before retiring to Patchogue on Long Island. Suffering from Bright's disease, George Zettlein died on May 23, 1905.

Epilogue

It is the month of April, the year 2000 in the "City of Churches," Brooklyn. I take the number 75 bus down to the ball grounds near the waterfront at the foot of Court Street in Red Hook. The several acres of Red Hood Park sprawl along the waterfront, as devoid of activity as the dilapidated grain elevators and warehouses along the harbor. Ball fields in various states of neglect are set up for baseball, football and soccer. I walk west, past what appears to have been a concession stand, boarded up for at least a decade or more, across a field of turf, sand, and fragments of broken glass. (What did T.S. Eliot say about the month of April?) As I continue walking I approach what I was looking for. At the southwestern corner of the park I approach a baseball field stretching beyond a rusting backstop, the outfield framed by silent docks and warehouses. This was surely the Excelsiors' grounds. As I look out I imagine what it was like 140 years earlier when thousands of enthusiastic baseball fans elbowed for space, even clung to the masts of ships in the harbor beyond the outfield, to watch Jim Creighton baffle an opposing team with his wily pitching. When I turn to leave, city park groundskeepers arrive to mend the backstop screen. In a few days the grounds will host a renewal of the rites of spring, the beginning of another baseball season.

I had decided to make a pilgrimage to the sites where baseball was first played in Brooklyn. My trips to Capitoline and Union grounds were disappointing. No traces remain of the first enclosed baseball parks in the country No plaques or historical markers at either location indicate that the best teams in baseball once played there. The 47th Regiment Armory, built in 1883 after Union Grounds' destruction, still stands at the site in Williamsburg. Apartment buildings and brownstones now cover what was Capitoline Grounds in the Bedford-Stuyvesant neighborhood.

At Washington Park, now Byrne Park, with some effort one can imagine what it was like when Adonis Terry pitched for the "Dodgers" in 1883. A replica of the Old Stone House, now an historical interpretive center, sits in what was right field. William Alexander Middle School now occupies the location of the main grandstand along the third base line. To the west, below the school and stone house, an open expanse of concrete stretches to Fourth Avenue. Grown men still play ball here, even pitch with an underhand delivery as Adonis Terry did in the 1880s. But, the game now played is softball.

South of Prospect Park, the Parade Grounds is the perhaps the best living memorial to the early days of baseball in the city. Each summer since 1869 the inhabitants of the old Flatbush neighborhood have heard the sound of the crack of the bat, as leather met wood, and now, regrettably to some, leather meets aluminum. The conditions of the ball fields, unfortunately, have suffered after many years of neglect. In the last year of the old millennium, the Parade Grounds was at the center of a controversy about a proposal that a professional baseball club, at least temporarily, make the hallowed grounds its home. The team was a low-level minor league franchise of the New York Mets. It is somewhat ironic that a number of players from the first New York Mets played at these grounds over a century before. In 1883, Brooklyn baseball fans welcomed the return of professional baseball, even if only at the minor league level, to the city. In the year 2000, however, a coalition of neighborhood groups, soccer moms and dads, and politicians blocked the effort, arguing that traffic congestion would make life unbearable for the local citizenry. For over a century Brooklynites were willing to dodge horse cars and later trolleys, but automobiles and trucks are another matter. Alas, the return of professional baseball, if but briefly, to the Parade Grounds was not to be. Meanwhile, construction began on a new stadium on the former site of the Steeplechase Amusement Park in Coney Island that would be home to what the press referred to as the "Mini-Mets." In the summer of the year 2001, truly the first year of the new millennium, professional baseball returned to Brooklyn. The team is called the Cyclones, in honor of the landmark Coney Island roller coaster. Regrettably, no one took the opportunity to remember the first great baseball clubs in Brooklyn. I can imagine no better means of honoring those players and clubs who forged our national pastime than to name the new club after the Atlantics or the Excelsiors. This would truly have been a living tribute to those who played in what Henry Chadwick called the "palmy days" when Brooklyn was the City of Baseball.

Home Grounds of
Brooklyn Baseball Clubs*

Enclosed Ball Grounds/Ballparks

A. Union Grounds: Located between Rutledge and Lynch streets and Harrison and Marcy avenues. Opening in 1862, originally the home of the Eckfords, Putnams, and Constellations; later the Mutuals and Atlantics.

B. Capitoline Grounds: Located between Nostrand and Marcy avenues and Putnam and Halsey avenues. Opening in 1864, originally the home of the Atlantics and Enterprise; later the Excelsiors and a host of amateur clubs.

C. Satellite Grounds: Located north of Meeker Avenue on the border of Williamsburg and Greenpoint. Opening date unknown, but likely replaced the open ballgrounds of the Manor House grounds sometime in the 1860s. Home of the Fultons and the location of games among black baseball clubs.

D. Washington Park I: Located between Third and Fifth streets and Fourth and Fifth avenues. From 1883 to 1890, home of the Brooklyn Grays (to become the Dodgers).

E. Washington Park II: Located between First and Third streets and Third and Fourth avenues. From 1898 to 1912, home of the Dodgers. Also home to the Tip Tops of the Federal League from 1914 to 1915.

F. Eastern Park: Located between Pitkin and Sutter avenues and Powell and Van Sinderen avenues. From 1891 to 1897, home of the Dodgers. Also home of the Wonders of the Players League in 1890.

---

*The locations of ballparks and ball grounds and their residents are derived from contemporary newspaper reports of ball games and from Michael Benson, Ballparks of North America: A Comprehensive Historical Reference to Baseball Grounds, Yards and Stadiums, 1845 to Present (Jefferson, N.C.: McFarland), 51–69. The presentation is intended to be illustrative and does not attempt to be comprehensive.

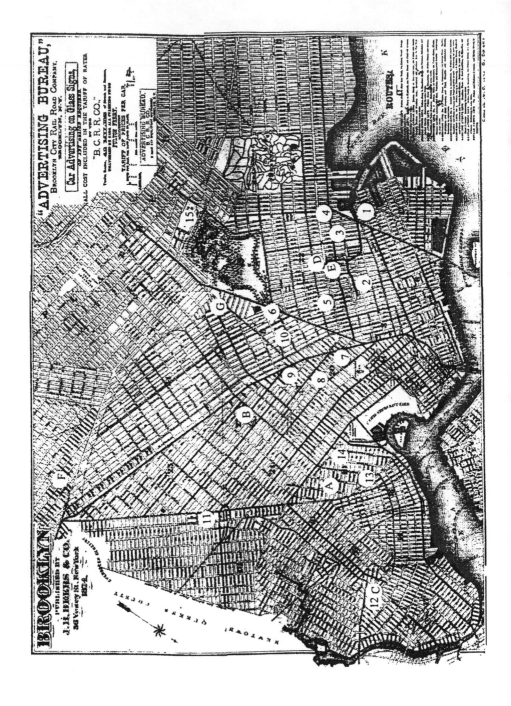

G. Ebbets Field: Located between Sullivan Place and Montgomery Street and McKeever Place and Bedford Avenue. From 1913 to 1957, home of the Dodgers. Also home of the Eagles of the Negro National League in 1935 and the Brown Dodgers of the United States League in 1945.

Open Ball Grounds

1. "Foot of Court Street": Excelsiors (the Stars played at Hamilton Avenue near Penny Bridge which was either the same location or nearby)
2. Carroll Park grounds (2 locations): Between Smith and Hoyt streets and Degraw and Sackett streets; and between Smith and Carroll streets and Hoyt and President streets: Excelsiors, Charter Oaks, Stars, Niagara
3. Third Avenue and Tenth Street: Exercise
4. Fourth Avenue and Sixteenth Street: E. Pluribus Unum
5. Fifth Avenue at Dean Street: Quickstep, Washington, Osceloa, American Eagle, Hiawatha, Favorita
6. Degraw Street at Flatbush and Nine Avenues: Albion, Tippecanoe
7. Oxford Street at Lafayette Avenue: Oneida
8. Washington at Dekalb Avenue: Ringold
9. Gates at Grand Avenue: Liberty
10. Bergen Street between Vanderbilt and Underhill avenues: Hickory
11. Broadway at Lafayette Avenue: Putnams, Constellations (Putnams also played on grounds nearby at Putnam Avenue near Broadway)
12. Manor House grounds, north of Meeker Avenue: Eckfords
13. Wheat Hill grounds, Marcy and Lee Avenues near Rush Street: Continentals
14. Penn Street at Bedford Avenue: Phoenix
15. Prospect Park Parade Grounds: Since 1869, continues to be the site of various sports including amateur baseball

Opposite: Map with locations of ball grounds in Brooklyn. The accompanying map is adapted from the Library of Congress's digitalized version of a street map of Brooklyn published by J.B. Beers & Company in 1874 for the Advertising Bureau, Brooklyn City Rail Road Company. (Library of Congress, "American Memory: Historical Collections for the National Digital Library," http://memory.loc.gov/ammem/amhome/html.)

Records of Brooklyn Clubs in the National Association of Base Ball Players (1857–68)*

Team	1857	1858	1859	1860	1861	1862	1863	1864	1865	1866	1867	1868
Atlantic	7–1–1	7–0	11–1	12–2–2	5–2	2–3	8–3	20–0	18–0	17–3	19–5–1	47–3
Eckford	2–5	5–1	11–3	15–2	8–4	14–2	10–0	1–4	8–6	9–8	6–16–1	23–12
Excelsior	1–2	8–5	12–3	18–2–1	4–1–1		5–4	8–3	4–3	13–6–1	11–5	4–5–1
Putnam	2–2	4–3	2–3	3–3								
Continental	1–3	3–3										
Star		8–1		0–5–1	4–2	4–2–1	5–5	3–4	4–5	8–6	6–4	9–10
Osceola		3–2										
Oriental		2–2										15–3
Pastime		2–3	2–6									
Charter Oak			1–3	5–2								
Enterprise				2–7	5–4			1–4	1–10	9–6		
Exercise					4–4							
Henry Eckford					3–3		4–8					
Hamilton					1–5							
Powhattan						0–1					0–4	
Resolute							3–6	3–11	0–7	5–4	0–3	
Mohawk										9–3	2–5	0–6
Independent										6–5	5–8	2–4
Contest										3–4		
Constellation										1–5		
Peconic										1–6	0–2	3–2–1
Greenwood										0–7		
Alpha											4–3	
Athletic												3–9
Alaska												1–3
Harmonic												1–6

Records of Brooklyn Clubs in the National Association of Base Ball Players (1869–70)*

Professional Clubs

| | 1869 | | 1870 | |
| | Professional | All | Professional | All |
Teams	Games	Games	Games	Games
Atlantics	15–6–1	40–6–2	20–16	41–17
Eckfords	15–8	47–8	2–12–1	13–16–1

Amateur Clubs

Teams	1869	1870
Star	16–6	24–9
Harmonic	9–9	3–9–1
Athletic	9–10–1	11–11
Excelsior	5–7	5–3–1
Powhattan	5–12–1	
Alpha	4–4	3–10
Union		3–5
Enterprise		2–5
Osceola		1–3

*In 1869 and 1870, the National Association of Base Ball Players made a distinction between professional clubs and amateur clubs.

Notes

Chapter One

1. Harold Seymour, *Baseball: the Early Years* (New York: Oxford University Press, 1960), 3–12; Victor Salvatore, "The Man Who Didn't Invent Baseball," *American Heritage* 34 (June/July 1983), 65–67.

2. George B. Kirsch, *The Creation of American Team Sports: Baseball and Cricket, 1838–72* (Urbana: University of Illinois Press, 1989), 1–20.

3. David Ment, *The Shaping of a City: A Brief History of Brooklyn* (Brooklyn: Brooklyn Educational and Cultural Alliance, 1979); Ellen M. Snyder-Grenier, *Brooklyn! An Illustrated History* (Philadelphia: Temple University Press, 1996); Henry R. Stiles, *History of the City of Brooklyn, Volume 2* (Brooklyn, 1869).

4. Edward Pessen, "A Social and Economic Portrait of Jacksonian Brooklyn: Inequality, Social Immobility, and Class Distinction in the Nation's Seventh City," *New York Historical Society Quarterly* 55 (1971), 329–330.

5. Ira Rosenwaike, *Population History of New York City* (Syracuse: Syracuse University Press), 51.

6. Rosenwaike, 32.

7. Pessen, 337.

8. Ment, 48–51.

9. Harold Coffin Syrett, *The City of Brooklyn, 1865–1898: A Political History* (New York: Columbia University Press, 1944), 25–40.

10. Benjamin G. Rader, "The Quest for Subcommunities and the Rise of American Sport," *American Quarterly* 29 (Fall 1977), 355–369.

11. Steven M. Gelber, "Their Hands Are All Out Playing: Business and Amateur Baseball, 1845–1917," *Journal of Sport History* 11 (Spring 1984), 5–27; Steven Gelber, "Working at Playing: the Culture of the Workplace and the Rise of Baseball," *Journal of Social History* 16 (Summer 1983), 3–22; Warren Goldstein, *Playing for Keeps: a History of Early Baseball* (Ithica: Cornell University Press, 1989), 4–5.

12. Gelber, *Journal of Social History*, 8.

13. Stiles, 571.

14. Donald E. Simon, *The Public Park Movement in Brooklyn, 1824–1873*,

Ph.D. Dissertation, New York University, 1972; Jacob Judd, *The History of Brooklyn, 1834–1855: Political and Administrative Aspects*, Ph.D. Dissertation, New York University, 1959.

15. George Thompson, a librarian at New York University, brought this article to my attention in the summer of 2000.

16. Seymour, 15–20.

17. Seymour, 15.

18. Charles H. Peverelly, *The Book of American Pastimes* (New York: published by the author, 1866), 346–348.

19. On the culture of the early game, see especially Warren Goldstein, 17–66.

20. Knickerbocker Game Book, Spalding Collection, New York Public Library.

21. *Brooklyn Daily Eagle*, October 3, 1861.

22. *New York Morning News*, October 22, 1845, reprinted in Dean A. Sullivan, *Early Innings: a Documentary History of Baseball, 1825–1908* (Lincoln: University of Nebraska Press, 1995), 11–12.

23. Michael Gershwin, *Diamonds: the Evolution of the Ballpark* (Boston: Houghton Mifflin, 1993), 7.

24. The dates of establishment for each of the early baseball clubs are printed in the first issue of *Beadle's Dime Base Ball Player* (1860).

25. Pessen, 350, lists for example the Suydam and Polhemus families among the wealthiest Brooklyn citizens in 1841.

26. James H. Bready, *Baseball in Baltimore* (Baltimore: Johns Hopkins University Press, 1998), 3–5.

27. Chadwick Scrapbooks, Spalding Collection.

28. Richard Goldstein in *Superstars and Screwballs: 100 Years of Baseball History* (New York: Dutton, 1991) is the only baseball historian who attempts to identify the exact location of the "foot of Court Street." He erroneously places the spot near Borough Hall in downtown Brooklyn. Stiles, 576–577, and *Porter's Spirit of the Times*, May 14, 1859, however, establish the Excelsiors' grounds at the "foot of Court Street" near the waterfront in Red Hook.

29. Eugene L. Armbruster, *Brooklyn's Eastern District* (Brooklyn: published by the author, 1942 [1928]), 42.

30. William Rankin, "The History of Baseball, Part III," *The Baseball Magazine* 3 (October 1909), 13–22.

31. Armbruster, 36.

32. *Spirit of the Times*, January 10, 1857.

33. Eleanora A. Schoenebaum, *Emerging Neighborhoods: The Development of Brooklyn's Fringe Areas, 1850–1930*, Ph.D. Dissertation, Columbia University, 1976, 43.

34. Ted Vincent, *Mudville's Revenge: the Rise and Fall of American Sport* (New York: Seaview, 1981), 25–26, 107.

35. Atlantics Game Book, Spalding Collection.

36. William Rankin, "The History of Baseball, Part II," *The Baseball Magazine* 3 (September 1909), 11–18; Atlantics Game Book.

37. Chadwick Scrapbooks.

38. Marshall D. Wright, *The National Association of Base Ball Players, 1857–1870* (Jefferson, N.C.: McFarland, 2000), 50, 58–59,

39. Wright, 60.

40. Seymour, 20.

41. Vincent, 101–103.

42. Melvin L. Adelman, *A Sporting Time: New York City and the Rise of Modern Athletics, 1820–70* (Urbana: University of Illinois Press, 1986), 154–156.

43. *Porter's Spirit of the Times.*

44. *Spirit of the Times,* January 31, 1857.

45. George B. Kirsch, ed., *Sports in North America. A Documentary History, Volume 3. The Rise of Modern Sports, 1840–1860* (Gulf Breeze, Fl.: Academic International Press, 1992), 79–85.

46. *New York Clipper,* December 12, 1863.

47. *New York Clipper,* December 24, 1964.

48. *Brooklyn Daily Eagle,* April 1862.

49. *Brooklyn Daily Eagle,* 1864.

50. Jeffrey A. Kroessler, "Baseball and the Blue Laws," *Long Island Historical Journal* 5, 168–177.

51. *Brooklyn Daily Eagle,* July 16, 1856.

52. See especially Jules Tiegel, *Past Time: Baseball as History* (New York: Oxford University Press, 2000), 15–34.

53. *Brooklyn Daily Eagle,* July 14, 1858.

54. *Spirit of the Times,* July 24, 1858.

55. *Brooklyn Daily Eagle,* July 21, 1858.

56. *Brooklyn Daily Eagle,* August 18, 1858.

57. *New York Clipper,* September 18, 1858

58. William Rankin, "The History of Baseball, Part V," *The Baseball Magazine* 3 (December 1909), 85–88.

59. Henry Chadwick, *The Game of Base Ball: How to Learn It, How to Play It, and How to Teach It, with Sketches of Noted Players* (Columbia, S.C.: Camden House, 1983 [originally published, New York: G. Munro, 1868]), 178–180.

Chapter Two

1. Chadwick Scrapbooks, Spalding Collection, New York Public Library.

2. *Brooklyn Daily Eagle,* November 3, 1861.

3. *New York Clipper,* October 3, 1863.

4. *Eagle,* October 31, 1864.

5. *Eagle,* April 30, 1860.

6. *Eagle,* July 9, 1860.

7. Henry Chadwick, *The Game of Base Ball: How to Learn It, How to Play It, and How to Teach It, with Sketches of Noted Players* (Columbia, S.C.: Camden House, 1983 [originally published, New York: G. Munro, 1868]), 32–33.

8. *Clipper,* August 2, 1862.

9. *Eagle,* May 26, 1860; June 9, 1860.

10. *Eagle,* July 16, 1860.

11. *Eagle,* July 20, 1860.

12. *Eagle,* August 10, 1860.

13. *Eagle,* August 10, 1860.

14. *Eagle,* August 17, 1860; August 21, 1860.

15. *Eagle,* August 22, 1860.

16. *Eagle,* August 24, 1860.

17. *Eagle,* September 1, 1860.

18. *Eagle,* September 3, 1860.

19. *Eagle,* September 25, 1860.

20. Marshall D. Wright, *The National Association of Base Ball Players, 1857–1870* (Jefferson, N.C.: McFarland, 2000), 43–44.

21. Albert G. Spalding, *America's National Game* (Lincoln: University of Nebraska Press, 1992[1911]), 101.

22. Chadwick Scrapbooks. According to Chadwick, ninety Excelsior Club members served in the Civil War.

23. *Clipper,* July 4, 1863.

24. *The Ball Player's Chronicle,* June 25, 1868, reported that after the war, Pearsall moved to Montgomery, Alabama, where he practiced medicine.

25. *Eagle,* September 3, 1861.

26. *Eagle,* September 24, 1861.

27. *Eagle,* October 10, 1861.

28. Chadwick Scrapbooks.

29. *Eagle,* October 23, 1861.

30. *Eagle,* October 4, 1861.

31. *Eagle,* October 17, 1861.

32. *Clipper,* April 19, 1862.

33. Eugene L. Armbruster, *Brooklyn's Eastern District* (Brooklyn: published by the author, 1942[1928]), 192; Chadwick Scrapbooks; *Clipper,* May 17, 1862.

34. By comparison, in 1862 the cheapest seat at an opera performance at the Brooklyn Academy of Music was 25 cents, *Brooklyn Daily Times,* February 10, 1862.

35. *Clipper,* July 12, 1862.

36. *Eagle,* July 22, 1862.

37. *Daily Times,* July 22, 1862.

38. *Daily Times,* July 22, 1862.

39. *Clipper,* September 22, 1862.

40. *Eagle,* August 25, 1862.

41. *Daily Times,* August 25, 1862.

42. *Daily Times,* September 23, 1862.

43. *Eagle,* June 27, 1862.

44. *Clipper,* July 12, 1862.

45. *Clipper,* July 12, 1862.

46. *Clipper,* August 2, 1862.

47. *Eagle,* October 6, 1862.

48. *Wilkes Spirit of the Times,* October 4, 1862.

49. *Eagle,* October 20, 1862.

50. *Clipper,* December 27, 1862.

51. *Eagle,* October 20, 1862.

52. *Eagle,* June 16, 1863.
53. *Eagle,* June 18, 1863.
54. *Daily Times,* June 18, 1863.
55. *Eagle,* June 19, 1863.
56. *Eagle,* June 20, 1863.
57. *Eagle,* July 23, 1863.
58. *Eagle,* August 4, 1863.
59. *Clipper,* August 15, 1863.
60. *Eagle,* August 4, 1863.
61. *Clipper,* August 15, 1863.
62. *Eagle,* August 26, 1863.
63. *Clipper,* September 5, 1863.
64. *Eagle,* September 9, 1863.
65. *Clipper,* October 3, 1863.
66. *Eagle,* October 7, 1863.
67. *Daily Times,* October 7, 1863.

Chapter Three

1. Michael Benson, *Ballparks of North America: A Comprehensive Historical Reference to Baseball Grounds, Yards and Stadiums, 1845 to Present* (Jefferson, N.C.: McFarland, 1989), 55.
2. *New York Clipper,* April 28, 1864
3. *Brooklyn Daily Eagle,* April 19, 1864.
4. *Eagle,* May 23, 1864.
5. *Eagle,* May 31, 1864.
6. *Eagle,* July 1, 1864.
7. *Eagle,* July 9, 1864.
8. *Brooklyn Daily Union,* August 5, 1864.
9. *Daily Union,* August 5, 1864.
10. *Eagle,* August 10, 1864.
11. *Daily Union,* August 12, 1864.
12. *Daily Union,* August 11, 1864.
13. *Daily Union,* August 11, 1864.
14. *Daily Union,* August 11, 1864.
15. *Daily Union,* August 11, 1864.
16. *Daily Union,* September 9, 1864.
17. *Daily Union,* September 24, 1864; September 36, 1864; *Clipper,* October 1, 1864.
18. *Daily Union,* September 26, 1864.
19. *Eagle,* October 22, 1864.
20. *Daily Union,* May 5, 1865.
21. *Daily Union,* July 29, 1865.
22. *Daily Union,* July 7, 1865.
23. *Eagle,* July 27, 1865.

24. *Daily Union*, July 29, 1865.
25. *Clipper*, November 11, 1865.
26. *Clipper*, November 11, 1865.
27. *Daily Union*, June 22, 1865.
28. *Eagle*, July 29, 1865.
29. *Eagle*, July 29, 1865.
30. *Daily Union*, July 29, 1865.
31. *Daily Union*, July 31, 1865.
32. *Daily Union*, July 31, 1865.
33. *Eagle*, July 31, 1865.
34. *Eagle*, August 4, 1865.
35. *Eagle*, August 4, 1865.
36. *Daily Union*, August 15, 1865.
37. *Eagle*, August 15, 1865.
38. *Daily Union*, August 15, 1865.
39. *Eagle*, August 19, 1865.
40. *Daily Union*, September 1, 1865.
41. *Eagle*, September 22, 1865.
42. *Eagle*, September 30, 1865.
43. Quoted in the *Eagle*, October 10, 1865.
44. *Eagle*, October 11, 1865.
45. *Eagle*, October 23, 1865.
46. *Eagle*, October 23, 1865.
47. *Eagle*, October 31, 1865.
48. *Eagle*, October 31, 1865.
49. *Eagle*, October 31, 1865.
50. *Eagle*, November 7, 1865.
51. *Eagle*, November 28, 1865.
52. *Eagle*, June 20, 1866.
53. *Eagle*, June 21, 1866.
54. *Eagle*, August 4, 1866.
55. *Eagle*, August 15, 1866.
56. William Arthur Cummings, "How I Pitched the First Curve," *The Base Ball Magazine* 1 (September 1908), 21.
57. *Eagle*, September 25, 1866.
58. *Eagle*, September 29, 1866.
59. *Eagle*, October 16, 1866.
60. *Eagle*, October 23, 1866.
61. *Eagle*, October 30, 1866.
62. Albert G. Spalding, *America's National Game* (Lincoln: University of Nebraska Press, 1992 [1911]), 102.
63. Chadwick Scrapbooks.
64. Frederick Ivor-Campbell, "George Wright," in *Baseball's First Stars*, edited by Frederick Ivor-Campbell et al. (Cleveland: Society for American Baseball Research, 1996), 177.
65. *Ball Player's Chronicle*, August 1, 1867.
66. Spalding, 122.

67. *American Chronicle of Sports and Pastimes*, January 9, 1868.

68. *Clipper*, April 27, 1867; July 5, 1867; July 20, 1867.

69. Marshal D. Wright, *The National Association of Base Ball Players, 1857–1870* (Jefferson, N.C.: McFarland, 2000), 148.

70. *Clipper*, October 5, 1867.

71. *Clipper*, October 5, 1867.

72. *Clipper*, October 19, 1867.

73. *Clipper*, October 23, 1867.

Chapter Four

1. Chadwick Scrapbooks, Spalding Collection, New York Public Library.

2. Chadwick Scrapbooks.

3. *New York Clipper*, September 5, 1868.

4. *Clipper*, September 5, 1868.

5. *Clipper*, September 5, 1868.

6. *Brooklyn Daily Eagle*, September 1, 1868.

7. *Eagle*, September 8, 1868.

8. *Eagle*, September 8, 1868.

9. *Eagle*, September 9, 1868.

10. *Eagle*, September 11, 1868.

11. *Eagle*, September 12, 1868.

12. *Eagle*, October 2, 1868.

13. *Eagle*, October 7, 1868.

14. *Clipper*, October 17, 1868.

15. *Eagle*, October 7, 1868.

16. *Eagle*, October 7, 1868.

17. *Eagle*, October 13, 1868.

18. *Clipper*, October 27, 1868.

19. *Eagle*, October 27, 1868.

20. *Eagle*, October 29, 1868.

21. *Clipper*, September 19, 1868; October 3, 1868.

22. *Clipper*, October 28, 1868.

23. *Clipper*, January 1, 1869.

24. *Clipper*, September 25, 1868.

25. *Clipper*, August 8, 1868; August 15, 1868; September 12, 1868.

26. Chadwick Scrapbooks.

27. *Eagle*, November 29, 1868.

28. *Eagle*, November 3, 1868.

29. *Eagle*, September 9, 1868.

30. *Clipper*, June 12, 1869.

31. On the history of the Red Stockings see especially Stephen D. Guschov, *The Red Stockings of Cincinnati: Base Ball's First All-Professional Team and Its Historic 1869 and 1870 Seasons* (Jefferson, N.C.: McFarland, 1998).

32. *Clipper*, February 11, 1871.

33. David Quentin Voigt, *American Baseball, Volume 1: From Gentleman's Sport to the Commissioner System* (University Park: Pennsylvania State University, 1983), 31.

34. *Clipper*, January 1, 1870.

35. *Clipper*, June 26, 1869.

36. *Eagle*, June 17, 1869.

37. *Eagle*, June 18, 1869.

38. *Clipper*, December 14, 1869.

39. *Clipper*, September 11, 1869.

40. *Clipper*, October 16, 1869.

41. *Clipper*, November 13, 1869.

42. *Eagle*, November 23, 1869.

43. *Eagle*, December 3, 1869.

44. *Eagle*, November 11, 1869.

45. Guschov, 133.

46. *Eagle*, May 30, 1870.

47. *Eagle*, June 14, 1870

48. *Eagle*, June 15, 1870.

49. *Clipper*, June 25, 1870.

50. *Eagle*, June 16, 1870.

51. Cincinnati and Chicago newspaper reports quoted in *Eagle*, June 17, 1870.

52. *Eagle*, September 1, 1870.

53. Guschov, 133–137.

54. *Eagle*, October 28, 1870.

55. *Eagle*, November 17, 1870.

56. Frank V. Phelps, "Richard J. Pearce," in *Nineteenth Century Stars*, edited by Robert L. Tiemann and Mark Rucker (Cleveland: Society for American Baseball Research, 1989), 101.

57. *Clipper*, July 30, 1881; August 27, 1881.

58. Joseph M. Overfield, "John Curtis Chapman," in *Nineteenth Century Stars*, 28.

59. Frank V. Phelps, "Robert V. Ferguson," in *Nineteenth Century Stars*, 43.

60. *Clipper*, February 11, 1871.

61. *Clipper*, April 3, 1869.

62. *Clipper*, December 10, 1870.

Chapter Five

1. *Brooklyn Daily Union*, April 3, 1864.

2. *Daily Union*, June 11, 1865.

3. *Brooklyn Daily Eagle*, October 8, 1868.

4. *New York Clipper*, July 24, 1869.

5. *Eagle*, December 18, 1865.

6. William Parry, *Life at the Old Stone House*, 1636–1852 (Brooklyn: First Battle Revival Alliance, 2000), 30.

7. *Eagle*, January 13, 1865.

8. *Brooklyn Daily Times*, January 9, 1862; February 3, 1862; February 11, 1862.

9. *Eagle*, December 18, 1865.

10. *Clipper*, February 8, 1862.

11. *Daily Times*, January 24, 1862.

12. *Eagle*, February 19, 1872.

13. *Clipper*, January 14, 1871; February 3, 1883.

14. *Clipper*, February 14, 1861.

15. *Eagle*, December 18, 1865.

16. *Eagle*, February 3, 1868.

17. *Harper's Weekly* (January 26, 1884), 63.

Chapter Six

1. On the history of the NAPBBP see especially William J. Ryczek, *Black-guards and Red Stockings: A History of Baseball's National Association, 1871–1875* (Jefferson, N.C.: McFarland, 1992). For player and team statistics, see *The Baseball Encyclopedia, 7th edition*, edited by Joseph L. Reichler (New York: Macmillan, 1988), 49–73.

2. *New York Clipper*, March 25, 1871.

3. *Brooklyn Daily Eagle*, September 8, 1871.

4. *Eagle*, September 12, 1871.

5. *Eagle*, April 24, 1871.

6. *Eagle*, May 3, 1871.

7. *Eagle*, May 3, 1871.

8. *Eagle*, September 8, 1871.

9. *Eagle*, September 8, 1871.

10. *Brooklyn Daily Times*, October 3, 1871.

11. *Eagle*, October 16, 1871.

12. *Eagle*, October 16, 1871.

13. *Eagle*, October 18, 1871.

14. *New York Daily Herald*, October 31, 1871.

15. *Eagle*, January 14, 1872.

16. *Clipper*, September 7, 1872.

17. *Eagle*, October 24, 1872.

18. In the 1890s, William Rankin of the *New York Clipper* interviewed several contemporaries of Pearce and Barlow, including John Chapman and Bob Ferguson, who claimed that Pearce's "fair-foul" hits were actually bunts. See Robert H. Schaefer, "Bunts and Fair-Foul Hits: Who was the First? Dickey Pearce or Tommy Barlow?" *The National Pastime: A Review of Baseball History* 20 (2000), 8–9. Adding to the confusion, *Total Baseball*'s list of "Famous Firsts" in baseball identifies Tommy Barlow as the Atlantic player who invented the bunt in 1866. Barlow, however, did not play for the Atlantics until 1872. See *Total Baseball: The Official Encyclopedia of Major League Baseball, 6th edition*, edited by John Thorn et al. (New York: Total Sports, 1999), 2507.

19. *Eagle*, September 22, 1873.

20. Ryczek (1992), 69.

21. *Clipper*, September 13, 1872.

22. Marshall D. Wright, *The National Association of Base Ball Players, 1857–1870* (Jefferson, N.C.: McFarland, 2000).

23. Joseph M. Overfield, "Alfred James Reach," in *Nineteenth Century Stars*, edited by Robert L. Tiemann and Mark Rucker (Cleveland: Society for American Baseball Research, 1989), 106.

24. Robert L. Tiemann, "James Leon Wood," in *Baseball's First Stars*, edited by Frederick Ivor-Campbell, Robert L. Tiemann and Mark Rucker (Cleveland: Society for American Baseball Research, 1996), 174.

25. William L. Armbruster, *Brooklyn's Eastern District* (Brooklyn: published by the author, 1942 [1928]), 109.

26. *Eagle*, July 23, 1873.

27. *Eagle*, July 26, 1873.

28. *Clipper*, February 21, 1874.

29. *Eagle*, July 25, 1873.

30. Richard Goldstein, *Superstars and Screwballs: 100 Years of Brooklyn Baseball* (New York: Dutton, 1991), 25.

31. *Clipper*, October 17, 1874.

32. *Clipper*, October 24, 1874.

33. *Clipper*, October 31, 1874.

34. Ryczek (1992), 220.

35. *Clipper*, February 1, 1876; April 8, 1876.

36. *Total Baseball*, 1280.

37. *Total Baseball*, 1916.

38. *Clipper*, April 4, 1877.

39. *Clipper*, May 5, 1877.

40. Harold Seymour, *Baseball: The Early Years* (New York: Oxford University Press, 1989), 86.

41. Chadwick Scrapbooks.

42. *Eagle*, May 26, 1869.

43. Chadwick Scrapbooks.

44. Chadwick Scrapbooks.

45. Chadwick Scrapbooks.

46. *Eagle*, May 12, 1872.

47. *Eagle*, May 20, 1872.

48. Chadwick Scrapbooks.

49. *Clipper*, April 12, 1879.

50. Jack Kavanaugh, "William Harrison Barnie," in *Baseball's First Stars*, edited by Frederick Ivor-Campbell, Robert L. Tiemann and Mark Rucker (Cleveland: Society for American Baseball Research, 1996), 6.

51. *Clipper*, May 3, 1879; May 10, 1879.

52. *Clipper*, April 16, 1881.

53. *Clipper*, July 8, 1881.

54. Seymour, 103.

55. Joseph M. Overfield, "Dennis Joseph Brouthers," in *Baseball's First Stars*, 11–12.

56. Richard Puff, "John W. Nelson," in *Baseball's First Stars*, 117.

57. Joseph M. Overfield, "Lipman Emanuel Pike," in *Nineteenth Century Stars*, edited by Robert L. Tiemann and Mark Rucker (Cleveland: Society for American Baseball Research, 1989), 103.

58. Bob Richardson, "Thomas Henry Bond," in *Nineteenth Century Stars*, 15.

59. *Clipper*, August 27, 1881.

60. *Clipper*, August 20, 1881.

61. Albert G. Spalding, *America's National Game* (Lincoln: University of Nebraska Press, 1992 [1911]), 239.

62. *Clipper*, November 5, 1881.

63. Robert F. Burk, *Never Just a Game: Players, Owners, and American Baseball to 1920* (Chapel Hill: University of North Carolina Press, 1994), 70–71.

64. *Clipper*, January 28, 1882.

65. *Clipper*, April 8, 1882.

66. *Clipper*, June 24, 1882.

67. *Clipper*, June 24, 1882.

68. *Clipper*, August 5, 1882.

Chapter Seven

1. Mary P. Ryan, *Womanhood in America: From Colonial Times to the Present*, 2nd ed. (New York: New Viewpoints Press, 1979), 75–118.

2. Gai Inham Berlage, *Women in Baseball: The Forgotten History* (Westport, Ct.: Praeger, 1994).

3. *Brooklyn Daily Eagle*, September 21, 1875.

4. *Eagle*, September 14, 1875.

5. *New York Clipper*, May 14, 1875.

6. See correspondence in Aileen S. Kraditor, ed., *Up from the Pedestal: Selected Writings in the History of American Feminism* (New York: Quadrangle, 1968), 123–131.

7. *Clipper*, August 29, 1868.

8. *Clipper*, August 29, 1868.

9. *Ball Player's Chronicle*, June 13, 1867.

10. *Brooklyn Daily Union*, July 22, 1865.

11. Reprinted in *Early Innings: A Documentary History of Baseball, 1825–1908*, compiled and edited by Dean A. Sullivan (Lincoln: University of Nebraska Press, 1995), 35.

12. "Dinah" was a dark-skinned female character in the popular black-face minstrel shows. See Alexander Saxton, "Blackface Minstrelsy and Jacksonian Ideology," *American Quarterly* 27 (March 1975), 23.

13. Craig Steven Wilder, *A Covenant with Color: Race and the History of Brooklyn*, Ph.D. Dissertation, Columbia University, 1994.

14. Kenneth L. Roff, "Brooklyn's Reaction to Black Suffrage in 1860," *Afro-Americans in New York Life and History* 2 (January 1978), 29–39.

15. Quoted by Roff, 31.

16. Ellen M. Snyder-Grenier, *Brooklyn! An Illustrated History* (Philadelphia: Temple University Press, 1996), 38–40.

17. *Eagle*, July 16, 1863.

18. Harold Seymour, *Baseball: The People's Game* (New York: Oxford University Press, 1990), 534–538.

19. George B. Kirsch, *The Creation of American Team Sports: Baseball and Cricket, 1838–72* (Urbana: University of Illinois Press, 1989), 126–127.

20. Melvin L. Adelman, *A Sporting Time: New York City and the Rise of Modern Athletics, 1820–70* (Urbana: University of Illinois Press, 1986), 138–144.

21. *Daily Union*, September 30, 1867.

22. *Ball Player's Chronicle*, October 3, 1867.

23. *Ball Player's Chronicle*, October 10, 1867.

24. *Daily Union*, October 4, 1867.

25. *Ball Player's Chronicle*, October 10, 1867.

26. *Ball Player's Chronicle*, October 31, 1867.

27. *Ball Player's Chronicle*, October 31, 1867.

28. *Ball Player's Chronicle*, December 19, 1867.

29. *Brooklyn Daily Times*, September 27, 1871.

30. *Daily Times*, September 29, 1871.

31. Sol White, *Sol White's History of Colored Base Ball, with Other Documents on the Early Black Game 1886–1936*, compiled and edited by Jerry Malloy (Lincoln: University of Nebraska Press, 1995 [1906]), 76.

32. Jules Tygiel, *Baseball's Great Experiment: Jackie Robinson and His Legacy*, expanded edition (New York: Oxford University Press, 1997), 10–12.

33. Daniel W. Zang, *Fleet Walker's Divided Heart: The Life of Baseball's First Black Major Leaguer* (Lincoln: University of Nebraska Press, 1995).

34. Quoted in Zang, 27.

35. *New York Sun*, June 18, 1884.

36. On the history of black baseball, see for example Mark Ribowsky, *A Complete History of the Negro Leagues, 1884–1955* (New York: Birch Lane Press, 1995); Robert Peterson, *Only the Ball Was White: A History of Legendary Black Players and All-Black Professional Teams* (Englewood Cliffs, N.J.: Prentice Hall, 1970); and others.

37. On Jackie Robinson's role in baseball history, see Jules Tygiel, *Baseball's Great Experiment: Jackie Robinson and His Legacy*, expanded edition (New York: Oxford University Press, 1997).

Chapter Eight

1. *New York Clipper*, March 4, 1889.

2. Andy McCue, "Charles H. Byrne," in *Baseball's First Stars*, edited by Frederick Ivor-Campbell, Robert L. Tiemann and Mark Rucker (Cleveland: The Society for American Baseball Research, 1996), 19.

3. *Clipper*, January 13, 1883.

4. *Clipper*, March 4, 1889.

5. Chadwick Scrapbooks, Spalding Collection, New York Public Library.

6. *Clipper*, January 27, 1883.

7. *Clipper*, January 20, 1883.

8. *Clipper*, February 3, 1883.

9. *Clipper*, April 7, 1883.

10. *Brooklyn Daily Eagle*, April 25, 1883.

11. *Eagle*, May 2, 1883.

12. *Clipper*, May 19, 1883.

13. *Eagle*, May 13, 1883.

14. *Clipper*, May 19, 1883.

15. Alan Trachtenberg, *Brooklyn Bridge: Fact and Symbol*, 2nd ed. (Chicago: University of Chicago Press, 1979).

16. *New York Times*, May 20, 1883.

17. Robert L. Tiemann, *Dodger Classics* (St. Louis: Baseball Histories, Inc., 1983), 4.

18. William E. McMahon, "William H. Terry," in *Baseball's First Stars*, 164.

19. *Clipper*, September 15, 1883.

20. *Clipper*, August 4, 1883.

21. *Clipper*, August 11, 1883.

22. *Clipper*, August 11, 1883.

23. Tiemann, 4–5.

Bibliography

Archival Materials and Special Collections

Brooklyn Collection, Brooklyn Public Library: Photograph collection.
Fales Special Collections, Bobst Library, New York University: *Harper's Weekly*
National Baseball Hall of Fame, Cooperstown, New York: *Beadle's Dime Base Ball Player*, edited by Henry Chadwick (New York: Irwin P. Beadle & Co., 186–1880).
Spalding Collection, Manuscripts & Archives Division, New York Public Library: Henry Chadwick Diaries, Henry Chadwick Scrapbooks, Atlantic Base Ball Club Game Book, Knickerbocker Base Ball Club Game Book
Spalding Collection photographs, Miriam & Ira D. Wallach Division of Art Prints and Photographs, New York Public Library
Transcendental Graphics. Photographs.

Contemporary Newspapers and Periodicals

Ball Player's Chronicle
Baseball Magazine
Brooklyn Daily Eagle
Brooklyn Daily Times
Brooklyn Daily Union
Chronicle of American Sports and Pastimes
Frank Leslie's Illustrated Newspaper
Harper's Weekly

National Advocate
New York Clipper
New York Herald
New York Sun
New York Times
Porter's Spirit of the Times
Spirit of the Times
Sporting News
Wilkes' Spirit of the Times

Books

Adelman, Melvin L. *A Sporting Time: New York City and the Rise of Modern Athletics, 1820–70* (Urbana: University of Illinois Press, 1986).

Armbruster, Eugene L. *Brooklyn's Eastern District* (Brooklyn: self-published, 1942 [1928]).

Baseball Encyclopedia, 7th edition, edited by Joseph L. Reichler (New York: MacMillan, 1988).

Baseball's First Stars, edited by Frederick Ivor-Campbell et al. (Cleveland: Society for American Baseball Research, 1996).

Benson, Michael. *Ballparks of North America: A Comprehensive Historical Reference to Baseball Grounds, Yards and Stadiums, 1845 to Present* (Jefferson, N.C.: McFarland, 1989).

Berlage, Gai Inham. *Women in Baseball: The Forgotten History* (Westport, Ct.: Praeger, 1994).

Bready, James H. *Baseball in Baltimore* (Baltimore: Johns Hopkins University Press, 1998).

Chadwick, Henry. *The Game of Base Ball: How to Learn it, How to Play it, and How to Teach it, With Sketches of Noted Players* (Columbia, S.C.: Camden House, 1983 [originally published, New York: G. Munro, 1868]).

Early Innings: a Documentary History of Baseball, 1825–1908, compiled and edited by Dean A. Sullivan (Lincoln: University of Nebraska Press, 1995).

Gershwin, Michael. *Diamonds: The Evolution of the Ballpark* (Boston: Houghton Mifflin, 1993).

Goldstein, Warren. *Playing for Keeps: A History of Early Baseball* (Ithaca: Cornell University Press, 1989).

Guschov, Stephen D. *The Red Stockings of Cincinnati: Base Ball's First All-Professional Team and Its Historic 1869 and 1870 Seasons* (Jefferson, N.C.: McFarland, 1998).

Kirsch, George B. *The Creation of American Team Sports: Baseball and Cricket, 1838–72* (Urbana: University of Illinois Press, 1989).

Ment, David. *The Shaping of a City: A Brief History of Brooklyn* (Brooklyn: Brooklyn Educational and Cultural Alliance, 1979).

Nineteenth Century Stars, edited by Robert L. Tiemann and Mark Rucker (Cleveland: Society for American Baseball Research, 1989).

Parry, William. *Life at the Old Stone House, 1636–1852* (Brooklyn: First Battle Revival Alliance, 2000).

Peterson, Robert. *Only the Ball Was White: A History of Legendary Black Players and All-Black Professional Teams* (Englewood Cliffs, N.J.: Prentice-Hall, 1970).

Peverelly, Charles H. *The Book of American Pastimes* (New York: self-published, 1866).

Ribowsky, Mark. *A Complete History of the Negro Leagues, 1884–1955* (New York: Birch Lane Press, 1995).

Rosenwaike, Ira. *Population History of New York City* (Syracuse: Syracuse University Press, 1972).

Ryan, Mary P. *Womanhood in America: From Colonial Times to the Present, 2nd edition* (New York: New Viewpoints Press, 1979).

Ryczek, William J. *Blackguards and Red Stockings: A History of Baseball's National Association, 1871–1875* (Jefferson, N.C.: McFarland, 1992).

Seymour, Harold. *Baseball: The Early Years* (New York: Oxford University Press, 1960).

_____. *Baseball: The People's Game* (New York: Oxford University Press, 1990).

Snyder-Grenier, Ellen M. *Brooklyn! An Illustrated History* (Philadelphia: Temple University Press, 1996).

Spalding, Albert G. *America's National Game* (Lincoln: University of Nebraska Press, 1992 [1911]).

Sports in America: A Documentary History, Volume 3. The Rise of Modern Sports, 1840–1860, edited by George B. Kirsch (Gulf Breeze, Fl.: Academic International Press, 1992).

Stiles, Henry. *History of the City of Brooklyn, Volumes 2 and 3* (Brooklyn, 1869).

Syrett, Harold Coffin. *The City of Brooklyn, 1865–1898: A Political History* (New York: Columbia University Press, 1944).

Tiemann, Robert L. *Dodger Classics* (St. Louis: Baseball Histories, Inc., 1983).

Total Baseball: The Official Encyclopedia of Major League Baseball, 6th edition, edited by John Thorn et al. (New York: Total Sports, 1999).

Trachtenberg, Alan. *Brooklyn Bridge: Fact and Symbol, 2nd edition* (Chicago: University of Chicago Press, 1979).

Tygiel, Jules. *Baseball's Great Experiment: Jackie Robinson and His Legacy*, expanded edition (New York: Oxford University Press, 1997).

_____. *Past Time: Baseball as History* (New York: Oxford University Press, 2000).

Up from the Pedestal: Selected Writings in the History of American Feminism, edited by Aileen S. Kraditor (New York: Quadrangle, 1968).

Vincent, Todd. *Mudville's Revenge: The Rise and Fall of American Sport* (New York: Seaview, 1981).

Voigt, David Quentin. *American Baseball, Volume 1: From Gentleman's Sport to the Commissioner System* (University Park: Pennsylvania State University Press, 1983).

White, Sol. *Sol White's History of Colored Base Ball, with Other Documents on the Early Black Game 1886–1936*, compiled and edited by Jerry Malloy (Lincoln: University of Nebraska Press, 1995 [1906]).

Wright, Marshall D. *The National Association of Base Ball Players, 1857–1870* (Jefferson, N.C.: McFarland, 2000).

Zang, Daniel W. *Fleet Walker's Divided Heart: The Life of Baseball's First Black Major Leaguer* (Lincoln: University of Nebraska Press, 1995).

Articles

Cummings, William Arthur. "How I Pitched the First Curve," *The Baseball Magazine* 1 (September 1908), 21–22.

Gelber, Steven M. "Their Hands Are All Out Playing: Business and Amateur Baseball, 1845–1917," *Journal of Sport History* 11 (Spring 1984), 5–27.

_____. "Working at Playing: The Culture of the Workplace and the Rise of Baseball," *Journal of Social History* 16 (Summer 1983), 3–22.

Kroessler, Jeffrey A. "Baseball and the Blue Laws," *Long Island Historical Journal* 5 (1993), 168–177.

Pessen, Edward. "A Social and Economic Portrait of Jacksonian Brooklyn:

Inequality, Social Immobility, and Class Distinction in the Nation's Seventh City," *New York Historical Society Quarterly* 55 (1971), 318–353.

Rader, Benjamin G. "The Quest for Subcommunities and the Rise of American Sport," *American Quarterly* 29 (Fall 1977), 355–369.

Rankin, William. "The History of Baseball, Part II," *The Baseball Magazine* 3 (September 1909), 11–18.

_____. "The History of Baseball, Part III," *The Baseball Magazine* 3 (October 1909), 13–22.

_____. "The History of Baseball, Part V," *The Baseball Magazine* 3 (December 1909), 85–88.

Roff, Kenneth L. "Brooklyn's Reaction to Black Suffrage in 1860," *Afro-Americans in New York Life and History* 2 (January 1978), 29–39.

Salvatore, Victor. "The Man Who Didn't Invent Baseball," *American Heritage* 34 (June/July 1983), 65–67.

Saxton, Alexander. "Blackface Minstrelsy and Jacksonian Ideology," *American Quarterly* 27 (March 1975),

Schaefer, Robert H. "Bunts and Fair-Foul Hits: Who was the First? Dickey Pearce or Tommy Barlow?" *The National Pastime: A Review of Baseball History* 20 (2000), 8–9.

Dissertations

Judd, Jacob. *The History of Brooklyn, 1834–1855: Political and Administrative Aspects.* Ph.D. dissertation, New York University, 1959.

Schoenebaum, Eleanora A. *Emerging Neighborhoods: The Development of Brooklyn's Fringe Areas, 1850–1930.* Ph.D. dissertation, Columbia University, 1976.

Simon, Donald E. *The Public Park Movement in Brooklyn, 1824–1873.* Ph.D. dissertation, New York University, 1972.

Wilder, Craig Steven. *A Covenant with Color: Race and the History of Brooklyn.* Ph.D. dissertation, Columbia University, 1994.

Index

Date Due

		2005	